ADVANCED CONCEPTS IN OPERATING SYSTEMS
Distributed, Database, and Multiprocessor Operating Systems

McGraw-Hill Series in Computer Science

Senior Consulting Editor

C. L. Liu, University of Illinois at Urbana-Champaign

Consulting Editor

Allen B. Tucker, Bowdoin College

Fundamentals of Computing and Programming
Computer Organization and Architecture
Systems and Languages
Theoretical Foundations
Software Engineering and Database
Artificial Intelligence
Networks, Parallel and Distributed Computing
Graphics and Visualization
The MIT Electrical Engineering and Computer Science Series

Systems and Languages

* **Abelson and Sussman:** *Structure and Interpretation of Computer Programs*
  Appleby: *Programming Languages, Paradigm and Practice*
* **Friedman, Wand, and Haynes:** *Essentials of Programming Languages*
  Kant: *Introduction to Computer System Performance Evaluation*
  Levi and Agrawala: *Real-Time System Design*
* **Liskov and Guttag:** *Abstraction and Specification in Program Development*
  Madnick and Donovan: *Operating Systems*
  Milenkovic: *Operating Systems: Concepts and Design*
  Singhal and Shivaratri: *Advanced Concepts in Operating Systems: Distributed, Database, and Multiprocessor Operating Systems*
* **Springer and Friedman:** *Scheme and the Art of Programming*
  Tucker: *Programming Languages*

* Co-published by The MIT Press and McGraw-Hill, Inc.

ADVANCED CONCEPTS IN OPERATING SYSTEMS

Distributed, Database, and Multiprocessor Operating Systems

Mukesh Singhal

Department of Computer and Information Science
The Ohio State University

Niranjan G. Shivaratri

NEC Systems Lab.
Princeton, NJ

McGraw-Hill, Inc.

New York   St. Louis   San Francisco   Auckland   Bogotá
Caracas   Lisbon   London   Madrid   Mexico City   Milan   Montreal
New Delhi   San Juan   Singapore   Sydney   Tokyo   Toronto

This book was set in Times Roman by Electronic Technical Publishing Services.
The editor was Eric M. Munson;
the production supervisor was Denise L. Puryear.
The cover was designed by Warren Infield;
cover photo by Tom Sanders/Stock Market.
Project supervision was done by Electronic Technical Publishing Services.
R. R. Donnelley & Sons Company was printer and binder.

ADVANCED CONCEPTS IN OPERATING SYSTEMS
Distributed, Database, and Multiprocessor Operating Systems

This book is printed on acid-free paper.

8 9 0 DOC DOC   0

ISBN 0-07-057572-X

Library of Congress Cataloging-in-Publication Data

Singhal, Mukesh.
  Advanced concepts in operating systems: distributed, database, and multiprocessor operating systems / Mukesh Singhal and Niranjan G. Shivaratri.
    p.   cm.
  Includes index.
  ISBN 0-07-057572-X
  1. Operating systems (Computers)   I. Shivaratri, Niranjan G.
  II. Title.
  QA76.76.063S565   1994
  005.4'3—dc20   93-29812

INTERNATIONAL EDITION

ABOUT THE AUTHORS

Mukesh Singhal is currently an associate professor of Computer and Information Science at The Ohio State University, Columbus. He received his Bachelor of Engineering degree in Electronics and Communication Engineering with high distinction from the University of Roorkee, Roorkee, India, in 1980, and his Ph.D. degree in Computer Science from the University of Maryland, College Park, in May 1986. His current research interests include distributed systems, operating systems, databases, and performance modeling. He has published in *IEEE Computer, IEEE Trans. on Computers, IEEE Trans. on Software Engineering, IEEE Trans. on Knowledge and Data Engineering, IEEE Trans. on Parallel and Distributed Systems, Journal of Parallel and Distributed Computing, Performance Evaluation, Information Processing Letters, Information Science, and Distributed Computing.*

Niranjan G. Shivaratri received a B.S. in Electrical Engineering from Mysore University, India, an M.S. degree in Computer Science from Villanova University, and a Ph.D. in Computer and Information Science from The Ohio State University in June 1994. Currently he is a principal engineer at NEC Laboratory in Princeton, NJ. From 1983 to 1987, he worked as a systems programmer for the Unisys Corporation, concentrating on network and operating systems software development. His research interests include distributed systems, operating systems, and performance evaluation. He was a recipient of a Presidential Fellowship at The Ohio State University.

To my daughter Priyanka.

M. S.

To my parents and brother.

N. G. S.

CONTENTS

Part II Distributed Operating Systems

Part IV   Failure Recovery and Fault Tolerance

12   Recovery

Part V   Protection and Security

Part VI   Multiprocessor Operating Systems

Part VII   Database Operating Systems

18   Introduction to Database Operating Systems

19   Concurrency Control: Theoretical Aspects

PREFACE

Computer Science and Computer Engineering departments in a large number of universities have been teaching a course on advanced operating systems for several years. Although the field of advanced operating systems is rapidly changing and operating systems design techniques have yet to be perfected, the topic is no longer in the state of infancy and a general consensus has developed as to what should be taught in such a course. Due to the lack of a centralized source of information, instructors for this course have generally relied on papers from the contemporary literature to teach the course. These two factors gave us the impetus to write this book to provide the much needed centralized source of information on advanced operating systems for use by instructors, students, researchers, practitioners, etc.

Operating systems first appeared in the late fifties. Until the early seventies, operating systems for mainframe systems were the main topic of research. Over the last two decades, considerable amounts of research has been done in "distributed operating systems," "database operating systems," and "multiprocessor operating systems." These topics form the basis of an advanced course in operating systems. Design issues of these operating systems and mechanisms to build these systems have been well investigated, have matured, and have stabilized (if not perfected yet) and it is imperative to teach them in an advanced course in operating systems. This book provides the information about these operating systems in a cohesive form.

We decided on the contents of the book after surveying about fifty top Computer Science/Engineering departments in the United States and abroad to determine the coverage in their graduate level courses in operating systems. Deciding on the contents was very difficult and the book contains a complete set of topics common to all of these departments. Most chapters of this book have been developed from the lecture notes used in teaching advanced operating systems and distributed computing courses at The Ohio State University over the past several years.

Most material in the book has been derived from their original sources (i.e., papers from contemporary literature). We have kept the presentation simple and stimulating;

nevertheless, the treatment of topics is detailed and up-to-date enough so that experts (researchers, etc.) in the field can use the book as a reference.

Chapters of the book include examples, figures, cases, and bibliography/references. "Suggested Further Readings" lists are also included so that interested readers can explore material beyond the scope of this book. Every chapter has a set of problems which include conceptual, descriptive, and design problems.

AUDIENCE

This book is intended for a second course on operating systems, for senior level under-graduates or graduate students, in computer science and engineering curriculum. The book is self-contained; nevertheless, having an introductory course in operating systems will be helpful. The book is intended to provide a basic foundation in the design of advanced operating systems. Therefore, rather than discussing the design and the structure of a specific operating system, the book emphasizes the fundamental concepts and mechanisms which form the basis of the design of advanced operating systems. The main emphasis of the book is on various alternative approaches to the solution of the problems encountered in the design of advanced operating systems. However, when we felt it appropriate, we have embedded relevant case studies to illustrate the fundamental concepts.

The book can also be used in a graduate course on "distributed computing systems" since Parts II, III, and IV of the book cover the fundamental concepts and issues underlying the design of distributed systems.

In addition, computer professionals such as researchers, practicing engineers, systems designers/programmers, and consultants in industry as well as in research should find the book a very useful reference because it contains state of the art techniques to address the various design issues in advanced operating systems.

ORGANIZATION OF THE BOOK

The book is divided into six parts. Each part consists of related chapters and focuses on a specific topic in advanced operating systems.

Chapter 1 gives an overview of the book. It introduces the concept of operating systems, of virtual machines, and of various types of operating system structures. It introduces the readers to advanced operating systems, gives the motivations for their design, and discusses the various types of advanced operating systems.

Part I deals with process management in a single machine operating system. Chapter 2 describes the concept of a process and illustrates several mechanisms for process synchronization. Chapter 3 focuses on process deadlocks explaining how to detect, avoid, and recover from deadlocks.

Part II introduces distributed operating systems. Chapter 4 introduces the architecture of distributed systems and the concept of distributed operating systems. It also ties in all the major components of a distributed operating system. It gives a global view of a distributed operating system and the role of each of the topics covered in Chapters 5 through 11 in a distributed operating system. Therefore, a reader not well versed with distributed operating systems should read Chapter 4 before proceeding to any of the Chapters 5 through 12. However, Chapters 5 through 12 are self contained and can be read in any order. Chapter 5 provides a theoretical foundation for distributed systems. Chapter 6 covers mutual exclusion and Chapter 7 covers deadlock detection in distributed systems. Chapters 6 and 7 are the distributed system's counterparts for process synchronization (Chapter 2) and for deadlock detection (Chapter 3) in nondistributed systems, respectively. Chapter 8 discusses the methods that processes in distributed systems use to arrive at a consensus under the occurrence of malicious failures.

Part III deals with resource management in distributed systems. Chapter 9 (Distributed File Systems), Chapter 10 (Distributed Shared Memory), and Chapter 11 (Global Scheduling) each describe the management of different resources in distributed systems.

In Part IV, Chapter 12 discusses various schemes for recovering from failures and Chapter 13 covers techniques for fault-tolerance in distributed systems.

Part V deals with security and protection in computer systems. Chapter 14 discusses various models and mechanisms for protection and security. Chapter 15 covers cryptographic techniques to protect the confidentiality of data.

Part VI is on Multiprocessor Operating Systems. Chapter 16 describes the architecture of multiprocessor systems. Chapter 17 discusses the design issues of a multiprocessor operating system and mechanisms used in building multiprocessor operating systems.

Finally, Part VII deals with database operating systems. Chapter 18 discusses the differences between general purpose and database operating systems. Chapter 19 introduces the concept of a transaction and gives a theoretical background for concurrency control. Chapter 20 discusses various algorithms for concurrency control.

ACKNOWLEDGMENTS

The authors wish to express their thanks to the following people who helped us at various capacities during the preparation of the text: Prof. Ken Birman of Cornell University, Prof. S. K. Tripathi of University of Maryland, Prof. David Finkel of Worcester Polytechnic Institute, Profs. Lionel Ni and M. Mutka of Michigan State University, Prof. Madalene Speziallete of Lehigh University, Prof. Miron Livny of University of Wisconsin, Prof. S. H. Son of University of Virginia, Prof. Akhil Kumar of Cornell University, Profs. Steve Bruell and Sukumar Ghosh of University of Iowa, Prof. Mustaque Ahamad of Georgia Institute of Technology, Prof. Larry Dowdy of Vanderbilt University, Prof. F. Mattern of University of Kaiserslautern, Prof. Richard Muntz of UCLA, Prof. Sol Shatz of University of Illinois at Chicago, Prof. M. Masaaki of Kansas State, Prof. K. Kant of Penn State, Prof. R. Finkel of University of Kentucky, Prof. Randy Chow of University of Florida, Prof. S. Cheung of Emory University, Prof. Ravi Sandhu of George Mason University, Prof. Venkatesan of University of Texas at Dallas, Prof. P. J. Denning of George Mason University, Prof. David Kotz of Dartmouth College, Prof. Steve Chapin of Kent State University, Prof. Alan Levis of Florida State University, Dr. Ajay Kshem Kalyani of IBM Corp., and Prof. M. Rasit Eskiciogln of University of New Orleans.

Prof. F. George Friedman of Univerity of Illinois at Urbana-Champaign read the manuscript and gave detailed feedback. Prof. Phil Krueger of Ohio State University made important contributions to Chapter 11. Dr. Martin Abadi of DEC SRC and Dr. Tom Woo of University of Texas gave comments on Chapter 15. Dr. B. Clifford Neuman of Information Science Institute, University of Southern California, gave several constructive comments on Chapters 14 and 15. We are thankful to Prof. Pankaj Jalote of Indian Institute of Technology, Kanpur, for commenting on the chapters on Recovery and Fault Tolerance.

We are also grateful to a large number of graduate students, especially Manas Mandal, Mahendra Ramachandran, and Dr. David Ebert at The Ohio State University for pointing out typos in the manuscript and for suggesting ways to improve the manuscript. Ravi Prakash of The Ohio State University went through the entire manuscript and made several useful suggestions.

The authors can be reached at singhal@cis.ohio-state.edu to report errors, comments, and suggestions.

We are greatly indebted to the staff of McGraw-Hill, especially Eric Munson, for providing us with professional help at various stages of the book. We are thankful to ETP Services for their excellent services in the production of this book. We are thankful to The Ohio State University for providing us with an excellent environment for the project.

Mukesh Singhal
Niranjan G. Shivaratri

the metric used to measure the load at nodes characterizes the load properly. The CPU queue length has been found to be a good load indicator.

Load distributing algorithms have been characterized as static, dynamic, or adaptive. Static algorithms do not make use of system state information in making decisions regarding the transfer of load from one node to another. On the other hand, dynamic algorithms do make use of system state information when making decisions. Therefore, these algorithms have a potential to outperform static algorithms. Adaptive algorithms are a special class of dynamic algorithms in that they adapt their activities, by dynamically changing the parameters of the algorithm, to suit the changing system state.

Load distributing algorithms can further be classified as load balancing or load sharing algorithms, based on their load distributing principle. Both types of algorithms strive to reduce the likelihood of an unshared state. Load balancing algorithms however, go a step further by attempting to equalize the loads at all computers. Because a load balancing algorithm transfers tasks at a higher rate than a load sharing algorithm, the higher overhead incurred by load balancing algorithms may outweigh this potential performance improvement.

Typically, load distributing algorithms have four policy components: (1) a transfer policy that determines whether a node is in a suitable state to participate in a task transfer, (2) a selection policy that determines *which* task should be transferred, (3) a location policy that determines to which node a task selected for transfer should be sent, and (4) an information policy which is responsible for triggering the collection of system state information.

Based on which type of nodes initiate load distributing actions, load distributing algorithms have been widely referred to as sender-initiated, receiver-initiated, and symmetrically initiated algorithms. In sender-initiated algorithms, senders (overloaded nodes) look for receivers (underloaded or idle nodes) to transfer their load. In receiver-initiated policies, receivers solicit load from senders. A symmetrically initiated policy is a combination of both, where load sharing actions are triggered by the demand for extra processing power or extra work.

The task transfers performed for load distributing can be of two types, nonpreemptive and preemptive. In nonpreemptive transfers, tasks that have not yet begun execution are transferred. Preemptive transfers involve the transfer of tasks that have already begun execution. These transfers are expensive compared to nonpreemptive transfers, because the state of the tasks must be transferred to the new location also.

In this chapter, we described several load sharing algorithms, their performance, and policies employed in several implementations of load distributing schemes. In addition, we discussed how several task migration implementations have tried to minimize the delay due to the transfer of state.

11.14 FURTHER READING

In [30], Rommel presents a general formula for the probability that any one node in the system is underloaded while some other node in the system is overloaded. This probability can be used to define the likelihood of load sharing success in a distributed system.

The availability of idle CPU cycles in a network of workstations is discussed by Mutka and Livny in [26] and by Mutka in [27].

A discussion on the selection of tasks suitable for remote execution can be found in [28]. Utopia [42] is a load sharing facility for large, heterogeneous distributed systems.

In [22], Lin and Keller present a gradient model load balancing method for a multiprocessor system. Tilborg and Wittie describe a wave scheduling scheme for a network of computers in [38]. In [2], Baumgartner and Wah present a load balancing scheme which has been implemented in a network of Sun workstations.

In [13], Hac discusses an algorithm for improving performance through file replication, file migration, and process migration.

In [17], Kremien and Kramer study the performance, efficiency, and stability of many load sharing algorithms.

In [5], Casavant and Kuhl describe a taxonomy of scheduling schemes for distributed systems. In [12], Eskicioglu presents a bibliography of process migration schemes. Smith discusses a survey of process migration schemes in [33]. Jacqmot and Milgrom present a survey of load distributing schemes that have been implemented on UNIX-based systems in [15].

PROBLEMS

11.1. Identify the actions that belong to the transfer policy actions in the load sharing of the V-System.

11.2. Identify the actions that belong to the location policy actions in the load sharing of the V-System.

11.3. Discuss how well the three load sharing implementations of Sec. 11.10 satisfy the scalability criterion.

11.4. Under what condition will process migration in the V-System fail to satisfy the stability criterion discussed in Sec. 11.5.

11.5. Predict the performance of the receiver-initiated load sharing algorithm when the entire system workload is generated at only a few nodes in the system instead of equally at all the nodes in the system. (Hint: performance depends on how successful receivers will be in locating senders.)

11.6. Identify all the overheads in a load sharing policy.

11.7. Sender-initiated algorithms cause system instability at high system loads. Predict, analytically, at what system load the instability will occur. Assume Probelimit = 5, average service requirement of a task = 1 second, overhead incurred by a processor to poll or to reply to a poll = 3 milliseconds.

REFERENCES

1. Artsy, Y., and R. Finkel, "Designing A Process Migration Facility: The Charlotte Experience," *IEEE Computer*, vol. 22, no. 9, Sept. 1989, pp. 47–56.
2. Baumgartner, J. M., and B. W. Wah, "GAMMON: A Load Balancing Strategy for Local Computer Systems with Multiaccess Networks," *IEEE Transactions on Computers*, vol. 38, no. 8, Aug. 1989, pp. 1098–1109.

3. Bryant, R. M., and R. A. Finkel, "A Stable Distributed Scheduling Algorithm," *Proceedings of the 2nd International Conference on Distributed Computing Systems*, Apr. 1981, pp. 314–323.

4. Cabrera, L., "The Influence of Workload on Load Balancing Strategies," *Proceedings of the Summer USENIX Conference*, June 1986, pp. 446–458.

5. Casavant, T. L., and J. G. Kuhl, "A Taxonomy of Scheduling in General-Purpose Distributed Computing Systems," *IEEE Transactions on Software Engineering*, vol. 14, no. 2, Feb. 1988, pp. 141–154.

6. Casavant, T. L., and J. G. Kuhl, "Effects of Response and Stability on Scheduling in Distributed Computing Systems," *IEEE Transactions on Software Engineering*, vol. 14, no. 11, Nov. 1988, pp. 1578–1587.

7. Chou, T. C. K., and J. A. Abraham, "Load Balancing in Distributed Systems," *IEEE Transactions on Software Engineering*, vol. 8, no. 4, July 1982.

8. Douglis, F., and J. Ousterhout, "Process Migration in the Sprite Operating System," *Proceedings of the 7th International Conference on Distributed Computing Systems*, Sept. 1987, pp. 18–25.

9. Douglis, F., and J. Ousterhout, "Transparent Process Migration: Design Alternatives and the Sprite Implementation," *Software Practice and Experience*, vol. 21, no. 8, Aug. 1991, pp. 757–785.

10. Eager, D. L., E. D. Lazowska, and J. Zahorjan, "A Comparison of Receiver-Initiated and Sender-Initiated Adaptive Load Sharing," *Performance Evaluation*, North-Holland, vol. 6, no. 1, March 1986, pp. 53–68.

11. Eager, D. L., E. D. Lazowska, and J. Zahorjan, "Adaptive Load Sharing in Homogeneous Distributed Systems," *IEEE Transactions on Software Engineering*, vol. 12, no. 5, May 1986, pp. 662–675.

12. Eskicioglu, M. R., "Process Migration: An Annotated Bibliography," *Newsletter, IEEE Computer Society Technical Committee on Operating Systems and Application Environments*, vol. 4, no. 4, Winter 1990.

13. Hac, A., "A Distributed Algorithm for Performance Improvement Through File Replication, File Migration, and Process Migration," *IEEE Transactions on Software Engineering*, vol. 15, no. 11, Nov. 1989, pp. 1459–1470.

14. Hagmann, R., "Process Server: Sharing Processing Power in a Workstation Environment," *Proceedings of the 6th International Conference on Distributed Computing Systems*, May 1986, pp. 260–267.

15. Jacqmot, C., and E. Milgrom, "UNIX and Load Balancing: A Survey," *European UNIX User Group, Spring Conference*, Apr. 1989, pp. 1–15.

16. Kleinrock, L., *Queueing Systems*, vol. 1: Theory, John Wiley & Sons, New York, 1975.

17. Kremien, O., and J. Kramer, "Methodical Analysis of Adaptive Load Sharing Algorithms," *IEEE Transactions on Parallel and Distributed Systems*, vol. 1, no. 2, Nov. 1992, pp. 747–760.

18. Krueger, P., *Distributed Scheduling for a Changing Environment*. PhD thesis, University of Wisconsin-Madison, available as Technical Report 780, June 1988.

19. Krueger, P., and R. Chawla, "The Stealth Distributed Scheduler," *Proceedings of the 11th International Conference on Distributed Computing Systems*, May 1991, pp. 336–343.

20. Krueger, P., and R. Finkel, "An Adaptive Load Balancing Algorithm for a Multicomputer," Technical Report 539, University of Wisconsin-Madison, Apr. 1984.

21. Krueger, P., and M. Livny, "The Diverse Objectives of Distributed Scheduling Policies," *Proceedings of the 7th International Conference on Distributed Computing Systems*, Sept. 1987, pp. 242–249.

22. Lin, F. C. H., and R. M. Keller, "The Gradient Model Load Balancing Method," *IEEE Transactions on Software Engineering*, vol. 13, no. 1, Jan. 1987, pp. 32–38.

23. Litzkow, M. J., M. Livny, and M. W. Mutka, "Condor—A Hunter of Idle Workstations," *Proceedings of the 8th International Conference on Distributed Computing Systems*, June 1988, pp. 104–111.

24. Livny, M., and M. Melman, "Load Balancing in Homogeneous Broadcast Distributed Systems," *Proceedings of the ACM Computer Network Performance Symposium*, Apr. 1982, pp. 47–55.

25. Mandelberg, K. I., and V. S. Sunderam, "Process Migration in UNIX Networks," *USENIX Winter Conference*, Feb. 1988, pp. 357–363.

26. Mutka, M., and M. Livny, "Profiling Workstation's Available Capacity for Remote Execution," *Proceedings of PERFORMANCE '87*, Dec. 1987, pp. 529–543.

27. Mutka, M. W., "Estimating Capacity for Sharing in a Privately Owned Workstation Environment," *IEEE Transaction on Software Engineering*, vol. 18, no. 4, Apr. 1992, pp. 319–328.

28. Osser, W., "Automatic Process Selection for Load Balancing," Technical Report UCSC-CRL-92-21, University of California, Santa Cruz, June 1992.

29. Ousterhout, J. K., A. R. Cherenson, F. Douglis, M. N. Nelson, and B. B. Welch, "The Sprite Network Operating System," *IEEE Computer*, Feb. 1988, pp. 23–35.

30. Rommel, C. G., "The Probability of Load Balancing Success in a Homogeneous Network," *IEEE Transactions on Software Engineering*, vol. 17, no. 9, Sept. 1991, pp. 922–933.

31. Shivaratri, N. G., and P. Krueger, "Two Adaptive Location Policies for Global Scheduling," *Proceedings of the 10th International Conference on Distributed Computing Systems*, May 1990, pp. 502–509.

32. Shivaratri, N. G., P. Krueger, and M. Singhal, "Load Distributing in Locally Distributed Systems," *IEEE Computer*, vol. 25, no. 12, Dec. 1992, pp. 33–44.

33. Smith, J. M., "A Survey of Process Migration Mechanisms," Technical Report CUCS-324-88, Columbia University, 1988. Also in *ACM SIGOPS Operating Systems Review*, July 1988, pp. 28–40.

34. Stankovic, J. A., and I. S. Sidhu, "An Adaptive Bidding Algorithms for Processes, Clusters, and Distributed Groups," *Proceedings of the 4th International Conference on Distributed Computing Systems*, May 1984, pp. 49–59.

35. Stumm, M., The Design and Implementation of a Decentralized Scheduling Facility for a Workstation Cluster. *Proceedings of the 2nd Conference on Computer Workstations,* March 1988, pp. 12–22.

36. Svensson, A., "History, an Intelligent Load Sharing Filter," *Proceedings of the 10th International Conference on Distributed Computing Systems*, May 1990, pp. 546–553.

37. Theimer, M. M., K. A. Lantz, and D. R. Cheriton, "Preemptable Remote Execution Facilities for the V-System," *Proceedings of the 10th ACM Symposium on Operating Systems Principles*, Dec. 1985, pp. 2–12.

38. Van Tilborg, A. M., and L. D. Wittie, "Wave Scheduling—Decentralized Scheduling of Task Forces in Multicomputers," *IEEE Transactions on Computers*, vol. 33, no. 9, Sept. 1984, pp. 835–844.

39. Zayas, E. R., "Attacking the Process Migration Bottleneck," *Proceedings of the 11th ACM Symposium on Operating Systems Principles*, Nov. 1987, pp. 13–24.

40. Zhao, W., and K. Ramamritham, "Distributed Scheduling Using Bidding and Focussed Addressing," *Proceedings of the Real-Time Systems Symposium*, Dec. 1985, pp. 103–111.

41. Zhou, S., "An Experimental Assessment of Resource Queue Lengths as Load Indices," *Proceedings of the 1987 Winter USENIX Conference, Washington, D.C.*, Jan. 1987, pp. 73–82.

42. Zhou, S., Z. Zheng, J. Wang, and P. Delisle, "Utopia: A Load Sharing Facility for Large, Heterogeneous Distributed Computer Systems," Technical Report M5S 1A1, Computer Systems Research Institute, University of Toronto, Apr. 1992.

PART
IV

FAILURE RECOVERY AND FAULT TOLERANCE

CHAPTER
12

RECOVERY

12.1 INTRODUCTION

Recovery in computer systems refers to restoring a system to its normal operational state. Recovery may be as simple as restarting a failed computer or restarting failed processes. However, from the following discussion, it will be clear that recovery is generally a very complicated process.

In general, resources are allocated to executing processes in a computer. For example, a process has memory allocated to it and a process may have locked shared resources, such as files and memory. Under such circumstances, if a process fails, it is imperative that the resources allocated to the failed process be reclaimed so that they can be allocated to other processes. If a failed process has modified a database, then it is important that all the modifications made to the database by the failed process are undone. On the other hand, if a process has executed for some time before failing, it would be preferable to restart the process from the point of its failure and resume its execution. By restarting from the point of failure, the situation of having to reexecute the process from the beginning is avoided, which may be a time consuming and expensive operation.

Distributed systems provide enhanced performance and increased availability (see Sec. 4.2). One way of realizing enhanced performance is through the concurrent execution of many processes, which cooperate in performing a task. If one or more of the cooperating processes fail, then the effects due to the interactions of the failed processes with the other processes must be undone, or every failed process would have to restart from an appropriate state. Increased availability in distributed systems is realized mainly through replication (e.g., data, processes, and hardware components can be replicated). If a site fails, copies of data stored at that site may miss updates, thus becoming inconsistent with the rest of the system when it becomes operational. Recovery in such cases involves the question of how not to expose the system to data inconsistencies and bring back the failed site to an up-to-date state consistent with the rest of the system.

In this chapter, (1) the basic causes that lead to failures and the types of failures that occur in a computer system are introduced. (2) The question of how a process can recover from failure when it does not interact with another process is discussed. (3) The effects of a process failing on other processes in concurrent systems, and techniques to recover cooperating processes without them having to resume execution from the beginning, are described. (4) Finally, recovery in distributed database systems is discussed.

12.2 BASIC CONCEPTS

A *system* consists of a set of hardware and software components and is designed to provide a specified service. The components of a system may themselves be systems together with interrelationships [32]. *Failure* of a system occurs when the system does not perform its services in the manner specified [32]. An *erroneous state* of the system is a state which could lead to a system failure by a sequence of valid state transitions [22]. A *fault* is an anomalous physical condition. The causes of a fault include design errors (such as errors in system specification or implementation), manufacturing problems, damage fatigue or other deterioration, and external disturbances (such as harsh environmental conditions, electromagnetic interference, unanticipated inputs or system misuse) [27]. An *error* is that part of the system state which differs from its intended value [32].

From the above definitions, it can be seen that *an error is a manifestation of a fault in a system, which could lead to system failure* (Fig. 12.1). Therefore, to recover from a system failure, we need to rid the system state of errors. In other words, *failure recovery* is a process that involves restoring an erroneous state to an error-free state.

12.3 CLASSIFICATION OF FAILURES

Failures in a computer system can be classified as follows:

PROCESS FAILURE. In a process failure, the computation results in an incorrect outcome, the process causes the system state to deviate from specifications, the process may fail to progress, etc. Examples of errors causing processes to fail are deadlocks, timeouts, protection violation, wrong input provided by a user, consistency violations (which can happen if an optimistic concurrency control technique is employed). Depending on the type of the error causing a process to fail, a failed process may be aborted or restarted from a prior state. For example, a deadlocked process can be restarted from a prior state, where it can try to acquire the resources again. On the other hand, a wrong input in the initial stages may require a process to be aborted. In this chapter, we do

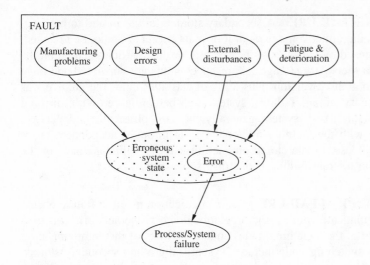

FIGURE 12.1
An error is a manifestation of fault and can lead to failure.

not consider process failures where processes behave maliciously. A discussion on that type of process behavior can be found in Chap. 8.

SYSTEM FAILURE. A system failure occurs when the processor fails to execute. It is caused by software errors and hardware problems (such as CPU failure, main memory failure, bus failure, power failure, etc.). In the case of a system failure, the system is stopped and restarted in a correct state. The correct state may be some predefined state or a prior state (checkpoint) of the system saved on nonvolatile storage. In this chapter, we assume that systems behave as fail-stop processors [33]. These type of systems have very simple failure mode operating characteristics. The only visible effects of a failure in such a system are: the system stops executing; and the internal state and contents of the volatile storage belonging to the system are lost.

A system failure can further be classified as follows [9].

- An *amnesia* failure occurs when a system restarts in a predefined state that does not depend upon the state of the system before its failure.

- A *partial-amnesia* failure occurs when a system restarts in a state wherein a part of the state is the same as the state before the failure and the rest of the state is predefined, i.e., it does not depend upon the state of the system before its failure. This type of failure typically occurs in file servers when a file server crashes and restarts, or when a system is restarted from a checkpoint.

- A *pause* failure occurs when a system restarts in the same state it was in before the failure.

- A *halting* failure occurs when a crashed system never restarts.

SECONDARY STORAGE FAILURE.   A secondary storage failure is said to have occurred when the stored data (either some parts of it or in its entirety) cannot be accessed. This failure is usually caused by parity error, head crash, or dust particles settled on the medium. In the case of a secondary storage failure, its contents are corrupted and must be reconstructed from an archive version, plus a log of activities since the archive was taken. To tolerate secondary storage failures, systems can be configured with mirrored disk systems [3]. A mirrored disk system generally has two physically independent disks that communicate with the memory and/or the CPU through independent buses and controllers. This enables the data stored on each disk to be a mirror image of the other. Thus, a system can tolerate failure of one disk subsystem.

COMMUNICATION MEDIUM FAILURE.   A communication medium failure occurs when a site cannot communicate with another operational site in the network. It is usually caused by the failure of the switching nodes and/or the links of the communicating system. The failure of a switching node includes system failure and secondary storage failure, and a link failure includes physical rupture and noise in the communication channels. Note that a communication medium failure (although it depends upon the topology and the connectivity) may not cause a total shut down of communication facilities. For example, a communication medium failure may simply cause a message loss, the receipt of a message with some errors, or the partition of a network where a subset of sites may be unable to communicate with the sites in another subset, though sites within a subset can communicate with each other.

12.4   BACKWARD AND FORWARD ERROR RECOVERY

Recall that an error is that part of the state that differs from its intended value and can lead to a system failure, and failure recovery is a process that involves restoring an erroneous state to an error-free state. There are two approaches for restoring an erroneous state to an error-free state [32]:

- If the nature of errors and damages caused by faults can be completely and accurately assessed, then it is possible to remove those errors in the process's (system's) state and enable the process (system) to move forward. This technique is known as *forward-error recovery*.
- If it is not possible to foresee the nature of faults and to remove all the errors in the process's (system's) state, then the process's (system's) state can be restored to a previous error-free state of the process (system). This technique is known as *backward-error recovery*.

Note that backward-error recovery is simpler than forward-error recovery as it is independent of the fault and the errors caused by the fault. Thus, a system can recover from an arbitrary fault by restoring to a previous state. This generality enables backward-error recovery to be provided as a general recovery mechanism to any type of system.

The major problems associated with the backward-error recovery approach are:

- Performance penalty: The overhead to restore a process (system) state to a prior state can be quite high.
- There is no guarantee that faults will not occur again when processing begins from a prior state.
- Some component of the system state may be unrecoverable. For example, cash dispensed at an automatic teller machine cannot be recovered.

The forward-error recovery technique, on the other hand, incurs less overhead because only those parts of the state that deviate from the intended value need to be corrected. However, this technique can be used only where the damages due to faults can be correctly assessed, and hence it is not a concept as general as the backward-error recovery and cannot be provided as a general mechanism for error recovery. In the forthcoming sections, we focus on backward-error recovery and several techniques to implement it in detail.

12.5 BACKWARD-ERROR RECOVERY: BASIC APPROACHES

In backward-error recovery, a process is restored to a prior state in the hope that the prior state is free of errors [32]. The points in the execution of a process to which the process can later be restored are known as *recovery points*. A recovery point is said to be restored when the current state of a process is replaced by the state of the process at the recovery point. The above concepts and the discussion that follow are also applicable at the system level. Recovery done at the process level is simply a subset of the actions necessary to recover the entire system. In a system recovery, all the user processes that were active need to be restored to their respective recovery points and data (in secondary storage) modified by the processes need to be restored to a proper state.

There are two ways to implement backward-error recovery, namely, the operation-based approach and the state-based approach [22]. These approaches are explained in the context of the following system model.

SYSTEM MODEL. The system is assumed to consist of a single machine. The machine is connected to a secondary storage system and a stable storage system (see Fig. 12.2). A storage that does not lose information in the event of system failure is referred to as a *stable* storage. Whenever a process accesses a data object stored on the secondary storage, the data object is brought into the main memory if it is not already there. If the access is a write operation, the copy of the object in the main memory is updated. The data object in the secondary storage is eventually updated when the copy of the object in the main memory is flushed to the disk by the paging scheme or when the process updating the object terminates. The stable storage is used to store the logs (defined later) and recovery points. The contents of both the stable storage and secondary storage survive system failures. However, the contents of the stable storage are much more

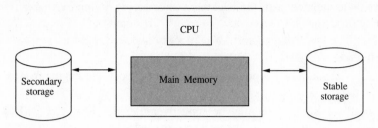

FIGURE 12.2
A system model.

secure than those of the secondary storage. It is assumed that the data on the secondary storage is archived periodically.

12.5.1 The Operation-based Approach

In the operation-based approach, all the modifications that are made to the state of a process are recorded in sufficient detail so that a previous state of the process can be restored by reversing all the changes made to the state. The record of the system activity is known as an *audit trail* or a *log* [32].

Consider a transaction based environment where transactions update a database. In such an environment, it is desirable to be able to commit or undo updates on a per-transaction basis. Commit is an action which indicates that the process or transaction updating the object has successfully completed, and therefore the changes done to the database can be made permanent. (Commit actions are explained in Chap. 13.) Note that even before a transaction commits, its updates may be recorded in the database because of the underlying paging scheme. Therefore, if a transaction does not commit, its database updates should be undone. Moreover, if a part of the database is lost due to a storage media error, it should be possible to reconstruct that part. We next describe the updating-in-place scheme proposed in [11], in which the above requirements can be satisfied.

UPDATING-IN-PLACE. Under the updating-in-place scheme, every update (write) operation to an object updates the object and results in a log to be recorded in a stable storage which has enough information to completely undo and redo the operation. The information recorded includes: (1) the name of the object, (2) the old state of the object (used for UNDO), and (3) the new state of the object (used for REDO). A recoverable update operation can be implemented as a collection of operations as follows:

- A *do* operation, which does the action (update) and writes a log record.
- An *undo* operation, which, given a log record written by a *do* operation, undoes the action performed by the *do* operation.
- A *redo* operation, which, given a log record written by a *do* operation, redoes the action specified by the *do* operation.
- An optional *display* operation, which displays the log record.

When a transaction is not committed or fails, the changes made by the transaction to the database can be undone by using *undo* operations. On the other hand, if a portion of the database is to be reconstructed, it can be reconstructed by performing *redo* operations on that previously archived portion of the database.

The major problem with the updating-in-place is that a *do* operation cannot be undone if the system crashes after an update operation but before the log record is stored. This problem is overcome by the write-ahead-log protocol [11].

THE WRITE-AHEAD-LOG PROTOCOL. In the write ahead log protocol, a recoverable update operation is implemented by the following operations:

- Update an object only after the *undo* log is recorded.
- Before committing the updates, *redo* and *undo* logs are recorded.

On restarting a system after failure (due to hardware failure or any other reason), it may be necessary to undo the changes made by the transactions that were in progress at the time of failure. Moreover, on restart, *redo* operations may have to be performed if the objects updated were still in the main memory at the time of the system failure. Therefore, both *undo* and *redo* actions should work properly, even under repetitive failures, whether updating-in-place or write-ahead-log protocol is used. Note also that writing a log record on every update operation is expensive in terms of storage requirement and CPU overhead incurred, especially if failures are rare.

12.5.2 State-based Approach

In the state-based approach for recovery, the complete state of a process is saved when a recovery point is established and recovering a process involves reinstating its saved state and resuming the execution of the process from that state [8, 32]. The process of saving state is also referred to as *checkpointing* or *taking a checkpoint*. The recovery point at which checkpointing occurs is often referred to as a *checkpoint*. The process of restoring a process to a prior-state is referred to as *rolling back* the process. Note that since rolling back a process and resuming its execution from a prior state incurs overhead and delays the completion of the process, it is desirable to rollback a process to a state as recent as possible. Therefore, it is customary to take many checkpoints over the execution of a process.

A NOTE. Readers should not construe that the state- and operation-based approaches are mutually exclusive. They can be combined together to minimize the amount of rollback in the event of a failure. Section 12.9 describes a technique that makes use of both approaches.

SHADOW PAGES. A special case of the state-based recovery approach is the technique based on shadow pages [21]. Under this technique, only a part of the system state is saved to facilitate recovery. Whenever a process wants to modify an object, the page containing the object is duplicated and is maintained on stable storage. From that point onwards, only one of the copies undergoes all the modifications done by the process. The other unmodified copy is known as the *shadow page*. If the process fails, the modified copy is discarded to restore the database to a proper state. If the process successfully commits, then the shadow page is discarded and the modified page is made part of the database.

12.6 RECOVERY IN CONCURRENT SYSTEMS

In concurrent systems, several processes cooperate by exchanging information to accomplish a task. The information exchange can be through a shared memory in the case of shared memory machines (e.g., multiprocessor systems) or through messages in the case of a distributed system. In such systems, if one of the cooperating processes fails and resumes execution from a recovery point, then the effects it has caused at other processes due to the information it has exchanged with them after establishing the recovery point will have to be undone. To undo the effects caused by a failed process at an active process, the active process must also rollback to an earlier state. Thus, in concurrent systems, all cooperating processes need to establish recovery points. Rolling back processes in concurrent systems is more difficult than in the case of a single process. The following discussion illustrates how the rolling back of processes can cause further problems.

12.6.1 Orphan Messages and the Domino Effect

Consider the system activity illustrated in Fig. 12.3. X, Y, and Z are three processes that cooperate by exchanging information (shown by the arrows). Each symbol '[' marks a recovery point to which a process can be rolled back in the event of a failure.

If process X is to be rolled back, it can be rolled back to the recovery point x_3 without affecting any other process. Suppose that Y fails after sending message m and is rolled back to y_2. In this case, the receipt of m is recorded in x_3, but the sending of m is not recorded in y_2. Now we have a situation where X has received message

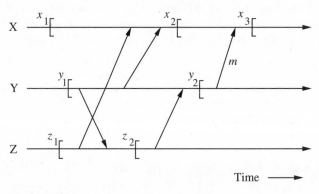

FIGURE 12.3
Domino effect.

m from Y, but Y has no record of sending it, which corresponds to an inconsistent state. Under such circumstances, m is referred to as an *orphan* message and process X must also roll back. X must roll back because Y interacted with X after establishing its recovery point y_2. When Y is rolled back to y_2, the event that is responsible for the interaction is undone. Therefore, all the effects at X caused by the interaction must also be undone. This can be achieved by rolling back X to recovery point x_2. Likewise, it can be seen that, if Z is rolled back, all three processes must roll back to their very first recovery points, namely, x_1, y_1, and z_1. This effect, where rolling back one process causes one or more other processes to roll back, is known as the *domino effect* [32], and orphan messages are the cause.

12.6.2 Lost Messages

Suppose that checkpoints x_1 and y_1 (Fig. 12.4) are chosen as the recovery points for processes X and Y, respectively. In this case, the event that sent message m is recorded in x_1, while the event of its receipt at Y is not recorded in y_1. If Y fails after receiving message m, the system is restored to state $\{x_1, y_1\}$, in which message m is *lost* as process X is past the point where it sends message m. This condition can also arise if m is lost in the communication channel and processes X and Y are in state x_1 and y_1, respectively. Both the above conditions are indistinguishable.

12.6.3 Problem of Livelocks

In rollback recovery, livelock is a situation in which a single failure can cause an infinite number of rollbacks, preventing the system from making progress [19]. A livelock situation in a distributed system is illustrated in Fig. 12.5.

Figure 12.5(a) illustrates the activity of two processes X and Y until the failure of Y. Process Y fails before receiving message n_1, sent by X. When Y rolls back to y_1, there is no record of sending message m_1, hence X must rollback to x_1. When process Y recovers, it sends out m_2 and receives n_1 (see Fig. 12.5(b)). Process X, after resuming from x_1, sends n_2 and receives m_2. However, because X rolled back, there is no record of sending n_1 and hence Y has to roll back for the second time. This forces X to rollback too, as it has received m_2, and there is no record of sending m_2 at Y. This situation can repeat indefinitely, preventing the system from making any progress.

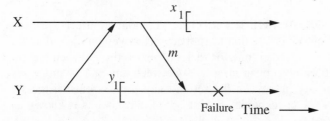

FIGURE 12.4
Message loss due to roll back recovery.

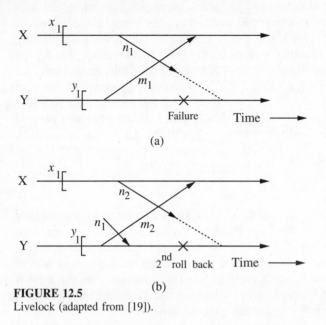

FIGURE 12.5
Livelock (adapted from [19]).

In view of these problems, operation-based or state-based recovery techniques are not adequate in locating and/or establishing usable recovery points for all the cooperating processes. There is a need for coordination among the processes, either at the time of establishing checkpoints or at the beginning of a recovery. We devote the rest of this chapter to the discussion of checkpointing and recovery in distributed systems.

12.7 CONSISTENT SET OF CHECKPOINTS

From the previous discussion, it is clear that checkpointing in distributed systems involves taking a checkpoint by all the processes (sites) or at least by a set of processes (sites) that interact with one another in performing a distributed computation. Typically, in distributed systems, all the sites save their local states, which are known as *local checkpoints,* and the process of saving local states is called *local checkpointing*. All the local checkpoints, one from each site, collectively form a *global checkpoint*.

STRONGLY CONSISTENT SET OF CHECKPOINTS. The domino effect is caused by orphan messages, which themselves are due to rollbacks. To overcome the domino effect, a set of local checkpoints is needed (one for each process in the set) such that no information flow takes place (i.e., no orphan messages) between any pair of processes in the set, as well as between any process in the set and any process outside the set during the interval spanned by the checkpoints. Such a set of checkpoints is known as a *recovery line* or a *strongly consistent set of checkpoints* [32].

In Fig. 12.6, the set $\{x_1, y_1, z_1\}$ is a *strongly* consistent set of checkpoints and the thinly dotted lines delineate the interval spanned by the checkpoints. A strongly

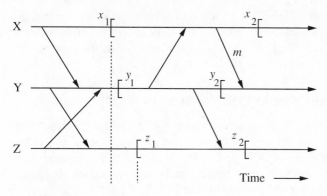

FIGURE 12.6
Consistent set of checkpoints.

consistent set of checkpoints corresponds to a strongly consistent global state (discussed in Sec. 5.6) wherein all messages have been delivered and processed, and no message is in transit. Notice that, processes X, Y, and Z can be rolled back to their respective checkpoints x_1, y_1, and z_1 and resume execution in the event of a failure. No further rollbacks due to the domino effect would be necessary as no information exchange took place in the interval spanned by the set of checkpoints. That is, no local checkpoint includes an effect whose cause would be undone due to the rollback of another process.

CONSISTENT SET OF CHECKPOINTS. Suppose that Y fails after receiving message m. If Y restarts from checkpoint y_2, message m is lost due to rollback. Note that the set $\{x_2, y_2, z_2\}$ is not a strongly consistent set of checkpoints, rather it is referred to as a *consistent set of checkpoints*. A consistent set of ckeckpoints is similar to a consistent global state (discussed in Sec. 5.6) in that it requires that each message recorded as received in a checkpoint (state) should also be recorded as sent in another checkpoint (state). Therefore, systems that do not establish a strongly consistent set of checkpoints have to deal with lost messages during roll back recovery. While the systems which establish strongly consistent set of checkpoints do not have to deal with lost messages during roll back recovery, they experience delays during the checkpointing process as processes cannot exchange messages while checkpointing is in progress.

12.7.1 A Simple Method for Taking a Consistent Set of Checkpoints

Assume that the action of taking a checkpoint and the action of sending or receiving a message are indivisible; that is, they are not interrupted by any other events. (See atomic actions in Sec. 13.3). If every process takes a checkpoint after sending every message, the set of the most recent checkpoints is always consistent. However, it is not strongly consistent [19]. The set of latest checkpoints is consistent because the latest checkpoint at every process corresponds to a state where all the messages recorded as received in it have already been recorded elsewhere as sent. Therefore, rolling back a process to its latest checkpoint would not result in any orphan messages, which would cause the system state to be inconsistent. However, taking a checkpoint after each message is sent is expensive, so one may attempt to reduce the overhead in the above method by taking a checkpoint after every K (K > 1) messages sent. This method, however, suffers from the domino effect (see Problem 12.2).

12.8   SYNCHRONOUS CHECKPOINTING AND RECOVERY

We now describe a checkpointing and recovery technique proposed by Koo and Toueg [19] that takes a consistent set of checkpoints and avoids livelock problems during recovery. The algorithm's approach is said to be *synchronous*, as the processes involved coordinate their local checkpointing actions such that the set of all recent checkpoints in the system is guaranteed to be consistent [17].

12.8.1   The Checkpoint Algorithm

The checkpoint algorithm assumes the following characteristics for the distributed system:

- Processes communicate by exchanging messages through communication channels.
- Channels are FIFO in nature. End-to-end protocols (such as sliding window protocols [41]) are assumed to cope with message loss due to rollback recovery (Fig. 12.4) and communication failure. (Another way to handle message loss is to have processes log messages in stable storage before sending them. A process encountering message loss due to a rollback can request the retransmission of the message. This scheme, however, requires that every process record the identity of the last message it has received from each process on stable storage.)
- Communication failures do not partition the network.

The checkpoint algorithm takes two kinds of checkpoints on stable storage, permanent and tentative. A permanent checkpoint is a local checkpoint at a process and is a part of a consistent global checkpoint. A tentative checkpoint is a temporary checkpoint that is made a permanent checkpoint on the successful termination of the checkpoint algorithm. Processes roll back only to their permanent checkpoint.

The checkpoint algorithm assumes that a single process invokes the algorithm, as opposed to several processes concurrently invoking the algorithm to take permanent checkpoints. Furthermore, the algorithm assures that no site in the distributed system fails during the execution of the algorithm.

The algorithm has two phases.

First Phase. An initiating process P_i takes a tentative checkpoint and requests all the processes to take tentative checkpoints. Each process informs P_i whether it succeeded in taking a tentative checkpoint. A process says "no" to a request if it fails to take a checkpoint, which could be due to several reasons, depending upon the underlying application. If P_i learns that all the processes have successfully taken tentative checkpoints, P_i decides that all tentative checkpoints should be made permanent; otherwise, P_i decides that all the tentative checkpoints should be discarded.

Second Phase. P_i informs all the processes of the decision it reached at the end of the first phase. A process, on receiving the message from P_i, will act accordingly. Therefore, either all or none of the processes take permanent checkpoints.

The algorithm requires that every process, once it has taken a tentative checkpoint, not send messages related to the underlying computation until it is informed of P_i's decision.

Correctness. A set of permanent checkpoints taken by this algorithm is consistent because:

- Either all or none of the processes take permanent checkpoints.
- A set of checkpoints will be inconsistent if there is a record of a message received but not of the event sending it. This will not happen as no process sends messages after taking a tentative checkpoint until the receipt of the initiating process's decision, by which time all processes would have taken checkpoints.

OPTIMIZATION. While the above protocol takes a consistent set of checkpoints, it may cause a process to take a checkpoint even when it is not necessary (note that taking a checkpoint is an expensive operation).

For example, consider the system activity shown in Fig. 12.7. The set $\{x_1, y_1, z_1\}$ is a consistent set of checkpoints. Suppose process X decides to initiate the check-pointing algorithm after receiving message m. It takes a tentative checkpoint x_2 and sends "take tentative checkpoint messages" to processes Y and Z, causing Y and Z to take checkpoints y_2 and z_2, respectively. Now $\{x_2, y_2, z_2\}$ forms a consistent set of checkpoints. Note, however, that $\{x_2, y_2, z_1\}$ also forms a consistent set of checkpoints. (The checkpoint algorithm uses the weaker definition of consistency which requires that every message recorded as "received" in a checkpoint should also be recorded as "sent" in another checkpoint, and not vice versa [19].) In our example, process Y should take

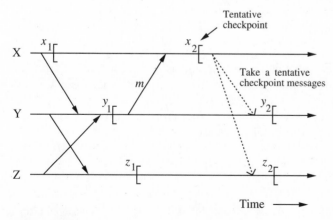

FIGURE 12.7
Checkpoints taken unnecessarily.

a checkpoint since x_2 records the receipt of message m, and y_1 does not record the sending of message m. However, there is no need for process Z to take checkpoint x_2 because Z has not sent any message since its last checkpoint. A process can decide whether it is necessary to take a checkpoint or not with the help of a labeling scheme described below.

Messages that are sent by the checkpointing or rollback-recovery algorithms (discussed later) are referred to as *control* messages. Messages that are sent as a part of the underlying computation are referred to as *messages*. Every outgoing message m has a field for a label, denoted by $m.l$. Each process uses monotonically increasing labels in its outgoing messages. The following terminology will be used in describing the algorithm:

$$\perp = \text{smallest label}$$
$$\top = \text{largest label.}$$

For any two processes X and Y, let m be the last message that X received from Y after X has taken its last permanent or tentative checkpoint. Then

$$last\_label\_rcvd_X[Y] = \begin{cases} m.l & \text{if } m \text{ exists} \\ \perp & \text{otherwise} \end{cases}$$

Let m be the first message that X sent to Y after X took its last permanent or tentative checkpoint. Then

$$first\_label\_sent_X[Y] = \begin{cases} m.l & \text{if } m \text{ exists} \\ \perp & \text{otherwise} \end{cases}$$

Whenever X requests Y to take a tentative checkpoint, X sends $last\_label\_rcvd_X[Y]$ along with its request; Y takes a tentative checkpoint only if

$$last\_label\_rcvd_X[Y] \geq first\_label\_sent_Y[X] > \perp$$

The above condition simply tells Y that the checkpoint at X has recorded the receipt of one or more messages sent by Y after Y took its last checkpoint. Therefore, Y should take a checkpoint to record the events that send those messages.

Finally, we define $ckpt\_cohort_X$ as the set of all processes that should be asked to take checkpoints when X decides to take a checkpoint.

$$ckpt\_cohort_X = \{Y \mid last\_label\_rcvd_X[Y] > \perp\}$$

This set simply indicates all the processes from which X has received messages after it has taken its last checkpoint. If X takes a checkpoint, then those processes should also take checkpoints to record the sending of those messages.

OUTLINE OF THE ALGORITHM

Initial state at all processes p:
>   for all processes q do $first\_label\_sent_p[q] := \bot$;
>
> $OK\_to\_take\_ckpt_p = \begin{cases} \text{``yes'' if } p \text{ is willing to take a checkpoint} \\ \text{``no'' \quad otherwise} \end{cases}$

At initiator process P_i:
>   for all processes $p \in ckpt\_cohort_{P_i}$ do
>   send $Take\_a\_tentative\_ckpt(P_i, last\_label\_rcvd_{P_i}[p])$ message;
>   if all processes replied "yes" then
>   for all processes $p \in ckpt\_cohort_{P_i}$ do
>   send $Make\_tentative\_ckpt\_permanent$;
>   else
>   for all processes $p \in ckpt\_cohort_{P_i}$ do
>   send $Undo\_tentative\_ckpt$.

At all processes p:
Upon receiving $Take\_a\_tentative\_ckpt(q, last\_label\_rcvd_q[p])$ message from q do
>   begin
>   if $OK\_to\_take\_ckpt_p$ = "yes" AND
> $last\_label\_rcvd_q[p] \geq first\_label\_sent_p[q] > \bot$ then
>   begin
>   take a tentative checkpoint;
>   for all processes $r \in ckpt\_cohort_p$ do
>   send $Take\_a\_tentative\_ckpt(p, last\_label\_rcvd_p[r])$ message;
>   if all processes $r \in ckpt\_cohort_p$ replied "yes" then
> $OK\_to\_take\_ckpt_p$:= "yes"
>   else
> $OK\_to\_take\_ckpt_p$:= "no"
>   end;
>   send $(p, OK\_to\_take\_ckpt_p)$ to q;
>   end;
Upon receiving $Make\_tentative\_ckpt\_permanent$ message do
>   begin
>   Make tentative checkpoint permanent;
>   For all processes $r \in ckpt\_cohort_p$ do
>   Send $Make\_tentative\_ckpt\_permanent$ message;
>   end;
Upon receiving $Undo\_tentative\_ckpt$ message do
>   begin
>   Undo tentative checkpoint;
>   For all processes $r \in ckpt\_cohort_p$ do
>   Send $Undo\_tentative\_ckpt$ message;
>   end;

12.8.2 The Rollback Recovery Algorithm

The rollback recovery algorithm assumes that a single process invokes the algorithm, as opposed to several processes concurrently invoking it to rollback and recover [19]. It also assumes that the checkpoint and the rollback recovery algorithms are not concurrently invoked. The rollback recovery algorithm has two phases.

First Phase. An initiating process P_i checks to see if all the processes are willing to restart from their previous checkpoints. A process may reply "no" to a restart request if it is already participating in a checkpointing or a recovering process initiated by some other process. If P_i learns that all the processes are willing to restart from their previous checkpoints, P_i decides that all the processes should restart; otherwise, P_i decides that all the processes should continue with their normal activities. (P_i may attempt a recovery at a later time.)

Second Phase. P_i propagates its decision to all the processes. On receiving P_i's decision, a process will act accordingly.

The recovery algorithm requires that every process not send messages related to the underlying computation while it is waiting for P_i's decision.

Correctness. All cooperating processes restart from an appropriate state because:

- All processes either restart from their previous checkpoints or continue with their normal activities.
- If processes decide to restart, then they resume execution in a consistent state, as the checkpoint algorithm (Sec. 12.8.1) takes a consistent set of checkpoints.

OPTIMIZATION. While the above protocol causes all the processes to restart from a consistent set of checkpoints (taken by the checkpointing algorithm), it causes all the processes to roll back irrespective of whether a process needs to roll back or not. For example, consider the process activity shown in Fig. 12.8. The above protocol, in the event of failure of process X, would require processes X, Y, and Z to restart from checkpoints x_2, y_2, and z_2, respectively. Note, however, that process Z need not have rolled back as there was no interaction between Z and the other two processes.

To minimize the number of process rollbacks, the rollback recovery algorithm uses the labeling scheme explained in Sec. 12.8.1. In addition to the terminology previously introduced, the following terminology is used in describing the rollback recovery algorithm: For any two processes X and Y, let m be the last message that X sent to Y before X takes its latest permanent checkpoint. Then

$$last\_label\_sent_X[Y] = \begin{cases} m.l & \text{if } m \text{ exists} \\ \top & \text{otherwise} \end{cases}$$

When X requests Y to restart from the permanent checkpoint, it sends $last\_label\_sent_X[Y]$ along with its request. Y will restart from its permanent checkpoint only if

$$last\_label\_rcvd_Y[X] > last\_label\_sent_X[Y]$$

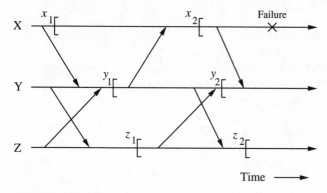

FIGURE 12.8
Unnecessary rollback.

When this condition holds, it indicates that X is rolling back to a state where the sending of one or more messages from X to Y is being undone.
We also define:

$$roll\_cohort_X = \{Y \mid X \ can \ send \ messages \ to \ Y\}$$

OUTLINE OF THE ALGORITHM

Initial state at all processes p:
$\qquad resume\_execution_p := \text{true};$
$\qquad$ for all processes q, do
$\qquad\qquad last\_label\_rcvd_p[q] := \top;$
$\qquad willing\_to\_roll_p = \begin{cases} \text{"yes" if } p \text{ is willing to roll back} \\ \text{"no"} \quad \text{otherwise} \end{cases}$

At initiator process P_i:
$\qquad$ for all processes $p \in roll\_cohort_{P_i}$ do
$\qquad\qquad$ send $Prepare\_to\_rollback(P_i, last\_label\_sent_{P_i}[p])$ message;
$\qquad$ if all processes replied "yes" then
$\qquad\qquad$ for all processes $p \in roll\_cohort_{P_i}$ do
$\qquad\qquad\qquad$ send $Roll\_back$ message;
$\qquad$ else
$\qquad\qquad$ for all processes $p \in roll\_cohort_{P_i}$ do
$\qquad\qquad\qquad$ send $Donot\_roll\_back$ message;

At all processes p:
$\qquad$ Upon receiving $Prepare\_to\_rollback(q, last\_label\_sent_q[p])$
$\qquad$ message from q do
$\qquad\qquad$ begin
$\qquad\qquad$ if $willing\_to\_roll_p$ AND $last\_label\_rcvd_p[q] > last\_label\_sent_q[p]$ AND
$\qquad\qquad (resume\_execution_p)$

then
    begin
    $resume\_execution_p := false$;
    for all processes $r \in roll\_cohort_p$ do
        send $Prepare\_to\_rollback(p, last\_label\_sent_p[r])$message;
    if all processes $r \in roll\_cohort_p$ replied "yes" then
        $willing\_to\_roll_p :=$ "yes"
    else
        $willing\_to\_roll_p :=$ "no"
    end;
Send($p, willing\_to\_roll_p$) message to q;
end;
Upon receiving $Roll\_back$ message AND if $resume\_execution_p$ = false do
    begin
    restart from p's permanent checkpoint;
    for all processes $r \in roll\_cohort_p$ do
        send $Roll\_back$ message;
    end;
Upon receiving $Donot\_roll\_back$ message do
    begin
    resume execution;
    for all processes $r \in roll\_cohort_p$ do
        send $Donot\_roll\_back$ message;
    end;

12.9 ASYNCHRONOUS CHECKPOINTING AND RECOVERY

While synchronous checkpointing simplifies recovery (because a consistent set of checkpoints is readily available), it has the following disadvantages [17]:

1. Additional messages are exchanged by the checkpoint algorithm when it takes each checkpoint.
2. Synchronization delays are introduced during normal operations. (Note that in the synchronous checkpointing algorithm described previously, no computational messages can be sent while the checkpointing algorithm is in progress.)
3. If failures rarely occur between successive checkpoints, then the synchronous approach places unnecessary burden on the system in the form of additional messages, delays, and processing overhead.

Under the asynchronous approach, checkpoints at each processor (or process) are taken independently without any synchronization among the processors [17]. Because of the absence of synchronization, there is no guarantee that a set of local checkpoints taken will be a consistent set of checkpoints. Thus, a recovery algorithm has to search

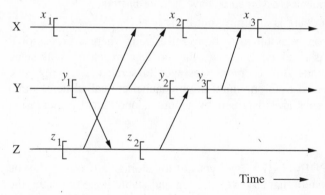

FIGURE 12.9
Asynchronous checkpointing may not result in a consistent set of checkpoints.

for the most recent consistent set of checkpoints before it can initiate recovery. For example, in Fig. 12.9, the latest set of checkpoints $\{x_3, y_3, z_2\}$ is not consistent. The most recent consistent set of checkpoints in Fig. 12.9 is $\{x_2, y_2, z_2\}$.

To minimize the amount of computation undone during a roll back, all incoming messages are logged (stored on stable storage) at each processor. The messages that were received after establishing a recovery point can be processed again in the event of a roll back to the recovery point. The messages received can be logged in two ways [17]: pessimistic and optimistic.

- In *pessimistic* message logging, an incoming message is logged before it is processed [7, 29]. A drawback of this approach is that it slows down the underlying computation, even when there are no failures.

- In *optimistic* message logging, processors continue to perform the computation and the messages received are stored in volatile storage, which are logged at certain intervals. In case of a system failure, an incoming message may be lost as it may not have been logged yet. Therefore, in the event of a rollback, the amount of computation redone during recovery is likely to be more in systems that make use of optimistic logging than in systems that make use of pessimistic logging. Optimistic logging, however, does not slow down the underlying computation during normal processing.

12.9.1   A Scheme for Asynchronous Checkpointing and Recovery

We now describe the algorithm of Juang and Venkatesan [17] for recovery in a system that employs asynchronous checkpointing. The algorithm makes the following assumptions about the underlying system:

1. The communication channels are reliable.
2. The communication channels deliver the messages in the order they were sent.

3. The communication channels are assumed to have infinite buffers.

4. The message transmission delay is arbitrary, but finite.

5. The underlying computation is assumed to be event-driven, where a processor P waits until a message m is received, processes the message m, changes its state, (say from s to s') and sends zero or more messages to some of its neighbors. (Processors directly connected by a communication channel are called neighbors.) The events at each processor are identified by unique monotonically increasing numbers (see Fig. 12.10).

ASYNCHRONOUS CHECKPOINTING. Two types of log storage are assumed to be available for logging in the system, namely, volatile log and stable log. Accessing the volatile log takes less time than accessing the stable log, but the contents of the volatile log are lost if the corresponding processor fails. The contents of the volatile log are periodically flushed to the stable storage and cleared.

Each processor, after an event, records a triplet $\{s, m, msgs\_sent\}$ in volatile storage where s is the state of the processor before the event, m is the message (including the identity of the sender) whose arrival caused the event, and $msgs\_sent$ is the set of messages that were sent by the processor during the event. Therefore, a local checkpoint at each processor consists of the record of an event occurring at the processor and it is taken without any synchronization with the other processors.

Notations and data structure. The following notations and data structure are used by the algorithm.

$RCVD_{i \leftarrow j}(CkPt_i)$ represents the number of messages received by processor i from processor j, per the information stored in the checkpoint $CkPt_i$.

$SENT_{i \rightarrow j}(CkPt_i)$ represents the number of messages sent by processor i to processor j, per the information stored in the checkpoint $CkPt_i$.

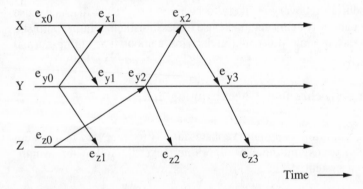

FIGURE 12.10
Event driven computation.

Basic idea. The fundamental issue in the recovery of a system based on asynchronous checkpointing is to find a consistent set of checkpoints to which the system can be restored. The basic idea of the recovery algorithm described next is as follows. Each processor keeps track of the number of messages it has sent to other processors as well as the number of messages it has received from other processors. Whenever a processor rolls back, it is necessary for all the other processors to find out whether any messages previously sent are now orphan messages. The existence of orphan messages is discovered by comparing the number of messages sent and received. If the number of messages received at a processor is greater than the number of messages sent (according to the state at other processors), it indicates that one or more messages are orphan messages and the processor (that has received more messages than that were sent) will have to roll back to a state where the number of messages received agrees with the number of messages sent.

For example, in Fig. 12.10, if Y rolls back to a state corresponding to e_{y1}, then according to this state Y has sent only one message to X. According to X's state, however, it has received two messages from Y thus far. Therefore, X has to roll back to a state preceding e_{x2} to be consistent with Y's state. For similar reasons, Z will also have to roll back.

THE ALGORITHM. The algorithm assumes that a processor, upon restarting, will broadcast a message that it had failed [17]. (This can be done using only O(|E|) messages where |E| is the total number of communication links [30].) The algorithm at a processor is initiated when it restarts after a failure or when it learns about another processor's failure. Because of the above broadcast, the algorithm will be initiated at all processors.

At processor i**:**

    (a) If i is a processor that is recovering after failure then

            $CkPt_i$:= latest event logged in the stable storage

      else

            $CkPt_i$:= latest event that took place in i;

                (* The latest event's log is either in stable/volatile storage *)

    (b) for k := 1 to N do (* N is the number of processors in the system *)

      begin

      for each neighboring processor j do

          send $ROLLBACK(i, SENT_{i \to j}(CkPt_i))$ message;

      wait for $ROLLBACK$ messages from every neighbor.

      (Note that, all the processors are executing the recovery procedure concurrently, and they would have sent $ROLLBACK$ messages to their neighbors as per step (b).)

For every $ROLLBACK(j, c)$ message received from a neighbor j,
i does the following:

if $RCVD_{i \leftarrow j}(CkPt_i) > c$ then
    (* Implies the presence of orphan messages *)
    begin
    find the latest event e such that $RCVD_{i \leftarrow j}(e) = c$;
    $CkPt_i := e$;
    end;

end; (* for k *)

Note that the procedure has $|N|$ iterations. During the kth iteration ($k \neq 1$), a processor i based on $CkPt_i$ determined in the $(k-1)$th iteration, computes $SENT_{i \rightarrow j}$ ($(CkPt_i)$) for each neighbor j and sends the value in a $ROLLBACK$ message to its neighbor and i processes $ROLLBACK$ messages sent to it by its neighbors. At the end of each iteration, at least one processor will rollback to its final recovery point unless the current recovery points are consistent.

Example 12.1. Figure 12.11 shows the activity of three processors. Suppose that processor Y fails and restarts from checkpoint y_1. Assuming event e_{y2} is the latest logged event in the checkpoint, Y will restart from the state corresponding to e_{y2}. Because of the broadcast protocol, the recovery algorithm is initiated at processors X and Z also. Initially, X, Y, and Z set $CkPt_X \leftarrow e_{x3}$, $CkPt_Y \leftarrow e_{y2}$, and $CkPt_Z \leftarrow e_{z2}$, respectively, and X, Y, and Z send the following messages during the first iteration. Y sends $ROLLBACK(Y, 2)$ to X and $ROLLBACK(Y, 1)$ to Z. X sends $ROLLBACK(X, 2)$ to Y and $ROLLBACK(X, 0)$ to Z. Z sends $ROLLBACK(Z, 0)$ to X and $ROLLBACK(Z, 1)$ to Y.

Since $RCVD_{X \leftarrow Y}(CkPt_X) = 3 > 2$ (2 is the number received in the $ROLL-BACK$ message from Y in the first iteration), X will set $CkPt_X$ to e_{x2} satisfying $RCVD_{X \leftarrow Y}(e_{x2}) = 2 = 2$. (Note that the second message received from Y is available in the log and can be processed again at X if e_{x2} is chosen as

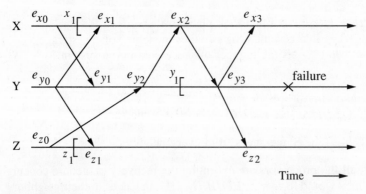

FIGURE 12.11
An example.

the recovery point in the end.) Since $RCVD_{Z \leftarrow Y}(CkPt_Z) = 2 > 1$, Z will set $CkPt_Z$ to e_{z1} satisfying $RCVD_{Z \leftarrow Y}(e_{z1}) = 1 \leq 1$. At Y, $RCVD_{Y \leftarrow X}(CkPt_Y)$ $= 1 < 2$ and $RCVD_{Y \leftarrow Z}(CkPt_Y) = 1 = SENT_{Z \rightarrow Y}(CkPt_Z)$. Hence, Y need not roll back further. In the second iteration, Y sends $ROLLBACK(Y, 2)$ to X and $ROLLBACK(Y, 1)$ to Z; Z sends $ROLLBACK(Z, 1)$ to Y and $ROLL - BACK(Z, 0)$ to X; X sends $ROLLBACK(X, 0)$ to Z and $ROLLBACK(X, 1)$ to Y. (Note that according to the state logged for e_{x2}, X has sent only one message to Y but it can resend the second message to Y as it is available from the log.) The second and third iteration will progress in a similar fashion. Notice that the set of recovery points chosen at the end of first iteration $\{e_{x2}, e_{y2}, e_{z1}\}$ is consistent, and no further rollbacks occur.

12.10 CHECKPOINTING FOR DISTRIBUTED DATABASE SYSTEMS

In previous sections of this chapter, we discussed the general concepts and techniques for checkpointing and recovering in distributed systems. In this section, we focus on a technique for taking checkpoints in a distributed database system (DDBS) where a set of data objects is partitioned among several sites. A checkpointing scheme for a DDBS should meet the following two basic objectives [37]:

- As checkpoints are taken during the normal operation of the system, it is highly desirable that normal operations be minimally interfered with by checkpointing.
- Since a process in a DDBS may update many different data objects at many different sites during the course of its execution, all sites should take local checkpoints recording the state of the local database. For fast recovery, it is desirable that the checkpoints taken are consistent.

THE NOTION OF CONSISTENCY IN A DDBS. The basic unit of user activity in a DDBS is a transaction. Therefore, consistency defined in terms of events pertaining to sending and receiving messages is not sufficient in a DDBS. In a DDBS, a consistent set of checkpoints requires that the updates of a transaction (which may be carried at many different sites) are included in all the checkpoints completely or not at all. Thus, the notion of consistency in a DDBS is much coarser than our previous definitions in the sense that a checkpoint in a DDBS should record all the events pertaining to a transaction or none of them.

Recall that taking a consistent checkpoint involves synchronization among all the sites during which sites may not exchange information related to the computation. In a DDBS, the exchange of information occurs through the database, where database updates of one transaction are read by the others. In other words, to take consistent checkpoints in a DDBS, transactions may have to be blocked while checkpointing is in progress, thereby interfering with normal operations. Thus, the objectives mentioned above conflict with each other.

ISSUES. In view of the requirements for checkpointing in a DDBS, the issues that need to be addressed by a checkpointing scheme for a DDBS are as follows:

- How sites decide or agree upon updates of what transactions are to be included in their checkpoints.
- How each site can take a local checkpoint in a noninterfering way. That is, a site should not block transactions while global checkpointing is in progress.

12.10.1 An Algorithm for Checkpointing in a DDBS

We now describe the Son and Agrawala [37] checkpointing algorithm, which is noninterfering and takes globally consistent checkpoints. The checkpointing algorithm makes the following assumptions about the underlying system:

1. The basic unit of user activity is a transaction.[†]
2. Transactions follow some concurrency control protocol.[‡]
3. Lamport's logical clocks (see Sec. 5.3) are used to associate each transaction with a timestamp. Thus, no two transactions have the same timestamp and only a finite number of transactions can have a timestamp less than that of a given transaction.
4. Site failures are detectable either by network protocols or by timeout mechanisms.
5. Network partitioning never occurs. (This assumption is reasonable in most local area networks.)

Basic idea. To decide the transactions whose updates are to be included in the checkpoint, all the participating sites agree upon a special timestamp known as the *global checkpoint number* (GCPN). The updates of the transactions, which have timestamps $\leq$ GCPN, are included in the checkpoint. These transactions are called *before-checkpoint-transactions* (BCPTs). The updates of the transactions which have timestamps $>$ GCPN are not included in the checkpoint. These transactions are called *after-checkpoint-transactions* (ACPTs).

To avoid interfering with the normal operations while checkpointing is in progress, each site maintains multiple versions of data items in volatile storage that are being updated by ACPTs. Thus, the state of the database is not disturbed once all the BCPTs terminate (at which time the database is consistent) until checkpointing completes. However, the ACPTs continue to access the database with the help of versions.

Data structures. The algorithm requires each site to maintain the following variables:

- *LC*: The local clock maintained as per Lamport's logical clock rules.

[†]Informally, a transaction consists of a sequence of read and write operations on the database and is the unit of user interaction with the database system. Transaction is a unit of consistency in the sense that when a transaction is executed alone in a database system, it maintains database consistency. (See Sec. 19.2.1.)

[‡]A database system must ensure that database consistency is maintained, even when several transactions are running concurrently. Concurrency control protocols ensure consistency of the database under such conditions. (See Chap. 20.)

- Local checkpoint number ($LCPN$): A number determined locally for the current checkpoint.

THE ALGORITHM. The checkpoint algorithm is initiated by a special process known as the checkpoint coordinator (CC). It takes a consistent set of checkpoints with the help of processes known as checkpoint subordinates (CS), running at every participating site. The CC process does not initiate checkpointing requests concurrently. The algorithm has two phases and the details of the steps are as follows.

Phase 1

At the checkpoint coordinator (CC) site:

1. The checkpoint coordinator broadcasts a Checkpoint_Request message with local timestamp LC_{CC}.
2. $LCPN_{cc} := LC_{CC}$.
3. $CONVERT_{CC} := false$. (Use of $CONVERT$ will become clear later.)
4. The checkpoint coordinator waits for replies (obtaining $LCPNs$) from all the subordinate sites.

At all the checkpoint subordinates (CS) sites:

1. On receiving a Checkpoint_Request message, a site m, updates its local clock as follows:
$$LC_m := \text{MAX}(LC_m, LC_{CC} + 1)$$
2. $LCPN_m := LC_m$
3. Site m informs $LCPN_m$ to the checkpoint coordinator.
4. $CONVERT_m := false$
5. Site m marks all the transactions with timestamps $\not> LCPN_m$ as BCPT, and marks the rest of the transactions as temporary-ACPT.

Once step 5 is executed at a site, all updates by temporary-ACPTs are stored in the buffers of the ACPTs. If a temporary-ACPT commits, the data objects updated by it are not flushed to the database, but rather are maintained as committed temporary versions (CTVs). If another transaction wishes to read an object for which a CTV exists, the data stored in the CTV is returned. Updates to an object that has a CTV creates yet another version of the object and the existing CTV is not overwritten.

Phase 2

At the checkpoint coordinator site:

Once all the replies for the Checkpoint_Request messages have been received, the coordinator broadcasts $GCPN$, which is decided as,
$$GCPN := \text{MAX}(LCPN_1, LCPN_2, ..., LCPN_n)$$
where n is the number of sites in the system.

At all sites:

1. On receiving GCPN, a site m marks all temporary ACPTs which satisfy the following condition as BCPT.

$$LCPN_m < \text{transaction's timestamp} \leq GCPN$$

The updates of these transactions, newly converted as BCPTs, are also included in the checkpoint. (The updates due to the remaining ACPTs will be flushed to the database after the current checkpointing is completed.)

2. $CONVERT_m := true$. When $CONVERT$ is true, it indicates that $GCPN$ is known and all BCPTs have been identified.

3. When all the BCPTs terminate and $CONVERT_m = true$, site m takes a local checkpoint by saving the state of the data objects.

4. When the local checkpoint is taken, the database is updated with the committed temporary versions and then the committed temporary versions are deleted.

Note that if a site m receives a new "initiate transaction" message for a new transaction whose timestamp is $\leq GCPN_m$ and the site m has already executed steps 1 and 2 of phase 2, then site m rejects the "initiate transaction" message.

In the algorithm described above, there are no restrictions on the order in which transactions can be executed. Under such conditions, it is possible that the algorithm may never terminate. To ensure that the algorithm terminates, a concurrency scheme that gives priority to older transactions is necessary. Since there are only a finite number of BCPTs when the checkpointing algorithm is initiated, and all of them will terminate in finite time, the checkpointing algorithm itself will terminate in finite time [37].

12.11 RECOVERY IN REPLICATED DISTRIBUTED DATABASE SYSTEMS

To enhance performance and availability, a distributed database system is replicated where copies of data objects are stored at different sites. Such a system is known as a replicated distributed database system (RDDBS). In RDDBS, transactions are allowed to continue despite one or more site failures as long as one copy of the database is available. The availability and performance of a database system is enhanced as the transactions are not blocked even when one or more sites fail. However, in the above scheme, copies of the database at the failed sites may miss some updates while the sites are not operational. These copies will be inconsistent with the copies at the operational sites. The goal of recovery algorithms in RDDBS is to hide such inconsistencies from user transactions, bring the copies at recovering sites up-to-date with respect to the rest of the copies, and enable the recovering sites to start processing transactions as soon as possible [6].

Two approaches have been proposed to recover failed sites. In one approach, message spoolers are used to save all the updates directed toward failed sites [13]. On recovery, the failed site processes all the missed updates before resuming normal operations. The other approach employs special transactions known as *copier* transactions. Copier transactions read the up-to-date copies at the operational sites and update the copies at recovering sites. Copier transactions run concurrently with user transactions. The recovery scheme should guarantee that: (1) the out-of-date replicas are not accessible to user transactions, and (2) once the out-of-date replicas are made up-to-date by copier transactions, they are also updated along with the other copies by the user transactions.

12.11.1 An Algorithm for Site Recovery

We next describe a recovery scheme proposed by Bhargava and Ruan [6], which is based on copier transactions. A limitation of this scheme is that it does not handle network partitions where sites of the database system are partitioned into different groups, and sites in different partitions cannot communicate with each other.

SYSTEM MODEL. The database is assumed to be manipulated through transactions (see Sec. 19.2.1) whose access to the database is controlled by a concurrency control algorithm (See Chap. 20). Transactions either run to completion or have no effect on the database (see Sec. 13.3). The semantics of read and write operations on the database are such that a read operation will read from any available copy and write operation updates all the available copies. All the out-of-date copies in the database are assumed to be marked "unreadable". We also assume that the database is fully replicated (i.e., every site has a copy of the database). A site may be in any one of the following states:

> **Operational/Up.** The site is operating normally and user transactions are accepted.
> **Recovering.** The recovery is still in progress at the site and the site is not ready to accept user transactions.
> **Down.** No RDDBS activity can be performed at the site.
> **Non-operational.** The site's state is either *recovering* or *down*.

An *operational session* of a site is a time period in which the site is *up*. Each operational session of a site is designated with a *session number* (an integer) which is unique in the site's history, but not necessarily unique systemwide. The session numbers are stored on nonvolatile storage so that a recovering site can use an appropriate new session number.

Data structures. Each site k maintains the following two data structures:

1. The session number of site k is maintained in a variable AS_k. AS_k is set to zero when site k is nonoperational.
2. PS_k is a vector of size n where n is the number of sites in the system. $PS_k[i]$ is the session number of site i as known to site k. Since the sites are up and down dynamically, a site's knowledge of the system is not always correct. Thus, PS_k gives the state of the system as perceived by k. $PS_k[i]$ is set to zero whenever k learns that site i is down or some other site informs k that site i is down.

We next describe how the system functions under normal conditions, failures, and during recovery.

User transactions. Each request that originates at a site i for reading or writing a data item at site k carries $PS_i[k]$. If $PS_i[k] \neq AS_k$ OR $AS_k = 0$ then the request is rejected by site k. Otherwise, there are three possible cases. (1) The data item is readable: the request is processed at site k. (2) The data item is marked unreadable and the operation is a write operation: the data item is modified and will be marked readable when the transaction commits. (3) The data item is marked unreadable and the operation is a read operation: a copier transaction is initiated by site k. The copier transaction uses the perceived session vector to locate a readable copy. A copy at site j is readable for a copier transaction from a site k if $PS_k[j] = AS_j$. The copier transaction uses the contents of the readable copy to renovate the local copy and removes the unreadable mark on the local copy. The user transaction may be blocked while the copier transaction is in progress or it can read some other copy. If the copier transaction cannot locate any readable copy, that data item is considered failed. A separate protocol is needed to resolve this problem, but this issue is beyond the scope of this book.

Copier transactions. Copier transactions may be initiated for all the data items marked unreadable when a site starts recovering. On the other hand, a copier transaction may be initiated on a demand basis, that is, whenever a read operation is received for individual data items marked unreadable. Copier transactions also follow the concurrency protocol used by the RDDBS.

Control transactions. Control transactions are special transactions that update AS and PS at all sites (including any recovering sites). When a recovering site (say k) decides that it is ready to change its state from recovering to operational, it initiates a type-1 control transaction. A type-1 control transaction performs the following operations:

- It reads PS_i from some reachable site i and refreshes PS_k.
- It chooses a new session number, sets $PS_k[k]$ to this new session number, and writes $PS_k[k]$ to all $PS_i[k]$ where $PS_k[i] \neq 0$ (i.e., at all sites that are perceived up by site k).

When a site discovers that one or more sites are down, it initiates a type-2 control transaction. For example, if site k learns that site m and n are down, then it initiates a type-2 control transaction which performs the following operations:

- It sets $PS_k[m]$ and $PS_k[n]$ to zero.
- For all i such that $PS_k[i] \neq 0$, it sets $PS_i[m]$ and $PS_i[n]$ to zero.

Control transactions also follow concurrency control and commit protocols (see Sec. 13.4) used by the RDDBS to control access to PS vectors. A control transaction may be aborted due to conflict with another control transaction or due to a write failure caused by another site failure.

THE SITE RECOVERY PROCEDURE. When a site k restarts after failure, the recovery procedure at site k performs the following steps:

1. It sets AS_k to zero. That is, site k is recovering and is not ready to accept user transactions.
2. It marks all the copies of data items unreadable.
3. It initiates a type-1 control transaction.
4. If the control transaction of step 3 successfully terminates, then the site copies the new session number from $PS_k[k]$ to AS_k. (Note that a new session number is set in $PS_k[k]$ by the type-1 control transaction.) Note that once $AS_k \neq 0$, the site is ready to accept user transactions.
5. If step 3 fails because of discovering that another site has failed, site k initiates a type-2 control transaction to exclude the newly failed site and then restarts from step 3.

In step 2, a recovering site will mark all the data items unreadable. However, only those data items that missed updates while the site was non-operational need to be marked unreadable.

12.12   SUMMARY

With the pervasion of computers that perform day-to-day tasks as well as critical tasks, it is very important that the work performed is not lost due to failures. It may not always be possible to avoid disruptions due to failures. However, it is very important that the work lost due to failures is minimal and the time for recovering from failures is minimal as well.

Since failures are caused by errors in the process (system) state (errors are caused by faults), failure recovery attempts to remove errors in the state. There are two approaches to remove errors from a process (system) state, namely, backward-error recovery and forward-error recovery. In backward-error recovery, a process (system) is restored to its prior state in the hope that it is error free and the execution is resumed from the prior state. In forward- error recovery, the errors in the process (system) state are removed and the process (system) resumes execution from that point. While the cost of recovery in backward-error recovery could be higher, it is a general mechanism applicable to any system. On the other hand, forward-error recovery may potentially be faster, but it is limited to situations where the nature of error and the extent of damages due to errors can be accurately assessed.

To facilitate quicker recovery in the case of backward-error recovery, a system saves its state (referred to as taking checkpoints) often. There are two approaches to take checkpoints in concurrent systems, namely, synchronous and asynchronous. In synchronous checkpointing, all the sites in the system coordinate in taking checkpoints, thereby assuring that the set of checkpoints taken by them will be consistent. To recover, the system will simply restart from the consistent state stored in the checkpoint. Delays due to coordination in synchronous checkpointing, however, can pose an undue burden on the system if failures are rare. In asynchronous checkpointing, sites take checkpoints without consulting each other. There is no guarantee that the set of checkpoints taken is consistent, and an attempt to restore the system to a prior state may cause the domino effect. Also, recovery has more overhead since a set of consistent checkpoints must be found before the system state can be restored to a previous state.

Checkpointing in transaction-oriented distributed database systems is further complicated by the need for transactions to complete quickly and recovery to be quick. We described one checkpointing scheme that takes consistent checkpoints, thereby enabling quick recovery. This scheme uses temporary versions of database objects to execute read and write operations while checkpointing is in progress, thus not interfering with the normal operations of user transactions.

In replicated distributed database systems (RDDBS), recovery is yet further complicated by the fact that copies at recovering sites may be inconsistent with the copies at operational sites and users must be protected from such inconsistencies. To recover a site in RDDBS, outdated copies at that site can be made up-to-date by refreshing them from other up-to-date copies with the help of copier transactions. User transactions at a recovering site can either be diverted to another site with up-to-date copy or provided with up-to-date data once the outdated copy is refreshed.

In this chapter, we discussed concepts and techniques for recovering from failures. These techniques, however, are only able to minimize disruptions due to failures. In the next chapter, we describe important techniques that deal with tolerating failures that attempt to prevent disruptions to users all together.

12.13 FURTHER READINGS

Koo and Toueg [19] have proposed extensions to the checkpointing and recovery algorithms of Sec. 12.8 to take care of failures during the execution of the algorithms as well as concurrent invocations of checkpointing and rollback recovery algorithms.

Checkpointing is a widely studied topic. Pilarski and Kameda [28] develop a general scheme from basics for taking checkpoints for distributed databases. The proposed scheme can be incorporated into most concurrency control protocols. Many approaches for synchronous checkpointing are proposed by Leu and Bhargava [23], Tamir and Se'quin [40], and Venkatesh et al. [42]. Also, many approaches for asynchronous checkpointing are proposed by Johnson and Zwaenepoel [16], Sistla and Welch [35], and Strom and Yemini [38].

In most recovery schemes, a failed process is restored to a checkpoint, and the process receives messages in the exact same order as it received them before failing. To recover messages lost due to failure, logging is the most commonly used technique. Jalote [15] shows that the above approach to recover messages is stricter than necessary, and proposes a scheme to implement fault-tolerant processes that can handle multiple process failures.

Hammer and Shipman [13] describe a recovery mechanism for distributed databases based on spoolers. Haskin et al. [14] have implemented recovery management based on logs in Quicksilver. Adam and Tewari [1] have discussed a scheme to dynamically regenerate copies of data objects in response to site failures and network partitions. More discussion on recovery approaches for databases can be found in [2, 4, 5, 12, 20, 25, 34, 36].

A checkpointing scheme to take consistent checkpoints and a recovery scheme for systems employing distributed shared memory is proposed by Wu and Fuchs in [43]. Tam and Hsu [39] have also proposed a scheme for recovery in systems with distributed shared virtual memory.

Distributed breakpoints is a concept related to consistent system state. Fowler and Zwaenepoel [10] and Miller and Choi [26] have discussed breakpoints for distributed systems and proposed algorithms for obtaining breakpoints in distributed systems.

Techniques for recovery in shared memory machines have been proposed in [18, 31]. Wu and Fuchs [44] propose a scheme for error recovery in shared memory multiprocessor machines with private caches. In [24], Liskov and Scheifler propose a programming language based mechanism for fault tolerance and error recovery in distributed systems.

PROBLEMS

12.1. Define livelocks. What is the difference between a deadlock and a livelock?

12.2. Show that when checkpoints are taken after every K ($K > 1$) messages are sent, the recovery mechanism can suffer from the domino effect. Assume that a process takes a checkpoint immediately after sending the Kth message but before doing anything else.

12.3. In the synchronous checkpointing algorithm of Sec. 12.8, a process, on receiving a Take_a_tentative_ckpt message, will send Take_a_tentative_ckpt messages to all the processes that are in its ckpt_cohort set. Why is this necessary?

12.4. What is the message complexity of the rollback recovery algorithm described in Sec. 12.9?

12.5. Give an example where the recovery algorithm of Sec. 12.9 will need to execute for |N| iterations where |N| is the number of processors in the system.

12.6. Give an example where the recovery algorithm of Sec. 12.9 can terminate after only one iteration.

REFERENCES

1. Adam, N. R., and R. Tewari, "Regeneration with Virtual Copies for Replicated Databases," *Proceedings of the 11th International Conference on Distributed Computing Systems*, May 1991, pp. 429–436.
2. Attar, R., P. A. Bernstein, and N. Goodman, "Site Initialization, Recovery, and Backup in a Distributed Database System," *IEEE Transactions on Software Engineering*, vol. 10, no. 6, Nov. 1984, pp. 645–650.
3. Banatre, M., G. Muller, B. Rochat, and P. Sanchez, "Design Decisions for the FTM: A General Purpose Fault Tolerant Machine," *Digest of Papers, Fault-Tolerant Computing: The 21st International Conference*, June 1991, pp. 71–78.
4. Bernstein, P. A., and N. Goodman, "The Failure and Recovery Problem for Replicated Database," *Proceedings of the ACM Symposium on Principles of Distributed Computing*, Aug. 1983, pp. 114–122.

5. Bernstein, P. A., and N. Goodman, "An Algorithm for Concurrency Control and Recovery in Replicated Distributed Databases," *ACM Transactions on Database Systems*, vol. 9, no. 4, Dec. 1984, pp. 596–615.

6. Bhargava, B., and Z. Ruan, "Site Recovery in Replicated Distributed Database Systems," *Proceedings of the 6th International Conference on Distributed Computing Systems*, May 1986, pp. 621–627.

7. Borg, A., J. Baumback, and S. Glazer, "A Message System Supporting Fault Tolerance," *Proceedings of the 9th ACM Symposium on Operating Systems Principles,* Oct. 1983, pp. 110–118. Also in ACM Operating System Review, vol. 21, no. 5, Oct. 1983, pp. 90–99.

8. Chandy, K. M., and L. Lamport, "Distributed Snapshots: Determining Global States of Distributed Systems," *ACM Transactions on Computer Systems*, Feb. 1985, pp. 63–75.

9. Cristian, F., "Understanding Fault-Tolerant Distributed Systems," *Communications of the ACM*, vol. 34, no. 2, Feb. 1991, pp. 56–78.

10. Fowler, J., and W. Zwaenepoel, "Causal Distributed Breakpoints," *Proceedings of the 10th International Conference on Distributed Computing Systems,* May 1990, pp. 134–141.

11. Gray, J. N., "Notes on Data Base Operating Systems," *Operating Systems An Advanced Course*, Springer-Verlag, New York, 1979, pp. 393–481.

12. Haerder, T., and A. Reuter, "Principles of Transaction-Oriented Database Recovery," *ACM Computing Surveys*, vol. 15, no. 4, Dec. 1983, pp. 287–317.

13. Hammer, M., and D. Shipman, "Reliablility Mechanisms for SDD-1: A System for Distributed Databases," *ACM Transactions on Database Systems*, vol. 5, no. 4, Dec. 1980, pp. 431–466.

14. Haskin, R., Y. Malachi, W. Sawdon, and G. Chan, "Recovery Management in QuickSilver," *ACM Transactions on Computer Systems*, vol. 6, no. 1, Feb. 1988, pp. 82–108.

15. Jalote, P., *Fault Tolerant Processes, Distributed Computing,* Springer-Verlag, New York, 1989, vol. 3: pp. 187–195.

16. Johnson, D., and W. Zwaenepoel, "Recovery in Distributed Systems Using Optimistic Message Logging and Checkpointing," *Proceedings of the 7th ACM Symposium on Principles of Distributed Computing*, Aug. 1988, pp. 171–180.

17. Juang, T., and S. Venkatesan, "Crash Recovery with Little Overhead," *Proceedings of the 11th International Conference on Distributed Computing Systems*, May 1991, pp. 454–461.

18. Kim, K. H., "Programmer-Transparent Coordination of Recovering Concurrent Processes: Philosophy and Rules for Efficient Implementation," *IEEE Transactions on Software Engineering*, vol. 14, no. 6, June 1988, pp. 810–821.

19. Koo, R., and S. Toueg, "Checkpointing and Rollback-Recovery for Distributed Systems," *IEEE Transactions on Software Engineering*, vol. 13, no. 1, Jan. 1987, pp. 23–31.

20. Kuss, H., "On Totally Ordering Checkpoints in Distributed Databases," *Proceedings of the ACM SIGMOD International Conference on Management of Data*, 1982, pp. 293–302.

21. Lampson, B. W., and H. E. Sturgis, "Crash Recovery in a Distributed Storage System," Unpublished report, Computer Sciences Laboratory, Xerox Palo Alto Research Center, Palo Alto, Ca, 1976.

22. Lee, P. A., and T. Anderson, *Fault Tolerance Principles and Practice*, 2d ed., Springler-Verlag, New York, 1990.

23. Leu, P., and B. Bhargava, "Concurrent Robust Checkpointing and Recovery in Distributed Systems," *Proceedings of the 4th International Conference on Data Engineering*, Feb. 1988, pp. 154–163.

24. Liskov, B., and R. Scheifler, "Guardians and Actions: Linguistic Support for Robust Distributed Programs," *Distributed Processing, IFIP*, North-Holland, 1988, pp. 355–369. Also in *ACM Transactions on Programming Languages and Systems*, vol. 5, no. 3, 1983, pp. 381-404.

25. McDermid, J., "Checkpointing and Error Recovery in Distributed Systems," *Proceedings of the 2nd International Conference on Distributed Computing Systems*, Apr. 1982, pp. 271–282.

26. Miller, B. P., and J. D. Choi, "Breakpoints and Halting in Distributed Programs," *Proceedings of the 8th International Conference on Distributed Computing Systems*, June 1988, pp. 141–150.

27. Nelson, V. P., "Fault-Tolerant Computing: Fundamental Concepts," *IEEE Computer*, vol. 23, no. 7, July 1990, pp. 19–25.

28. Pilarski, S., and T. Kameda, "Checkpointing for Distributed Databases: Starting from the Basics," *IEEE Transactions on Parallel and Distributed Systems*, vol. 3, no. 5, Sept. 1992, pp. 602–610.

29. Powell, M. L., and D. Presotto, "Publishing: A Reliable Broadcast Communication Mechanism," *Proceedings of the 9th ACM Symposium on Operating Systems Principles*, pp. 110–118. 1983, Also in *ACM Operating System Review* vol. 21, no. 5, Oct. 1983, pp. 100–109.

30. Ramarao, K. V. S., and S. Venkatesan, "Design of Distributed Algorithms Resilient to Link Failures," Technical report, University of Pittsburgh, 1987.

31. Randell, B., "System Structure for Software Fault Tolerance," *IEEE Transactions on Software Engineering*, vol. 1, June 1975, pp. 226–232.

32. Randell, B., "Reliable Computing Systems," *Operating Systems: An Advanced Course*, Springer-Verlag, New York, 1979, pp. 282–391.

33. Schlichting, R. D., and F. B. Schneider, "Fail-Stop Processors: An Approach to Designing Fault-Tolerant Computing Systems," *ACM Transactions on Computing Systems*, vol. 1, no. 3, Aug. 1983, pp. 222–238.

34. Schumann, R., R. Kroger, M. Mock, and E. Nett, "Recovery-Management in the RelaX Distributed Transaction Layer," *Proceedings of the 8th Symposium on Reliable Distributed Systems*, Oct. 1989, pp. 21–28.

35. Sistla, A. P., and J. Welch, "Efficient Distributed Recovery Message Logging," *Proceedings of the Principles of Distributed Computing*, 1989.

36. Son, S. H., and A. K. Agrawala, "An Algorithm for Database Reconstruction in Replicated Environments," *Proceedings of the 6th International Conference on Distributed Computing Systems*, May 1986, pp. 532–539.

37. Son, S. H., and A. K. Agrawala, "Distributed Checkpointing for Globally Consistent States of Databases," *IEEE Transactions on Software Engineering*, vol. 15, no. 10, Oct. 1989, pp. 1157–1167.

38. Strom, R. E., and S. Yemini, "Optimistic Recovery in Distributed Systems," *ACM Transactions on Computing Systems*, vol. 3, no. 3, 1985, pp. 204–226.

39. Tam, V. O., and M. Hsu, "Fast Recovery in Distributed Shared Virtual Memory Systems," *Proceedings of the 10th International Conference on Distributed Computing Systems*, May 1990, pp. 38–45.

40. Tamir, Y., and C. H. Se'quin, "Error Recovery in Multicomputers Using Global Checkpoints," *Proceedings of the 13th International Conference on Parallel Processing*, 1984.

41. Tanenbaum, A. S., *Computer Networks*, Prentice-Hall, Englewood Cliffs, 1981.

42. Venkatesh, K., T. Radhakrishnan, and H. F. Li, "Optimal Checkpointing and Local Recording for Domino-Free Rollback Recovery," *Information Processing Letters*, vol. 25, no. 5, 1987, pp. 295–304.

43. Wu, K. L., and W. K. Fuchs, "Recoverable Distributed Shared Virtual Memory: Memory Coherence and Storage Structures," *Proceedings of the 19th IEEE International Symposium on Fault-Tolerant Computing*, 1989, pp. 520–527.

44. Wu, K. L., and W. K. Fuchs, "Error Recovery in Shared Memory Multiprocessors Using Private Caches," *IEEE Transactions on Parallel and Distributed Systems*, vol. 1, no. 2, Apr. 1990, pp. 231–240.

CHAPTER
13

FAULT TOLERANCE

13.1 INTRODUCTION

In the previous chapter, several techniques to recover from failures were discussed. However, the disruptions caused during failures can be especially severe in many cases (for example: on-line transaction processing, process control, and computer based communication user communities, etc.) [14]. To avoid disruptions due to failures and to improve availability, systems are designed to be fault-tolerant.

A system can be designed to be fault-tolerant in two ways [14]. A system may *mask* failures or a system may exhibit a *well defined failure behavior* in the event of failure. When a system is designed to mask failures, it continues to perform its specified function in the event of a failure. A system designed for well defined behavior may or may not perform the specified function in the event of a failure, however, it can facilitate actions suitable for recovery. An example of well defined behavior during a failure is: the changes made to a database by a transaction are made visible to other transactions only if the transaction successfully commits; if the transaction fails, the changes made to the database by the failed transaction are not made visible to the other transactions, thus not affecting those transactions.

One key approach used to tolerate failures is *redundancy*. In this approach, a system may employ a multiple number of processes, a multiple number of hardware components, multiple copies of data, etc., each with independent failure modes (i.e., failure of one component does not affect the operation of other components).

In this chapter, we discuss widely used techniques, such as commit protocols and voting protocols, used in the design of fault-tolerant systems. Commit protocols implement well defined behavior in the event of failure, such as the one described in the above example. Voting protocols, on the other hand, mask failures in a system. To implement a fault-tolerant distributed system, processes in the system should be able to tolerate system failures and communicate reliably. We describe two techniques that have been used to implement processes that are resilient to system failures. In addition, we describe a technique to send messages reliably among processes. Finally, we close this chapter by presenting a case study of a fault-tolerant system.

13.2 ISSUES

Since a fault-tolerant system must behave in a specified manner in the event of a failure, it is important to study the implications of certain types of failures.

PROCESS DEATHS. When a process dies, it is important that the resources allocated to that process are recouped, otherwise they may be permanently lost. Many distributed systems are structured along the client-server model in which a client requests a service by sending a message to a server. If the server process fails, it is necessary that the client machine be informed so that the client process, waiting for a reply can be unblocked to take suitable action. Likewise, if a client process dies after sending a request to a server, it is imperative that the server be informed that the client process no longer exists. This will facilitate the server in reclaiming any resources it has allocated to the client process.

MACHINE FAILURE. In the case of machine failure, all the processes running at the machine will die. As far as the behavior of a client process or a server process is concerned, there is not much difference in their behavior in the event of a machine failure or a process death. The only difference lies in how the failure is detected. In the case of a process death, other processes including the kernel remain active. Hence, a message stating that the process has died can be sent to an inquiring process. On the other hand, an absence of any kind of message indicates either process death or a failure due to machine failure.

NETWORK FAILURE. A communication link failure can partition a network into subnets, making it impossible for a machine to communicate with another machine in a different subnet. A process cannot really tell the difference between a machine and a communication link failure, unless the underlying communication network (such as a slotted ring network) can recognize a machine failure. If the communication network cannot recognize machine failures and thus cannot return a suitable error code (such as Ethernet), a fault-tolerant design will have to assume that a machine may be operating and processes on that machine are active.

13.3 ATOMIC ACTIONS AND COMMITTING

Typically, system activity is governed by the sequence of primitive or atomic operations it is executing. Usually, a machine level instruction, which is indivisible, instantaneous, and cannot be interrupted (unless the system fails) corresponds to an atomic operation. However, it is desirable to be able to group such instructions that accomplish a certain task and make the group an atomic operation.

For example, suppose two processes P_1 and P_2 share a memory location X and both modify X as shown in Fig. 13.1. Suppose P_1 succeeds in locking X before P_2, then P_1 updates X and releases the lock, making it possible for P_2 to access X. If P_1 fails after P_2 has seen the changes made to X by P_1, then P_2 will also have to be aborted or rolled back. Thus, what is necessary is that P_2 should not be able to interact with P_1 through X until it can do so safely. In other words, P_1 should be atomic. Its effect on X should not be visible to P_2 or any other process until P_1 is guaranteed to finish. In essence, the effect of P_1 on the system (even though it executes concurrently with P_2) should look like an undivided and uninterrupted operation.

Atomic actions extend the concept of atomicity from one machine instruction level to a sequence of instructions or a group of processes that are themselves to be executed atomically. Atomic actions are the basic building blocks in constructing fault-tolerant operations. They provide a means to a system designer to specify the process interactions that are to be prevented to maintain the integrity of the system. Atomic actions have the following characteristics [29, 39].

- An action is atomic if the process performing it is not aware of the existence of any other active processes, and no other process is aware of the activity of the process during the time the process performs the action.
- An action is atomic if the process performing it does not communicate with other processes while the action is being performed.
- An action is atomic if the process performing it can detect no state changes except those performed by itself, and if it does not reveal its state changes until the action is complete.
- Actions are atomic if they can be considered, so far as other processes are concerned, to be indivisible and instantaneous, such that the effects on the system are as if they were interleaved as opposed to concurrent.

A transaction groups a sequence of actions (for example, on a database) and the group is treated as an atomic action to maintain the consistency of a database. (The concept of a transaction is discussed in Sec. 19.2.1.) At some point during its

Process P_1	**Process** P_2
–	–
–	–
Lock(X);	Lock(X);
X := X + Z;	X := X + Y;
Unlock(X);	Unlock(X);
–	–
–	–
failure	

FIGURE 13.1
Process interaction.

execution, the transaction decides whether to commit or abort its actions. A *commit* is an unconditional guarantee (even in the case of multiple failures) that the transaction will be completed. In other words, the effects of its actions on the database will be permanent. An *abort* is an unconditional guarantee to back out of the transaction, and none of the effects of its actions will persist [44].

A transaction may abort due to any of the following events: deadlocks, timeouts, protection violation, wrong input provided by user, or consistency violations (which can happen if an optimistic concurrency control technique is employed). To facilitate backing out of an aborting transaction, the write-ahead-log protocol (discussed in Sec. 12.5.1) or shadow pages (discussed in Sec. 12.5.1) can be employed.

In distributed systems, several processes may coordinate to perform a task. Their actions may have to be atomic with respect to other processes. For example, transaction may spawn many processes that are executed at different sites. As another example, in distributed database systems, a transaction must be processed at every site or at none of the sites to maintain the integrity of the database. This is referred to as *global atomicity*. The protocols that enforce global atomicity are referred to as *commit protocols*. Given that each site has a recovery strategy (e.g., the write-ahead-log protocol or the shadow page protocol) at the local level, commit protocols ensure that all the sites either commit or abort the transaction unanimously, even in the presence of multiple and repetitive failures [44]. Note that commit protocols fall into the second class of fault-tolerant design techniques in that they help the system behave in a certain way in the presence of failures. We next present several commit protocols.

13.4 COMMIT PROTOCOLS

The following situation illustrates the difficulties that arise in the design of commit protocols [20].

THE GENERALS PARADOX. There are two generals of the same army who have encamped a short distance apart. Their objective is to capture a hill, which is possible only if they attack simultaneously. If only one general attacks, he will be defeated. The two generals can communicate only by sending messengers. There is a chance that these messengers might lose their way or be captured by the enemy. The challenge is to use a protocol that allows the generals to agree on a time to attack, even though some messengers do not get through.

A simple proof shows that there exists no protocol which sends the messengers a fixed number of times to solve the above problem. Let P be the shortest protocol. Suppose the last messenger in P does not make it to the destination. Then either the message carried by the messenger is useless or one of the generals does not get the needed message. Since P is the minimal length protocol by our assumption, the message that was lost was not a useless message and hence one of the generals will not attack. This contradiction proves that there exists no such protocol P of fixed length.

The situation faced by the generals is very similar to the situation that arises in the commit protocols. The goal of commit protocols is to have all the sites (generals) agree either to commit (attack) or to abort (do not attack) a transaction. By relaxing the requirement that the number of messages employed by a commit protocol be bounded by a fixed number of messages, a commit protocol can be designed. We next describe a famous protocol by Gray [20], which has been referred to as the two-phase commit protocol.

13.4.1   The Two-Phase Commit Protocol

This protocol assumes that one of the cooperating processes acts as a coordinator. Other processes are referred to as cohorts. (Cohorts are assumed to be executing at different sites.) This protocol assumes that a stable storage is available at each site and the write-ahead log protocol is active. At the beginning of the transaction, the coordinator sends a start transaction message to every cohort.

Phase I. *At the coordinator:*

1. The coordinator sends a COMMIT-REQUEST message to every cohort requesting the cohorts to commit.
2. The coordinator waits for replies from all the cohorts.

At cohorts:

1. On receiving the COMMIT-REQUEST message, a cohort takes the following actions. If the transaction executing at the cohort is successful, it writes UNDO and REDO log on the stable storage and sends an AGREED message to the coordinator. Otherwise, it sends an ABORT message to the coordinator.

Phase II. *At the coordinator:*

1. If all the cohorts reply AGREED and the coordinator also agrees, then the coordinator writes a COMMIT record into the log. Then it sends a COMMIT message to all the cohorts. Otherwise, the coordinator sends an ABORT message to all the cohorts.
2. The coordinator then waits for acknowledgments from each cohort.
3. If an acknowledgment is not received from any cohort within a timeout period, the coordinator resends the commit/abort message to that cohort.
4. If all the acknowledgments are received, the coordinator writes a COMPLETE record to the log (to indicate the completion of the transaction).

At cohorts:

1. On receiving a COMMIT message, a cohort releases all the resources and locks held by it for executing the transaction, and sends an acknowledgment.
2. On receiving an ABORT message, a cohort undoes the transaction using the UNDO log record, releases all the resources and locks held by it for performing the transaction, and sends an acknowledgment.

When there are no failures or message losses, it is easy to see that all sites will commit only when all the participants (including the coordinator) agree to commit. In the case of lost messages (sent from either cohorts or the coordinator), the coordinator simply resends messages after the timeout. Now we shall attempt to show that this protocol results in all participants either committing or aborting, even in the case of site failures.

SITE FAILURES. For site failures, we look at the following cases:

- Suppose the coordinator crashes before having written the COMMIT record. On recovery, the coordinator broadcasts an ABORT message to all the cohorts. All the cohorts who had agreed to commit will simply undo the transaction using the UNDO log and abort. Other cohorts will simply abort the transaction. Note that all the cohorts are blocked until they receive an ABORT message.

- Suppose the coordinator crashes after writing the COMMIT record but before writing the COMPLETE record. On recovery, the coordinator broadcasts a COMMIT message to all the cohorts and waits for acknowledgments. In this case also the cohorts are blocked until they receive a COMMIT message.

- Suppose the coordinator crashes after writing the COMPLETE record. On recovery, there is nothing to be done for the transaction.

- If a cohort crashes in Phase I, the coordinator can abort the transaction because it did not receive a reply from the crashed cohort.

- Suppose a cohort crashes in Phase II, that is, after writing its UNDO and REDO log. On recovery, the cohort will check with the coordinator whether to abort (i.e., perform an undo operation) or to commit the transaction. Note that committing may require a redo operation because the cohort may have failed before updating the database.

While the two-phase commit protocol guarantees global atomicity, its biggest drawback is that it is a blocking protocol. Whenever the coordinator fails, cohort sites will have to wait for its recovery (see Problem 13.1). This is undesirable as these sites may be holding locks on the resources. (Note that transactions lock the resources to maintain the integrity of resources. See Chap. 20.) In the event of message loss, the two-phase protocol will result in the sending of more messages. We next discuss nonblocking commit protocols that do not block in the event of site failures.

13.5 NONBLOCKING COMMIT PROTOCOLS

If transactions must be resilient[†] to site failures, the commit protocols must not block in the event of site failures. To ensure that commit protocols are nonblocking in the event

---

[†]Progress despite failures.

of site failures, operational sites should agree on the outcome of the transaction (while guaranteeing global atomicity) by examining their local states. In addition, the failed sites, upon recovery must all reach the same conclusion regarding the outcome (abort or commit) of the transaction. This decision must be consistent with the final outcome at the sites that were operational. If the recovering sites can decide the final outcome of the transaction based solely on their local state (without contacting the sites that were operational), the recovery is referred to as *independent recovery* [44]. Skeen [43, 44] proposed nonblocking commit protocols that tolerate site failures. Before describing a nonblocking protocol, it is first necessary to discuss the conditions that cause a commit protocol to block and then discuss how a failed site can recover to an appropriate state.

ASSUMPTIONS. The communication network is assumed to have the following characteristics:

- The network is reliable and point-to-point communication is possible between any two operational sites.
- The network can detect the failure of a site (for example by a timeout) and report it to the site trying to communicate with the failed site.

DEFINITIONS

Synchronous protocols. A protocol is said to be *synchronous* within one state transition if one site never leads another site by more than one state transition during the execution of the protocol. In other words, $\forall i, j, |t_i - t_j| \leq 1$, where $1 \leq i, j \leq n, n$ is the total number of sites, and t_k is the total number of state transitions that have occurred thus far at site k. A state transition (change in the state) occurs in a process participating in the two-phase commit protocol whenever it receives and/or sends messages (see Fig. 13.2). With the help of a finite state automaton (FSA), we will see that the two-phase commit protocol satisfies the above definition (see Fig. 13.2).

Whenever the coordinator is in state q, all the cohorts are either in state q or a. When the coordinator is in state w, a cohort can either be in state q, w, or a, which is at most one state transition behind or ahead of the coordinator's state in the FSA. When the coordinator is in state a/c, a cohort is in state w or a/c depending on whether it has received a message (Abort/Commit) from the coordinator.

Likewise, whenever a cohort is in state q: some cohorts may be in state w/q if they have or have not received the Commit_Request message yet; and some cohorts may be in state a depending on whether a cohort has received an Abort message or not. Whenever a cohort is in state a/c, other cohorts may be in state a or c, depending on whether they have received an Abort or Commit message, respectively; otherwise, they are in state w. Note that a site is never in state c when another site is in state q, which means that a site never leads another site by two or more state transitions.

Concurrency set. Let s_i denote the state of site i. The set of all the states of every site that may be concurrent with it is known as the concurrency set of s_i (denoted by $C(s_i)$). For example, consider a system having two sites. If site 2's state is w_2, then

Coordinator

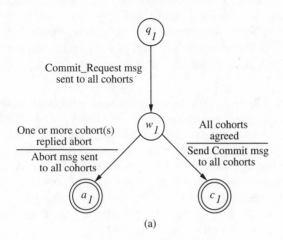

(a)

Cohort i (i = 2, 3, ..., n)

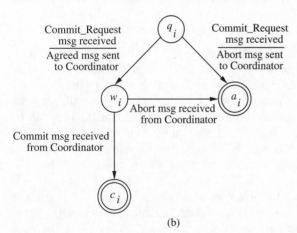

(b)

FIGURE 13.2
Finite state automata illustrating the
2-phase commit protocol (adapted
from [43]).

$C(w_2) = \{c_1, a_1, w_1\}$. Likewise, $C(q_2) = \{q_1, w_1\}$. Note that, $a_1, c_1 \notin C(q_2)$ because the two-phase commit protocol is synchronous within one state transition.

Sender set. Let s be an arbitrary state of a site, and let M be the set of all messages that are received in state s. The sender set for s, denoted by $S(s)$, is

$$\{i \mid \text{site } i \text{ sends } m \text{ and } m \in M\}$$

13.5.1 Basic Idea

We first consider the simple case where at most *one* site fails during a transaction execution. We begin by describing the conditions that cause blocking in two-phase commit protocols. We then discuss how to overcome them. Next, we explain how a decision regarding the final outcome of the transaction is made at a site that is recovering after failure. Finally, we describe how operational sites deal with a site failure.

CONDITIONS THAT CAUSE BLOCKING. We now present some observations that lead to the conditions under which the two-phase commit protocol blocks [44]. Consider a simple case where only one site remains operational and all other sites have failed. This site has to proceed based solely on its local state. Let s denote the state of the site at this point. If $C(s)$ contains both commit and abort states, then the site cannot decide to abort the transaction because some other site may be in the commit state. On the other hand, the site cannot decide to commit the transaction because some other site may be in the abort state. In other words, the site has to block until all the failed sites recover. The above observation leads to the following lemma [44]:

Lemma 13.1. If a protocol contains a local state of a site with both abort and commit states in its concurrency set, then under independent recovery conditions it is not resilient to an arbitrary single failure.

HOW TO ELIMINATE BLOCKING. We now address the question of how to modify the two-phase commit protocol to make it a nonblocking protocol. Notice that in Fig. 13.2, only states w_i ($i \neq 1$) have both abort and commit states in their concurrency sets. To make the two-phase commit protocol a nonblocking protocol, we need to make sure that $C(w_i)$ does not contain both abort and commit states. This can be done by introducing a buffer state p_1 in the finite state automaton of Fig. 13.2(a). We also introduce a buffer state p_i for the cohorts. (The reason for adding p_i, $i \neq 1$ will become clear later.) The resulting finite state automata are shown in Fig. 13.3. Now, in a system containing only two sites, $C(w_1) = \{q_2, w_2, a_2\}$, and $C(w_2) = \{a_1, p_1, w_1\}$.

This extended two-phase commit protocol is nonblocking in case of a single site failure and a failed site can perform independent recovery. Independent recovery is possible mainly because a site can make unilateral decisions regarding the global outcome of a transaction. Also, when a site fails, other sites can make decisions regarding the global outcome of the transaction based on their local states.

FAILURE TRANSITIONS. In order to perform independent recovery at a failed site, the failed site should be able to reach a final decision based solely on its local state. The decision making process is modeled in the FSA using *failure transitions*. A failure transition occurs at a failed site at the instant it fails (or immediately after it recovers from the failure). The local state resulting due to the state change caused by the failure transition will initially be occupied by the site upon recovery. The failure transitions are performed according to the following rule [44].

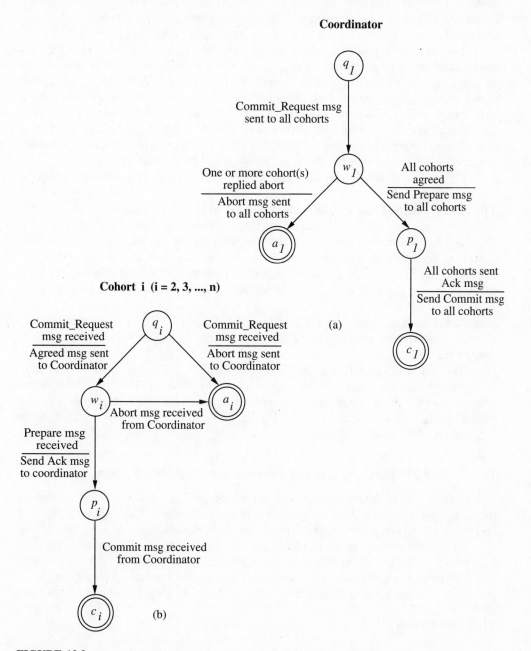

FIGURE 13.3
Finite state automata illustrating 3-phase commit protocol (adapted from Skeen [44]).

Rule 1. For every nonfinal state s (i.e., q_i, w_i, p_i) in the protocol: if $C(s)$ contains a commit, then assign a failure transition from s to a commit state in its FSA; otherwise, assign a failure transition from s to an abort state in its FSA.

The intuition behind this rule is straightforward. Note that, p_i $(i \neq 1)$ is the only state which has a commit state in its concurrency set. When site i is in state p_i, all the sites including i have agreed to commit. Thus, if site i fails in state p_i (recall our assumption that only one site fails during a transaction execution), there is no problem if it commits the transaction on recovery. On the other hand, all states other than p_i have the abort state in their concurrency sets. Hence, if a site fails in any state other than p_i and c_i, then it is not safe for the failed site to recover and commit the transaction unilaterally. Therefore, the failed site on recovery aborts the transaction.

Figure 13.4 illustrates the FSA resulting from the failure and timeout transitions.

TIMEOUT TRANSITIONS. We now consider what an operational site does in the event of another site's failure. If site i is waiting for a message from site j (i.e., $j \in S(i)$) and site j has failed, then site i times out. Based on the type of message expected from j, we can determine in what state site j failed. Once the state of j is known, we can determine the final state of j due to the failure transition at j. This observation leads to the timeout transitions in the commit protocol at the operational sites [44].

Rule 2. For each nonfinal state s, if site j is in $S(s)$, and site j has a failure transition to a commit(abort) state, then assign a timeout transition from state s to a commit (abort) state in the FSA.

The rationale behind this rule is as follows. The failed site makes a transition to a commit (abort) state using the failure transition (Rule 1). Therefore, operational sites must make the same transition in order to ensure that the final outcome of the transaction is identical at all the sites. Figure 13.4 illustrates the FSA resulting from the timeout transitions.

13.5.2   The Nonblocking Commit Protocol for Single Site Failure

It is assumed that each site uses the write-ahead-log protocol. It is also assumed that, at most, one site can fail during the execution of the transaction. The following protocol is a modified version of the protocol proposed by Skeen and Stonebraker [44].

Before the commit protocol begins, all the sites are in state q. If the coordinator fails while in state q_1, all the cohorts timeout, waiting for the Commit_Request message, and they perform the timeout transition, thus aborting the transaction. Upon recovery, the coordinator performs the failure transition from state q_1, also aborting the transaction.

THE PROTOCOL

Phase I. The first phase of the nonblocking protocol is identical to that of the two-phase commit protocol (see Sec. 13.4.1) except in the event of a site's failure. During the first phase, the coordinator is in state w_1, and each cohort is either in state a (in which case the site has already sent an Abort message to the coordinator) or w or q

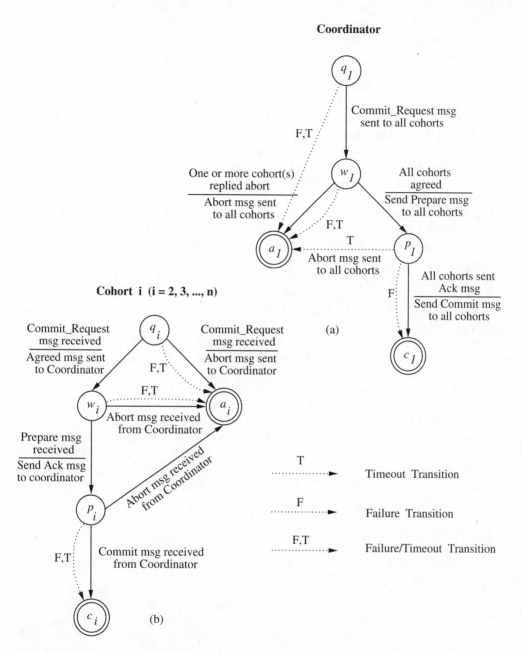

FIGURE 13.4
Finite state automata illustrating timeout and failure transitions (adapted from Skeen [44]).

depending on whether it has received the Commit_Request message or not. If a cohort fails, the coordinator times out waiting for the Agreed message from the failed cohort. In this case, the coordinator aborts the transaction and sends abort messages to all the cohorts.

Phase II. In the second phase, the coordinator sends a Prepare message to all the cohorts if all the cohorts have sent Agreed messages in phase I. Otherwise, the coordinator will send an Abort message to all the cohorts. On receiving a Prepare message, a cohort sends an acknowledge message to the cohort. If the coordinator fails before sending Prepare messages (i.e., in state w_1), it aborts the transaction upon recovery, according to the failure transition. The cohorts time out waiting for the prepare message, and also abort the transaction as per the timeout transition.

Phase III. In the third phase, on receiving acknowledgments to the Prepare messages from all the cohorts, the coordinator sends a Commit message to all the cohorts. A cohort, on receiving a Commit message, commits the transaction. If the coordinator fails before sending the Commit message (i.e., in state p_1), it commits the transaction upon recovery, according to the failure transition from state p_1. The cohorts time out waiting for the Commit message. They commit the transaction according to the timeout transition from state p_i. However, if a cohort fails before sending an acknowledgment message to a Prepare message, the coordinator times out in state p_1. The coordinator aborts the transaction and sends Abort messages to all the cohorts. The failed cohort, upon recovery, will abort the transaction according to the failure transition from state w_i.

Now, to clarify why state p_i was added to the FSA of cohorts (see Fig. 13.4), consider a system with three sites. Suppose the state p_i is not present. Under this case, if the coordinator is in state p_1 waiting for an acknowledgment message. Let cohort 2 (in state w_2) acknowledge and commit the transaction. Suppose cohort 3 (in state w_3) fails, then both the coordinator and cohort 3 (upon recovery as per the failure transition) will abort the transaction, thus, causing an inconsistent outcome for the transaction. By adding state p_i ($i \neq 1$), we ensure that no state has both abort and commit states in its concurrency set.

CORRECTNESS

Theorem 13.1. Rules 1 and 2 are sufficient for designing commit protocols resilient to a single site failure during a transaction [44].

Proof. The proof is by contradiction. Let P be a protocol that abides by Rules 1 and 2. Assume that protocol P is not resilient to all single site failures. Also, assume that the system has only two sites. Without loss of generality, let site 1 fail in state s_1, and let site 2 be in state s_2 when site 1 fails. Let site 1 make a failure transition to state f_1, and let site 2 make a timeout transition to state f_2. Suppose that the global state of the system, wherein site 1 is in state f_1 and site 2 is in state f_2, is inconsistent. Depending on whether s_2 is a final state (abort/commit) or a nonfinal state (all states other than abort and commit), we have the following two cases:

Case 1. s_2 is a final state. This implies that $f_2 \in C(s_1)$. If f_2 is a commit(abort) state, and f_1 is an abort(commit) state, then Rule 1 has been violated.

Case 2. s_2 is a nonfinal state. By the definition of the commit protocol, site 1 belongs to the sender set $S(s_2)$ of site 2. Hence, if f_2 is a commit(abort) state, and f_1 is an abort(commit) state, then Rule 2 has been violated.

13.5.3 Multiple Site Failures and Network Partitioning

We now discuss independent recovery under multiple site failures and network partitioning. We state the results by Skeen and Stonebraker [44] without giving the proof. Note that a protocol is resilient to a given condition only if it is nonblocking under that condition.

Theorem 13.2. There exists no protocol using independent recovery that is resilient to arbitrary failures by two sites.

Theorem 13.3. There exists no protocol resilient to network partitioning when messages are lost.

Theorem 13.4. There exists no protocol resilient to multiple network partitionings.

13.6 VOTING PROTOCOLS

A common approach to provide fault tolerance in distributed systems is by replicating data at many sites. If a site is not available, the data can still be obtained from copies at other sites. Commit protocols can be employed to update multiple copies of data. While the nonblocking protocol of the previous section can tolerate single site failures, it is not resilient to multiple site failures, communication failures, and network partitioning. In commit protocols, when a site is unreachable, the coordinator sends messages repeatedly and eventually may decide to abort the transaction, thereby denying access to data. However, it is desirable that the sites continue to operate even when other sites have crashed, or at least one partition should continue to operate after the system has been partitioned. Another well known technique used to manage replicated data is the voting mechanism. With the voting mechanism, each replica is assigned some number of votes, and a majority of votes must be collected from a process before it can access a replica. The voting mechanism is more fault-tolerant than a commit protocol in that it allows access to data under network partitions, site failures, and message losses without compromising the integrity of the data. We next describe static and dynamic voting mechanisms.

13.6.1 Static Voting

The static voting scheme is proposed by Gifford [19].

System model. The replicas of files are stored at different sites. Every file access operation requires that an appropriate lock is obtained. The lock granting rules allow either 'one writer and no readers' or 'multiple readers and no writers' to access a file simultaneously. It is assumed that at every site there is a lock manager that performs the lock related operations, and every file is associated with a version number, which gives the number of times the file has been updated. The version numbers are stored on stable storage, and every successful write operation on a replica updates its version number.

Basic idea. The essence of a voting algorithm which controls access to replicated data is as follows. Every replica is assigned a certain number of votes. This information is stored on stable storage. A read or write operation is permitted if a certain number of votes, *read quorum or write quorum*, respectively, are collected by the requesting process.

THE VOTING ALGORITHM.   When a process executing at site i issues a read or write request for a file, the following protocol is initiated.

1. Site i issues a Lock_Request to its local lock manager.
2. When the lock request is granted, site i sends a Vote_Request message to all the sites.
3. When a site j receives a Vote_Request message, it issues a Lock_Request to its local lock manager. If the lock request is granted, then it returns the version number of the replica (VN_j) and the number of votes assigned to the replica (V_j) to site i.
4. Site i decides whether it has the quorum or not, based on the replies received within a timeout period as follows (P denotes the set of sites which have replied).
   If the request issued was a read,

$$V_r = \sum_{k \in P} V_k$$

If $V_r \geq r$, where r is the read quorum, then site i has succeeded in obtaining the read quorum.
   If the request issued was a write,

$$V_w = \sum_{k \in Q} V_k$$

where the set of sites Q is determined as follows:

$$M = \max\{VN_j : j \in P\}$$
$$Q = \{j \in P : VN_j = M\}$$

In other words, the largest version number M denotes the version number of the current copy, and only the votes of the current replicas are counted in deciding the write quorum. If $V_w \geq w$, where w is the write quorum, then site i has succeeded in obtaining the write quorum.

5. If site i is not successful in obtaining the quorum, then it issues a Release_Lock to the local lock manager as well as to all the sites in P from whom it has received votes.

6. If site i is successful in obtaining the quorum, then it checks whether its copy of the file is current. A copy is current if its version number is equal to M. If the copy is not current, a current copy is obtained from a site that has a current copy. Once a current copy is available locally, site i performs the next step.

7. If the request is a read, site i reads the current copy available locally. If the request is a write, site i updates the local copy. Once all the accesses to the copy are performed, site i updates VN_i, and sends all the updates and VN_i to all the sites in Q. Note that a write operation updates only current copies. Site i then issues a Release_Lock request to its local lock manager as well as to all the sites in P.

8. All the sites receiving the updates perform the updates on their local copy, and on receiving a Release_Lock request, release the locks.

VOTE ASSIGNMENT. Let v be the total number of votes assigned to all the copies. The values for r (read quorum) and w (write quorum) are selected such that:

$$r + w > v \; ; \; w > \frac{v}{2}$$

The values selected for r and w combined with the fact that write operations update only the current copies guarantee the following:

- None of the obsolete copies are updated due to a write operation.
- There is a subset of replicas that are current and whose votes total to w.
- There is a nonnull intersection between every read quorum and write quorum. Hence, in any read quorum gathered, irrespective of the sites that participate in the quorum, there will be at least one current copy, which is selected for reading.
- Write quorum w is high enough to disallow simultaneous writes on two distinct subsets of replicas.

A note. In the above scheme, it is not necessary to count votes from current replicas only to obtain a write quorum. In addition, obsolete replicas can be updated whenever a write operation is performed. These steps will improve the performance of the system.

A highlight of the voting scheme is that the performance and reliability characteristics of a system can be altered by judiciously assigning the number of votes to each replica and carefully selecting the values for r and w [19]. Consider a system having four replicas stored at four different sites. The votes assigned to each replica and the disc latency at each replica is shown in Fig. 13.5. For the sake of simplicity, it is assumed that the communication delay between sites is negligible.

Suppose $r = 1$ and $w = 5$. Then the read access time is 75 milliseconds and the write access time is 750 milliseconds. While read operations perform well with this configuration, the inaccessibility of any one site will make the system unavailable for writes.

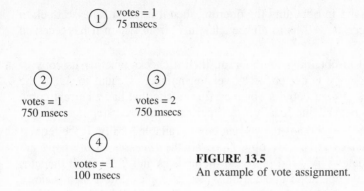

FIGURE 13.5
An example of vote assignment.

Suppose that for the configuration shown in Fig. 13.5, the quorums are changed to $r = 3$ and $w = 3$. The read access time is still 75 milliseconds. In addition, the system is unavailable for writes only when two sites (site 3 and any one of the other three) or any three sites (excluding site 3) are inaccessible simultaneously. Hence, by carefully selecting the values for quorums, the configuration has been made much more reliable than the previous configuration.

Suppose that site 4 is known to be more reliable compared to the other three, the voting configuration is changed as shown in Fig. 13.6, and the quorums are $r = 3$ and $w = 3$. Now the system is unavailable for writes only when two sites (site 4 and any one of the other three) or any three sites (excluding site 4) are inaccessible simultaneously. Since site 4 is known to be reliable, the system's fault tolerance is much higher compared to the previous two configurations. Therefore, a system's ability to tolerate faults can be increased by assigning a higher number of votes to reliable sites.

The voting scheme described above is referred to as a static scheme because both criteria that decide the majority and the number of votes assigned to each replica remain unchanged, irrespective of the system state.

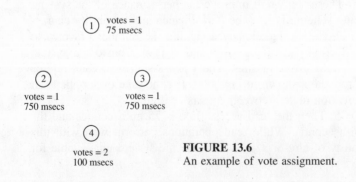

FIGURE 13.6
An example of vote assignment.

13.7   DYNAMIC VOTING PROTOCOLS

Suppose that in the system shown in Fig. 13.6, site 4 becomes unreachable from the rest of the sites due to its failure or due to a network partition. Sites 1, 2, and 3 can still collect a quorum (also referred to as majority) while site 4 (if operating) cannot collect a quorum. If another partition or a failure of a site occurs, making any site unavailable, the system cannot serve any read or write requests as a quorum cannot be collected in any partition. In other words, the system is completely unavailable—a serious problem indeed. Dynamic voting protocols solve this problem by adapting the number of votes or the set of sites that can form a quorum, to the changing state of the system due to site and communication failures. From the previously proposed dynamic protocols, two approaches to enhance availability can be identified.

- Majority based approach—the set of sites that can form a majority to allow access to replicated data changes with the changing state of the system.
- Dynamic vote reassignment—the number of votes assigned to a site changes dynamically.

We next describe two voting protocols that illustrate the above techniques.

13.8   THE MAJORITY BASED DYNAMIC VOTING PROTOCOL

In the majority based approach, the set of sites that can form a majority is dynamically altered to enhance availability in the event of site or communication failure. The set of sites that can form a majority are those that were updated when the most recent update was performed. A partition graph is used to represent the history of the network's failure and recovery. In a partition graph, nodes correspond to partitions and edges represent further partitioning of the network or recovery. In case of recovery, two or more partitions are merged into single partition.

In Fig. 13.7, the root node corresponds to a system with five copies stored on five sites which form a single partition. This indicates that all the sites are connected and that all the replicas are mutually consistent. The initial single partition is fragmented into two partitions ABD and CE. Later D is isolated from ABD and B is isolated from AB. Finally, partition A and CE merge to from a single partition ACE. In the voting protocol of Sec. 13.6.1, only ABCDE, ABD, and ACE partitions allow data access, assuming each copy has one vote.

In the majority based approach, once a system is partitioned, the protocol selects one of the partitions where read and write operations can continue. The partition selected is the one which could have formed a majority in the configuration that existed before the partitioning. Sites that belong to the selected partition will be able to collect quorums, whereas sites in the partitions not selected will not be able to collect quorums. Given this approach, sites in the partitions ABCDE, ABD, AB, A, and ACE will be able to obtain quorums.

A majority based dynamic voting protocol proposed by Jajodia and Mutchler [23] is now described. It is assumed that each replica is stored on a distinct site. The protocol

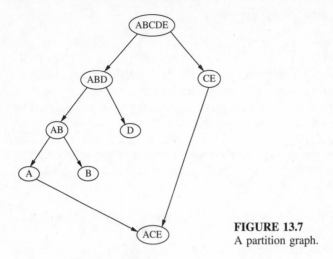

FIGURE 13.7
A partition graph.

requires that the replicas are linearly ordered a priori. The ordering is used to break ties among partitions. Each replica is associated with three variables: the version number, the number of replicas updated, and the distinguished site list.

Version number. The version number of a replica at a site i is an integer (denoted by VN_i) that counts the number of successful updates to the replica at i. VN_i is initially set to zero and is incremented by one at every successful update.

Number of replicas updated. It is an integer (denoted by RU_i at site i) that almost always reflects the number of replicas participating in the most recent update. RU_i is initially equal to the total number of replicas.

Distinguished sites list. The distinguished sites list at a site i is a variable (denoted by DS_i) that stores ID's of one or more sites. The contents of DS_i depend on RU_i. When RU_i is even, DS_i identifies the replica that is greater (as per the linear ordering) than all the other replicas that participated in the most recent update of the replica at site i; When RU_i is odd, DS_i is nil except when $RU_i = 3$, in which case DS_i lists the three replicas that participated in the most recent update from which a majority is needed to allow access to data. (The reason for this special case will become clear later.)

Before describing the details of the protocol, we give an example that illustrates how the protocol works.

Example 13.1. Suppose there are five replicas of a file stored at sites A, B, C, D, and E. The state of the system is represented by the following table, where each replica has already been updated three times. $\forall i$, $RU_i = 5$ (i.e., all the sites are accessible to every site), and the DS values are irrelevant here.

	A	B	C	D	E
VN	3	3	3	3	3
RU	5	5	5	5	5
DS	–	–	–	–	–

Suppose B receives an update request and finds that it can communicate only with sites A and C. B determines that the latest version of replicas in its partition (i.e., ABC) is version 3, and the number of replicas associated with version 3 is 5. Since partition ABC has 3 of the 5 copies, site B decides that it belongs to the distinguished partition (the partition that has more than half of the current replicas) and processes the update. Because three sites participated in the update, RU is changed to 3. Since $RU = 3$, DS lists the IDs of the three sites that participated in the update, namely, A, B, and C. The state at this point is as follows:

	A	B	C	D	E
VN	4	4	4	3	3
RU	3	3	3	5	5
DS	ABC	ABC	ABC	–	–

Suppose C receives an update and finds that it can communicate only with B. It discovers that the latest version is 4 and since $RU_c = 3$, the protocol chooses the static voting protocol (see Sec. 13.6.1). The reason for using static voting is that when the number of replicas is three, Jajodia and Mutchler [23] found that the static voting performs better than dynamic voting. Given $DS_c = ABC$, B and C form a majority among ABC and therefore, C processes the update. The state changes to the following:

	A	B	C	D	E
VN	4	5	5	3	3
RU	3	3	3	5	5
DS	ABC	ABC	ABC	–	–

Note that sites B and C do not change RU or DS as they are using the static voting protocol. Suppose D receives an update and discovers that it can communicate with B, C, and E. The latest version in the partition BCDE is 5 with $RU = 3$. So a majority from $DS = ABC$ is sought, which is available. Since the partition BCDE has four sites, RU is set to 4. Since RU is even, DS is set to B, which has the highest order (assuming the lexicographic ordering was used to linearly order the copies). The current state is as follows:

	A	B	C	D	E
VN	4	6	6	6	6
RU	3	4	4	4	4
DS	ABC	B	B	B	B

Suppose C receives an update and discovers that it can communicate only with B. Since partition BC contains exactly half the sites in the partition and contains the distinguished site B (DS is used to break the tie), the update is carried out in partition BC and the state changes to the following:

	A	B	C	D	E
VN	4	7	7	6	6
RU	3	2	2	4	4
DS	ABC	B	B	B	B

We now describe the steps of the majority based dynamic voting protocol.

OUTLINE OF THE PROTOCOL.   When site i receives an update, it executes the following protocol [23]:

1. Site i issues a Lock_Request to its local lock manager.
2. If the lock is granted, i sends a Vote_Request message to all the sites.
3. When a site j receives the Vote_Request message, it issues a Lock_Request to its local lock manager. If the lock is granted, j sends the values of VN_j, RU_j, and DS_j to site i.
4. From all the responses, site i decides whether it belongs to the distinguished partition, described shortly.
5. If i does not belong to the distinguished partition, it issues a Release_Lock request to its local lock manager and sends Abort messages to all the other sites that responded. A site, on receiving a Abort message, issues a Release_Lock request to its local lock manager.
6. If i belongs to the distinguished partition, it performs the update if its local copy is current. Otherwise, i obtains a current copy from one of the other sites and then performs the update. Note that along with the replica update, VN_i, RU_i, and DS_i are also updated (described shortly under **update**). Site i then sends a Commit message to all the participating sites along with the missing updates and values of VN_i, RU_i, and DS_i. It then issues a Release_Lock request to the local lock manager.
7. When a site j receives a commit message: it updates its replica, updates the variables VN_j, RU_j, and DS_j, and issues a Release_Lock request to its local lock manager.

Distinguished partition.   Note that when this procedure is invoked, the invoking site i has collected the responses for its Vote_Request messages. Let P denote the set of responding sites.

1. The site i calculates the following values:

$$M = \max\{VN_j : j \in P\}$$
$$Q = \{j \in P : VN_j = M\}$$
$$N = RU_j, \text{ where } j \in Q$$

Note that M gives the most recent version in the partition; Q gives the set of those sites containing the version M; N gives the number of sites that participated in the latest update indicated by version number M.

2. If Cardinality(Q) $> N/2$, then site i is a member of the distinguished partition, because it has collected votes from the majority of members that participated in the latest updates.

    Otherwise, if Cardinality(Q) $= N/2$, then the tie needs to be broken. Arbitrarily select a site $j \in Q$; If $DS_j \in Q$, then i belongs to the distinguished partition. Note that when N is even, RU_j is also even and DS_j contains the site with the highest order in the linear order (see **Update**). In other words, site i is in the partition containing the distinguished site.

3. Otherwise, if $N = 3$, and if P contains two or all three sites indicated by the DS variable of the site in Q, then i belongs to the distinguished partition. Note that since step 2 did not apply and $N = 3$, there is only one site in Q.

4. Otherwise, i does not belong to the distinguished partition.

Update. Update is invoked when a site is ready to commit. The variables associated with the replica at site i are updated as follows:

$$VN_i = M + 1$$
$$RU_i = \text{Cardinality(P)}$$

DS_i is updated as follows when $N \neq 3$, since static voting protocol is used when $N = 3$.

$$DS_i = \begin{cases} K \text{ if } RU_i \text{ is even, where } K \text{ is the site with the highest order} \\ P \text{ if } RU_i = 3 \end{cases}$$

Note that this protocol can deadlock because it employs locks. In case of a deadlock, the deadlock must be resolved (see Chap. 7 for deadlock detecting and resolving algorithms). Stochastic analysis of this algorithm can be found in [24].

13.9 DYNAMIC VOTE REASSIGNMENT PROTOCOLS

In dynamic vote reassignment protocols, the number of votes assigned to a site changes dynamically. We first illustrate this concept with the help of an example. Let both read and write quorums be three (i.e., $r = w = 3$) for the system shown in Fig. 13.8. If a network partition separates site 4 from the rest of the system, then sites 1, 2, and 3 can still collect a quorum (or a majority) while site 4 cannot. If another partition occurs and separates site 3 from its group (i.e., we have three partitions consisting of sites {1,2}, {3}, and {4}) then no partition will be able to collect a quorum and the system cannot execute any read or write request. Note that the above situation can also occur if sites 3 and 4 both fail. We can reduce the likelihood of the above situation by increasing the number of votes assigned to the group {1,2,3} before the second partition or failure occurs. That is, after any failure, the majority group if any (in this example, the group {1,2,3}) dynamically reassigns the votes in order to increase its voting power and increase the system's chances of surviving subsequent failures. For instance, the votes assigned to sites 1, 2, and 3 can each be changed to five making the total number of votes in the system seventeen. Now after the second failure, the group {1,2} has ten votes out of a total of seventeen, and therefore a quorum can still be collected.

The idea of dynamic vote reassignment was first suggested by Gifford [19]. However, dynamic vote reassignment was discussed in complete detail by Barbara, Garcia-Molina, and Spauster [8] on which the following discussion is based. Barbara et al. categorized the dynamic vote reassignment into two types:

Group Consensus. The sites in the active (majority) group agree upon the new vote assignment using either a distributed algorithm or by electing a coordinator to perform the task. Sites outside the majority group do not receive any votes.

Because this method relies on the active group's participation, the current system topology will be known before deciding the vote assignments. By using that information, this method can make an intelligent vote assignment that is more resilient to future failures. However, deciding the vote assignment and installing it are quite complicated. Moreover, a good vote assignment requires accurate information on the current topology.

Autonomous Reassignment. Each site uses a view of the system to make a decision about changing its votes and picking a new vote value without regard to the rest of the sites. In this method, a site essentially tries to obtain all or part of the votes of a site (or sites) that have been separated from the majority group. Before the change is made final, the site must obtain approval for its vote change from a majority to ensure that the mutual exclusion provided by the voting mechanism is not compromised. Since each site operates on its own, the global vote assignment may not be as effective compared to the vote assignment in the group consensus method. However, this method is quicker, simpler, and more flexible.

In the following, only the autonomous method is described. Interested readers are referred to [6] for techniques to determine vote assignments for a given topology. Algorithms for arriving at a consensus can be found in [17, 18].

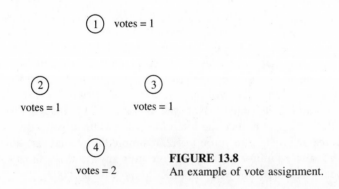

FIGURE 13.8
An example of vote assignment.

13.9.1 Autonomous Vote Reassignment

The autonomous vote reassignment protocol is initiated when a site chooses a new vote value. The way in which a site picks a new vote value is a policy decision and is discussed later. The protocol allows the increasing as well as the decreasing of the vote value assigned to a site. The protocol uses a vote changing protocol to install the new vote value. The vote changing protocol invokes a vote collecting protocol to ensure that it has approval from a majority. The vote collecting protocol is also used by other operations (such as updates) that require majority approval. We next describe the data structures used by the protocol.

DATA STRUCTURES. At each site i, a vector V_i is maintained in the stable storage, which represents what site i believes to be the global vote assignment. $V_i[j]$, an element of V_i, indicates the number of votes of site j according to site i. Another vector maintained at each site i is v_i, where $v_i[j]$ indicates the votes of site j as determined by site i upon the collection of votes. It will be clear later from the protocols that the values of $v_i[j]$ and $V_i[j]$ are not necessarily the same. As both the increasing and the decreasing of vote values assigned to a site are allowed, it is necessary to keep track of the currency of the vote values. This is done by maintaining a version vector N at each site. $N_i[j]$ represents the version number of $V_i[j]$ at site i.

Vote increasing protocol. When site i wishes to increase its vote value, it takes the following steps.

1. Site i sends V_i and N_i along with the new vote value to the sites with which it can communicate.
2. Site i waits for a majority of the sites to respond with their votes (see the vote collecting protocol below).
3. If a majority of votes were collected (see the vote collecting protocol), then site i performs the following:

$$V_i[i] := new\ value\ ;\ N_i[i] := N_i[i] + 1$$

A site j on receiving the message sent in step 1 performs the following actions:

- $V_j[i] :=$ new vote value of site i
- $N_j[i] := N_i[i] + 1$

Vote decreasing protocol. Suppose site i wishes to decrease its vote value. A decrease in vote value implies that a site is relinquishing some (or all) of its voting power, which does not endanger mutual exclusion [8]. This fact yields a simple protocol where site i need not obtain a majority before changing its vote value. Site i takes the following steps.

1. Set $V_i[i]$ to the new value.
2. $N_i[i] := N_i[i] + 1$
3. Send the vectors V_i and N_i to the other sites in the system.

A site j, on receiving the above message, will perform the following actions:

- $V_j[i] := V_i[i]$
- $N_j[i] := N_i[i]$

Vote collecting protocol. Suppose site i is collecting votes to decide upon an event (read, write, vote reassignment). Each voting site j will send V_j and N_j to site i. After receiving the responses, the following protocol is followed at i:

1. For each reply (V_j and N_j) received, site i performs the following actions.
   - $v_i[j] := V_j[j]$
   - If $V_j[j] > V_i[j]$ OR ($V_j[j] < V_i[j]$ AND $N_j[j] > N_i[j]$) then

   $$V_i[j] := V_j[j]; \quad N_i[j] := N_j[j]$$

   Note that $V_j[j] > V_i[j]$ implies that site j has increased its votes since site i last determined $V_i[j]$ and site i has to update its vector $V_i[j]$ to reflect this fact.
   On the other hand, ($V_j[j] < V_i[j]$ AND $N_j[j] > N_i[j]$) implies that site j has decreased its votes and site i has to update its vector $V_i[j]$ to reflect this change.

2. If site i does not receive a reply from some site j, then it performs the following actions:
   - Determines k such that $k \in G$ and $N_k[j] = \max\{N_p[j] : p \in G\}$, where G is the set of all the sites from which site i has received replies. The site k has the latest information on the votes assigned to site j.
   - $v_i[j] := V_k[j]$
     $V_i[j] := V_k[j]$
     $N_i[j] := N_k[j]$

3. Site i decides whether it has the majority of votes or not as follows: Let K denote the set of all the sites in the system and G denote the set of the sites that responded. The total number of votes in the system is computed as:

$$TOT := \sum_{k \in K} v_i[k]$$

The total number of votes received is computed as:

$$RCVD := \sum_{k \in G} v_i[k]$$

If $RCVD > TOT/2$, then site i has collected a majority.

13.9.2   Vote Increasing Policies

Vote increasing policies are concerned with how to pick a new vote value for a site in a systematic way. Barbara et al. [8] divide vote increasing policies into two strategies, namely, the overthrow technique and the alliance technique.

THE OVERTHROW TECHNIQUE.   After a failure (or a number of failures), one site in the active group takes on more votes. To decide which site should increase its voting power, any election algorithm can be employed. For example, in a token passing mechanism the site with the token will increase its votes. Another scheme to select the site is to linearly order the sites a priori. In case of a failure, the site with the highest order in the majority group will increase its votes.

Let T be the total number of votes in the system, and assume that it is an odd number. Then $M = (T + 1)/2$ is the minimum number of votes required for the majority. Let us also assume that site i has failed and the rest of the sites in the system are operational. Let j be the site selected for increasing its voting power. If j increases its voting power by $2V_i$ where V_i is the voting power of site i, then we have

$$T' = T + V_i, \text{ and } M' = M + V_i$$

where T' is the total voting power in the new system configuration and M' is the number of votes required for the majority. With this voting configuration, all the groups that could obtain a majority with site i can still obtain a majority using the votes of site j (see Problem 13.2). Note that the increase in the number of votes should be at least $2V_i$ and M should be changed to M' to ensure that the mutual exclusion is not compromised when site i becomes available again. By increasing the number of votes by $2V_i$, we counteract against those votes that site i holds and would have contributed if it were in an active group.

THE ALLIANCE TECHNIQUE.   With this technique, if a failure occurs or a number of failures occur, all the sites in the active group increase their votes. Again the increase in the number of votes should be at least twice the number of votes held by the unavailable site(s). There are many possibilities to increase the votes under this technique. Suppose site i becomes unavailable: (1) all sites will increase their voting power by $\lceil 2V_i/N \rceil$ where N is the number of sites in the majority group, or (2) all sites will increase their voting power by $2V_i$ votes.

Irrespective of whether the alliance or the overthrow technique is used to increase votes in the system, some disparity in voting power among the sites will result. This will of course affect availability, which depends on the availability of sites with higher voting power. Also, when the token passing mechanism is used in the overthrow scheme, if the token ends up in a site that belongs to a partition that does not form a majority, the votes are not increased. This means that no partition will have the majority, thus affecting availability. Over a period of time, with many increases in voting power, the imbalance in voting power may reach a point where it will be desirable to balance the voting power of sites.

13.9.3   Balance of Voting Power

There are two approaches to restore the balance of voting power among the sites [8]:

- A site that has been out of the active group can "catch up" when it returns to the active group, in other words, it increases its votes. For an example of this technique, readers are referred to [8].

- When a site that has been out of the active group returns, the sites that have increased their votes can relinquish them, that is, decrease their votes. This technique requires that each site remember the number of additional votes it has taken for each site's absence.

13.10   FAILURE RESILIENT PROCESSES

The fundamental unit of execution is a process. Hence, in order for any system to be fault-tolerant, the processes of that system must be resilient to system failures. A process may recover immediately upon recovery of the system and continue execution from where it was interrupted due to the failure. We do not call such a process a resilient process, because the system may be unavailable for a long duration, thereby disrupting the service provided by the process. A process is said to be resilient if it masks failures and guarantees progress despite a certain number of system failures. In other words, a minimum disruption is caused to the service provided by the process in the event of a system failure.

Two approaches have been proposed to implement resilient processes: backup processes and replicated execution.

13.10.1   Backup Processes

In the backup processes approach, each resilient process is implemented by a primary process and one or more backup processes. The primary process executes while the backup processes are inactive. If the primary process terminates because of a failure, one of the backup processes becomes active and takes over the functions of the primary process. To facilitate this takeover and minimize the computation that has to be redone by the backup process, the state of the primary process is stored (checkpointed) at appropriate intervals. The checkpointed state is stored in a suitable place such that the failure of the primary process's machine does not affect the checkpoint's availability. Checkpointing is also referred to as the synchronization of the primary and backup processes. An attractive feature of this scheme is that very little system resources are consumed by the backup processes as they are inactive. However, the computation may be delayed because the checkpointing is done during the normal operation of the system. Moreover, there will be a delay before a backup process can take over for the failed primary process for the following reasons. (1) The termination of the primary process must be detected before a secondary process can begin execution. The termination detection in distributed systems typically involves timeouts, which causes delays. (2) When a backup process begins execution, it may have to perform some amount of recomputation as the checkpoint does not always reflect the state of the primary process at the time of its termination.

The recomputation by a backup process to catch up with the primary process introduces additional complexities. The backup process should take care not to reissue IOs and resend messages that are already sent by the primary process. In addition, messages that were processed by the primary process since the latest checkpoint must to be available for the backup process during the recomputation phase.

When a primary process fails, the issue of which backup process will take over the primary process functions needs to be resolved. This issue can be handled through election algorithms in which one of the backup processes is elected as the new primary. However, a simpler method has been used, wherein the processes are logically arranged as a ring. When the primary process fails, a neighbor process in the ring is chosen to be the next primary process [10, 32].

13.10.2 Replicated Execution

In the replicated execution approach, several processes execute the same program concurrently. As long as one of the processes survives failures, the computation or the service continues. A significant advantage of replicated execution is that it can be used to increase *reliability* as well as *availability*. The reliability of a computation can be increased by taking a majority consensus among the results generated by all the process. This final result can then be used in subsequent computations. If replicated execution is used only to increase availability, the output of any one of the processes can be used as the final result. The main disadvantage of replicated execution is that a number of CPUs must be made available for a single computation.

If the computation performs nonidempotent operations, problems may arise. (An operation is idempotent if the effect of executing it several times on the system state is identical to the effect of executing it only once.) For example, if the computation uses random number generating routines, then problems arise as each process can use a different random number, resulting in different outputs by the processes. Consider a distributed computation where several processes cooperate by exchanging messages in performing the computation. Suppose these processes are implemented as resilient processes through replicated execution. In this case, only one of the replicated processes should be allowed to send messages to the other resilient processes. Also note that the messages exchanged may arrive in different orders at different processes. Under such circumstances, it must be ensured that all the replicas of a resilient process choose the same communicant for their next message [31].

Similarly, if the computation must communicate to the outside world, only one of the messages generated by the replicated processes should be allowed to communicate to the outside world.

13.11 RELIABLE COMMUNICATION

Consider a system that maintains replicated data. (Replicated data may be maintained by a system for higher availability and/or for higher reliability). Assume that at each site, there is a data manager process responsible for maintaining the replica at that site. Suppose a process p wishes to update a replicated data item. The following three scenarios can occur if p sends the update message and then fails [9]:

- A data manager receives the update and then learns of the failure of p.
- A data manager learns of the failure of p before receiving the update.
- A data manager neither receives the update nor learns of p's failure.

Under these circumstances, if a system must be fault-tolerant (i.e., behave in a certain way or mask failures), it is necessary that all the data managers behave identically. To ensure this, all the data managers are required to have an identical view of the events occurring in the system. Note that even under normal operating conditions, it is necessary that all the data managers carry out the updates in the same order to prevent inconsistencies among the replicas. All the data managers in the system can have an identical view if the following conditions are met. (1) The messages received at them are identically ordered, (Identical ordering helps to process messages in the same order at all data managers.) (2) Each message is either received at every data manager or at none of them (i.e., atomic broadcast). We next describe a communication protocol proposed by Birman and Joseph [9] that satisfies these conditions.

13.11.1 Atomic Broadcast

The protocol has two phases, and it assumes that there is a queue associated with each process to store the received messages (see Fig. 13.9).

Phase I

1. A process (sender) wishing to send a message to a group of destinations (receivers) multicasts the message to the group. (The ids of the receivers are also part of the message.)
2. On receiving the message, a receiver:
   - Assigns a priority (highest among all the buffered messages' priorities) to the message, marks it *undeliverable*, and buffers the message in the message queue. (Note that a local timestamp based on the Lamport's Clocks can be used as a unique priority.)
   - It then informs the sender of the priority assigned to the message.

FIGURE 13.9
Data structure used by the reliable communication protocol.

Phase II

1. On receiving the responses from all the destinations, the sender:
   - Chooses the highest priority assigned by all the receivers as the final priority for the message.
   - It then multicasts the final priority of the message to all the receivers.
2. On receiving the final priority for a message, a receiver:
   - Assigns the priority to the corresponding message.
   - Marks the message as *deliverable*.
   - Orders the messages in the message queue based on the increasing order of priorities.
   - The message will be delivered when it reaches the head of the queue and has been marked as deliverable.

If a receiver detects that it has a message marked undeliverable, whose sender has failed, it performs the following steps as a coordinator to complete the protocol:

1. It interrogates all the receivers about the status of the message. A receiver may respond in one of the following three ways:
   - The message is marked undeliverable and the priority assigned by it to the message.
   - The message is marked deliverable and the final priority of the message.
   - It has not received the message.
2. After collecting all the responses, the coordinator will perform the following steps:
   - If the message was marked deliverable at any of the receivers, the final priority assigned to the message is multicasted. On receiving this message, receivers will perform the steps of phase II.
   - Otherwise, the coordinator reinitiates the protocol from phase I.

Note that this protocol requires that receivers retain messages even after they are delivered. A scheme to discard delivered messages can be found in [9].

13.12   CASE STUDIES

13.12.1   Targon/32: Fault Tolerance Under UNIX

Targon/32 is a fault-tolerant version of UNIX for distributed systems developed at Nixdorf Computer [10]. Providing fault-tolerance with complete transparency is the goal of this system. Targon/32 implements fault-tolerant user processes that employ the technique of backup processes. Once a user or the system administrator specifies which processes are to be backed up, the rest is completely transparent. Programs need no modification in order to be backed up.

SYSTEM ARCHITECTURE.   The system consists of a local area network of two to sixteen machines connected via a fast dual bus. Each machine is a shared memory multiprocessor consisting of three processors. Each processor runs an operating system kernel that is responsible for the creation and scheduling of processes and for inter-process communication. One of the three processors is responsible for the creation, maintenance, and recovery of backup processes. The other two processors are available for executing user processes.

There is one *process server* per system. It is responsible for keeping track of the current system configuration. There are many *page servers* in the system whose number is configuration dependent. A page server is mainly responsible for backing up the virtual memory space of a subset of primary processes in the system. It also maintains the virtual memory space as well as checkpoints for the backup processes. Other servers in the system are file servers, TTY servers (that manage communication with terminals and related devices), and Raw servers (that manage unrestrained access to disk and tape servers).

Processes communicate through channels which have queues to hold unread mes-sages. A user process views a channel as just another UNIX-style file. A channel is opened to establish connection, a message is sent by writing into the channel, and a message is read by reading the channel.

FAILURE RESILIENT PROCESSES.   Targon/32 employs a backup processes scheme to implement failure resilient processes. It uses one inactive process as a backup for the primary process. The backup process is maintained on a machine different from that of the primary process. The process server (which is also backed up) is responsible for deciding on which machines a primary process and its backup will be located. It is also possible to specify when and where a new backup process is created after a crash occurs. In one scheme, a primary process runs with a backup until a crash occurs, but no new backup is created after the crash. In another scheme, a new backup is created after a crash only when the machine in which the original primary or backup process resided returns to service.

The state of a primary process is periodically checkpointed with the help of an operation referred to as a *sync* operation. However, messages received by a primary process after the most recent sync operation must also be made available to the backup in the event of primary process termination. These messages are made available in the following manner.

Whenever a sender sends a message to a receiver, the message is also sent to the sender's backup and the receiver's backup. For this purpose, a three way atomic broadcast is used to ensure that either all three destinations, or none of them, receive the message. The messages are saved at the receiver's backup until the next sync operation. A variable called *write_since_sync* is used at the sender's backup process to keep track of the number of messages sent by the primary process.

Whenever the primary process's machine fails, its backup is activated (see "Crash Detection and Handling" and "Process Recovery" later in this section). It demand pages the state of the primary and begins execution from that state on. The backup process reads the same messages that were read by the primary process, and it avoids resending messages by using the *write_since_sync* count. Once the backup process catches up with the primary process, the saved messages are discarded and the *write_since_sync* count is set to zero.

If a primary process forks off a child process, a *birth notice* is sent to the backup's machine. On receiving the birth notice, the kernel sets up the necessary data structures for the child process's backup to hold the messages that are sent to it.

Kernel interaction. Whenever a backup process takes over for its primary process, every interaction between the backup and the kernel on its machine must appear to the backup as it did to the primary. Therefore, the system should insulate the backup process from any differences between the kernel at the backup's machine and the kernel at the primary process. In other words, system calls by a backup process should return the same information as they would have returned at the primary process's location.

In Targon/32, many types of information (such as the process *id*, the priority of the process, etc.) are directly returned by the local kernel at the primary process. These types of information are maintained at the backup process's kernel also, to ensure that they can be returned as replies to system calls by the backup in the event of a primary process's machine failure.

SYNC OPERATION. The state of the primary process and its backup process are made identical by the sync operation. The sync operation is automatically initiated by the kernel whenever the number of messages read by the primary process exceeds a certain number, or the primary process has executed for a duration longer than a threshold since the previous sync operation. Normally, a sync operation is initiated immediately before the return from a system call, a page fault, or at the beginning of a new time slice. This facilitates the reconstruction of the primary process's kernel stack for the backup process, without relying on the local kernel's data (e.g., physical addresses). If a sync operation must be performed while a system call is in progress (this might be necessary while awaiting a response from a slow device such as a terminal), the process's state is saved as though it were just about to enter the system call. This also makes the reconstruction of the kernel's stack straightforward [10].

The sync operation is handled in two stages at the primary process's machine. In the first stage, a normal paging mechanism, is used to send all the dirty pages (via a message) to the page server and to the page server's backup. A dirty page is one that has not been sent to the page server since its last modification. The primary process's stack (if it has changed since the last sync operation) is also saved through the paging mechanism, as the stack is kept in pages owned by the process rather than in the kernel's space. The page server, upon receiving these pages, adds them to the primary process's page account.

The second stage of the sync operation constructs a sync message. This message contains [10]:

- All machine independent information about the primary process's state, such as the virtual address of the next instruction to be executed, register values, etc.
- Information about all the open channels and the number of messages read from each channel since the last sync operation.

- A small amount of information allowing the construction of the kernel stack on recovery so that the process appears to be just entering or just returning from a system call.

Once the sync message is constructed, it is sent to the primary process's backup, the page server, and the page server's backup, using the atomic message delivery mechanism. The primary process resumes normal operation immediately upon queuing the sync message. Any messages sent by the primary process will not be delivered before the sync message, as the communication channels are FIFO. If the primary process crashes before the sync message leaves the machine, the backup process starts execution from the state saved by the previous sync operation.

The page server, upon receiving the sync message, makes the backup process's page account identical to the page account of the primary process and frees up any pages that are no longer needed.

The machine on which the backup process is running, upon receiving the sync message, updates the backup's state and deletes all the messages (previously received and already read by the primary) saved since the last sync operation. (Recall that any message sent to a primary process is also sent to its backup.) Also, the variable *write_since_sync* is reset to zero.

DETERMINISTIC EXECUTION IN THE PRESENCE OF SIGNALS. Whenever a signal is generated in UNIX (e.g., kill, alarm expiration, or typing certain control characters at the terminal), it generates a message to the process server requesting that a signal be sent. The signal is sent to both the primary process and its backup. The signal is queued at the backup process. Signals are special in the sense they must be dealt with—ignored or handled—immediately on their arrival, unlike regular messages which can be queued for later consumption. It is generally difficult to inform the backup process of the exact point at which the primary process dealt with a signal, especially when failures occur. Hence to make sure that the backup deals with the signal at the same point as the primary process, Targon/32 designers made the primary machine initiate a sync operation just before handling any signal. This guarantees that, on recovery, the backup will find the signal pending and will handle it at exactly the same place as the primary process did. It is necessary to guarantee that a backup ignores the same signals ignored by the primary. Thus, whenever a message is sent by the primary, the count of ignored signals since the last message send is piggybacked on the message. This count is used in the backup's machine to remove ignored signals. This ensures that only those signals handled by the primary process are available at the backup's machine.

CRASH DETECTION AND HANDLING. Crash detection in Targon/32 is based on the protocol proposed in [47]. The machines are organized as a virtual ring. Each machine periodically sends a report that it is alive to the neighbor to its right. Each machine expects a report periodically from the neighbor to its left. Should a machine fail to report, the neighbor to its right attempts to communicate with it. If its efforts fail, it takes the following actions [10]:

- It determines whether it can communicate with any other machine in the system. If not, it assumes that it must crash, otherwise it assumes that its neighbor to the left has crashed. It sends a message that orders its neighbor to the left to crash, in case its neighbor can receive messages and is not aware of its problem. This step becomes tricky when there are only two machines operating in the system.
- It broadcasts a machine-dead message that the neighbor to its left has crashed.
- It locates a new neighbor to its left.

A machine, on receiving a machine-dead message, will stop trying to communicate with the failed machine. It puts the message at the end of the message queue for the backup processes located in the machine. Thus, backups are sure to deal with any sync messages that have previously arrived but are yet to be handled.

PROCESS RECOVERY. Once the news of the primary process's termination (through a machine-dead message) reaches its backup process, it must be activated. This is done by the kernel as follows [10]:

- It allocates and initializes the data structures needed for the local kernel state and memory mapping.
- It requests a list of the pages held by the page server so that memory mapping tables can be correctly initialized.
- It sets up the kernel stack from the latest sync information.
- It puts the backup process on the run queue.

At this point, the backup process is ready to begin execution. In the user mode, the process executes as its primary process would execute. While the backup process is catching up with the primary process, a backup process may act differently from its primary process (only in the kernel mode) under the following circumstances:

- When the backup process attempts to send a message, if the kernel finds the *writes_since_sync* count greater than zero, it decrements the count by one and discards the message. By using this technique, the backup process avoids resending a message that has already been sent by the primary process.
- When the backup process attempts to fork off a child process, the kernel checks for the existence of a birth notice. If one exists, the child process *id* is retrieved from the birth notice and is returned to the backup process.
- Finally, the backup process is not allowed to sync until it has completely caught up with the primary process.

PERFORMANCE. A Targon/32 system user whose primary process dies experienced a delay of five to fifteen seconds. The performance of a fault-tolerant two-machine Targon/32 system is 1.6 times that of a standard UNIX running on a single machine.

13.13 SUMMARY

Fault-tolerant computer systems prevent the disruption of services provided to users. A system can be designed to be fault-tolerant in two ways: a system may mask failures or it may exhibit a well defined failure behavior in the event of a failure. When a system is designed to mask failures, it continues to perform its specified function despite failures. On the other hand, a system designed to behave in a well defined manner may or may not perform the specified function during failures, but it may facilitate actions suitable for recovery.

In this chapter, we discussed commit protocols and voting protocols, two widely used techniques in the design of a fault-tolerant system. Commit protocols implement a well defined behavior in the event of failures. Voting protocols, on the other hand, mask failures in a system in the event of failures.

Two-phase commit protocols block in the event of site failure. Nonblocking commit protocols under independent recovery conditions are only resilient to single site failures. Voting protocols are much more fault resilient than commit protocols. They can tolerate multiple site failures and communication failures as long as quorums can be obtained. Dynamic voting protocols provide higher availability than static voting protocols by adapting the number of votes assigned to sites or the set of sites that can form a majority to the changing state of the system.

To implement a fault-tolerant distributed system, processes in the system should be able to tolerate system failures and communicate reliably. Two techniques were described that have been used to implement processes that are resilient to system failures. In one technique, backup processes stand by to take over the function of a failed process. In the second technique, a multiple number of processes execute simultaneously. As long as one of the processes survives, the system can tolerate failures. In addition, we described a technique based on a two-phase commit protocol to send messages reliably among processes.

13.14 FURTHER READING

Chang and Gouda [11] provide a theoretical treatment of recovery in distributed systems. They discuss the conditions necessary for independent recovery in the case of site failures where a site does not coordinate recovery activity with the other sites in the system.

Ramarao [38] derives characterizations of commit protocols that are resilient to a prescribed number of failures (site and link faults not leading to network partition). He also investigates the effects of the architecture of the underlying distributed system on the commit protocols. Based on these observations, two nonblocking commit protocols are designed.

In [28], Levy, Korth, and Silberschatz propose an optimistic commit protocol to overcome the blocking problem of two-phase commit protocol in the event of failures. In this protocol, locks are released as soon as a site agrees to commit a transaction. If the transaction must eventually be aborted, its effects are undone using a compensation transaction.

The static voting of Sec. 13.6.1 requires a minimum of three replicas to be useful, which can be expensive in terms of storage requirement. Paris [34] replaces some replicas by mere records of the current state of the data, thus reducing the storage requirements but not decreasing the availability of data. The reliability of voting mechanisms is discussed by Barbara and Garcia-Molina in [7]. In [46], Tong and Kain present different algorithms to assign votes to replicas aimed at maximizing reliability. Agrawal and Jalote [2] have proposed an efficient voting protocol that requires only $O(\sqrt{N})$ messages for an operation where N is the number of nodes in the system. Agrawal and Bernstein [1] have proposed a nonblocking quorum consensus to reduce delays in accessing databases while collecting a quorum.

Ahamad and Ammar [3] present a multidimensional voting scheme. In this scheme, the vote assignment to each replica and the quorums are k-dimensional vectors of nonnegative integers. Each dimension of the vote and quorum assignment is similar to voting, and the quorum requirements in different dimensions can be combined in a number of ways. This makes multidimensional voting more powerful than static voting. Akhil Kumar [27] has presented a randomized algorithm for vote assignment. The availability obtained by using this algorithm is shown to be close to those produced by optimal assignments.

A majority based dynamic voting protocol presented in Sec. 13.8 does not keep track of network partitions that occur between two successive initiations of the majority determination, thus reducing availability under certain conditions. In [45], Tang and Natarajan propose a dynamic voting scheme to overcome the above problem. In [16], yet another dynamic voting scheme is presented by Davcev.

In [22], Huang and Li propose a quorum based commit and termination protocol to provide improved availability of data in the presence of concurrent site failures, lost messages, and network partitioning.

In [37], Ramarao discusses the necessary and sufficient conditions for the implementation of atomic transactions in the presence of network partitions. He reports that protocols to implement atomic actions despite network partitions exist only under unrealistically strong conditions.

Replication is a key method employed to achieve fault tolerance. In [26], Joseph and Birman describe how replicated data is maintained in the ISIS system. Oki and Liskov present a replication method based on the primary copy technique to achieve fault tolerance, that causes little delay to user's computation [33]. In [30], Misra, Peterson, and Schlichting propose a scheme to implement fault-tolerant replicated objects using an IPC protocol that explicitly preserves the partial order of messages exchanged among processes. On the other hand, Jalote [25] proposes a scheme that exploits properties of broadcast networks to implement resilient objects in distributed systems.

Replicated execution provides fault tolerance by having a multiple number of processes execute the same program concurrently. However, many processes executing the same program introduce consistency problems. In [42], Shi and Belford explain why inconsistencies arise and propose algorithms to ensure that computation replicas behave consistently. In [31], Natarajan and Tang propose a synchronization scheme to prevent inconsistencies among computation replicas.

In order to design a fault-tolerant system, it is important to be able to detect failures. In [40], Ricciardi and Birman discuss the 'group membership problem,' which relates to failure detection in distributed systems.

Delivering messages reliably enhances the fault tolerance capability of distributed systems. In [15], Dasser describes an enhanced version of the reliable communication protocol described in Sec. 13.11 to cut down the time that expires from the moment a site receives a message to the moment it effectively delivers this message to the user. There are many other schemes to deliver messages reliably and these can be found in [5, 12, 35, 41]. In real-time systems, it is critical that messages are delivered reliably and in a timely manner. In [36], Ramanathan and Shin propose a scheme to deliver messages before their deadlines and reduce overhead incurred by the system as a result of untimely message deliveries.

Many distributed systems have been designed with fault tolerance as one of their goals. Rose [32] is a reliable distributed operating system developed at the University of Illinois at Urbana-Champaign. It makes use of both backup processes and replicated execution to implement fault-tolerant processes. In [4], Ahamad, Dasgupta, LeBlanc, and Wilkes discuss features provided in the Clouds operating systems for fault-tolerant computing. A discussion on reliability mechanisms provided in SDD1 (system for distributed databases) can be found in [21].

A comprehensive bibliography for fault-tolerant distributed computing can be found in [13].

PROBLEMS

13.1. Consider a system with three sites employing two-phase commit protocols. Illustrate a situation wherein a site may not be able to arrive at a consistent decision concerning the outcome of the transaction in the event of site failures. Assume that a site can communicate with any other operating site to check the outcome of a transaction.

13.2. Consider a system using the dynamic vote reassignment protocol (Sec. 13.9.2) with an overthrow technique to increase the voting power of a site. Show that if a site j increases its voting power by twice the number of votes of the failed site i, all the majority groups that used i can still form a majority group using site j instead.

13.3. The two-phase commit protocol of Sec. 13.4.1 is a centralized protocol where the decision to abort or commit is taken by the coordinator. Design a decentralized two-phase commit protocol where no site is designated to be a coordinator.

13.4. Design a decentralized two-phase commit protocol where no site is designated to be a coordinator which uses only $O(\sqrt{N})$ messages where N is the number of sites in the system. (Hint: See Maekawa's Mutual Exclusion algorithm.)

REFERENCES

1. Agrawal, D., and A. J. Bernstein, "A Nonblocking Quorum Consensus Protocol for Replicated Data," *IEEE Transactions on Parallel and Distributed Systems*, vol. 2, no. 2, Apr. 1991, pp. 171–179.

2. Agrawal, G., and P. Jalote, "An Efficient Protocol for Voting in Distributed Systems," *Proceedings of the 12th International Conference on Distributed Computing Systems*, June 1992, pp. 640–647.

3. Ahamad, M., and M. H. Ammar, "Multidimensional Voting," *ACM Transactions on Computer Systems*, vol. 9, no. 4, Nov. 1991, pp. 399–431.

4. Ahamad, M., P. Dasgupta, R. J. LeBlanc, and C. T. Wilkes, "Fault Tolerant Computing in Object Based Distributed Operating Systems," *Proceedings of the 6th Symposium on Reliability in Distributed Software and Database Systems*, March 1987, pp. 115–125.

5. Atkins, M. S., G. Haftevani, and W. S. Luk, "An Efficient Kernel-level Dependable Multicast Protocol for Distributed Systems," *Proceedings of the 8th Symposium on Reliable Distributed Systems*, Oct. 1989, pp. 94–101.

6. Barbara, D., and H. Garcia-Molina, "Optimizing the Relibility Provided by Voting Mechanisms," *Proceedings of the 4th International Conference on Distributed Computing Systems*, Oct. 1984, pp. 340–346.

7. Barbara, D., and H. Garcia-Molina, "The Reliability of Voting Mechanisms," *IEEE Transactions on Computers*, vol. 36, no. 10, Oct. 1987, pp. 1197–1208.

8. Barbara, D., H. Garcia-Molina, and A. Spauster, "Increasing Availability Under Mutual Exclusion Constraints with Dynamic Vote Reassignment," *ACM Transactions on Computer Systems*, vol. 7, no. 4, Nov. 1989, pp. 394–426.

9. Birman, K., and T. Joseph, "Reliable Communications in the Presence of Failures," *ACM Transactions on Computer Systems*, vol. 5, no. 1, Feb. 1987, pp. 47–76.

10. Borg, A., W. Blau, W. Graetsch, F. Herrmann, and W. Oberle, "Fault Tolerance Under UNIX," *ACM Transactions on Computer Systems*, vol. 7, no. 1, Feb. 1989, pp. 1–24.

11. Chang, C. K., and M. G. Gouda, "On the Minimum Requirements for Independent Recovery in Distributed Systems," *Information Processing Letters*, vol. 37, no. 1, 1991, pp. 1–7.

12. Chang, J. M., and N. F. Maxemchuk, "Reliable Broadcast Protocols," *ACM Transactions on Computer Systems*, vol. 2, no. 8, Aug. 1984, pp. 251–273.

13. Coan, B. A., "Bibliography for Fault-Tolerant Distributed Computing," *Lecture Notes in Computer Science*, vol. 448, Springler-Verlag, New York, 1990, pp. 274–298.

14. Cristian, F., "Understanding Fault-Tolerant Distributed Systems," *Communications of the ACM*, vol. 34, no. 2, Feb. 1991, pp. 56–78.

15. Dasser, M., "TOMP A Total Ordering Multicast Protocol," *Operating Systems Review*, vol. 26, no. 1, Jan. 1992, pp. 32–40.

16. Davcev, D., "A Dynamic Voting Scheme in Distributed Systems," *IEEE Transactions of Software Engineering*, vol. 15, no. 1, Jan. 1989, pp. 93–97.

17. Garcia-Molina, H., "Elections in a Distributed Computing System," *IEEE Transactions on Computers*, vol. 31, no. 1, Jan. 1982, pp. 48–59.

18. Garcia-Molina, H., "Reliability Issues for Fully Replicated Distributed Databases," *IEEE Computer*, vol. 15, no. 9, Sept. 1982, pp. 34–42.

19. Gifford, D. K., "Weighed Voting for Replicated Data," *Proceedings of the 7th ACM Symposium on Operating System Principles*, Dec. 1979, pp. 150–162.

20. Gray, J. N., "Notes on Data Base Operating Systems," *Operating Systems An Advanced Course*, Springer-Verlag, 1979, New York, pp. 393–481.

21. Hammer, M., and D. Shipman, "Reliablility Mechanisms for SDD-1: A System for Distributed Databases," *ACM Transactions on Database Systems*, vol. 5, no. 4, Dec. 1980, pp. 431–466.

22. Huang, C. L., and V. O. K. Li, "A Quorum-based Commit and Termination Protocol for Distributed Database Systems," *Proceedings of the 4th International Conference on Data Engineering*, Feb. 1988, pp. 136–143.

23. Jajodia, S., and D. Mutchler, "Integrating Static and Dynamic Voting Protocols to Enhance File Availability," *Proceedings of the 4th International Conference on Data Engineering*, Feb. 1988, pp. 144–153.

24. Jajodia, S., and D. Mutchler, "Dynamic Voting Algorithms for Maintaining the Consistency of a Replicated Database," *ACM Transactions on Database Systems*, June 1990, pp. 230–280.

25. Jalote, P., "Resilient Objects in Broadcast Networks," *IEEE Transactions on Software Engineering*, vol. 15, no. 1, January 1989, pp. 68–72.

26. Joseph, T., and K. P. Birman, "Low Cost Management of Replicated Data in Fault-Tolerant Distributed Systems," *ACM Transactions on Computer Systems*, vol. 4, no. 1, Feb. 1986, pp. 54–70.

27. Kumar, A., "A Randomized Voting Algorithm," *Proceedings of the 11th International Conference on Distributed Computing Systems*, May 1991, pp. 412–419.

28. Levy, E., H. F. Korth, and A. Silberschatz, "An Optimistic Commit Protocol for Distributed Transaction Management," *Proceedings of the ACM SIGMOD, International Conference on Data Management*, 1991.

29. Lomet, D. B., "Process Structuring, Synchronization, and Recovery Using Atomic Actions," *Proceedings of the ACM Conference on Language Design for Reliable Software, SIGPLAN*, Notices 12, 3, March 1977, pp. 128–137.

30. Mishra, S., L. L. Peterson, and R. D. Schlichting, "Implementing Fault-Tolerant Replicated Objects Using Psync," *Proceedings of the 8th Symposium on Reliable Distributed Systems*, Oct. 1989, pp. 42–52.

31. Natarajan, N., and J. Tang, "Synchronization of Redundant Computation in a Distributed System," *Proceedings of the 6th Symposium on Reliability in Distributed Software and Database Systems*, March 1987, pp. 139–148.

32. Ng, T. P., "The Design and Implementation of a Reliable Distributed Operating System—Rose," *Proceedings of the 9th Symposium on Reliable Distributed Systems*, Oct. 1990.

33. Oki, B. M., and B. H. Liskov, "Viewstamped Replication: A New Primary Copy Method to Support Highly-Available Distributed Systems," *Proceedings of the 7th ACM Symposium on Principles of Distributed Computing*, Aug. 1988, pp. 8–17.

34. Paris, J. F., "Voting With Witnesses: A Consistency Scheme for Replicated Files," *Proceedings of the 4th International Conference on Distributed Computing Systems*, May 1986, pp. 606–612.

35. Rajagopalan, B., and P. K. McKinley, "A Token-Based Protocol for Reliable, Ordered Multicast Communication," *Proceedings of the 8th Symposium on Reliable Distributed Systems*, Oct. 1989, pp. 84–93.

36. Ramanathan, P., and K. G. Shin, "Delivery of Time-Critical Messages Using a Multiple Copy Approach," *ACM Transactions on Computer Systems*, vol. 10, no. 1, May 1992, pp. 144–166.

37. Ramarao, K. V. S., "Transaction Atomicity in the Presence of Network Partitions," *Proceedings of the 4th International Conference on Data Engineering*, Feb. 1988, pp. 512–519.

38. Ramarao, K. V. S., "Design of Transaction Commitment Protocols," *Information Sciences*, vol. 55, nos. 1,2, and 3, Jun 1991, pp 129–149.

39. Randell, B., "Reliable Computing Systems," *Operating Systems: An Advanced Course*, Springer-Verlag, New York, 1979, pp. 282–391.

40. Ricciardi, A., and K. Birman, "Using Process Groups to Implement Failure Detection in Asynchronous Environments," *Proceedings of the 10th Annual ACM Symposium on Principles of Distributed Computing*, 1991, pp. 341–353.

41. Schneider, F. B., D. Gries, and R. D. Schlichting, "Fault-Tolerant Broadcasts," *Science of Computer Programming*, vol. 4, no. 1, Apr. 1984, pp. 1–15.

42. Shi, S. S. B., and G. G. Belford, "Consistent Replicated Transactions: A Highly Reliable Program Execution Environment," *Proceedings of the 8th Symposium on Reliable Distributed Systems*, Oct. 1989, pp. 30–41.

43. Skeen, D., "Nonblocking Commit Protocols," *Proceedings of the ACM SIGMOD International Conference on Management of Data*, 1981, pp. 133–142.

44. Skeen, D., "A Formal Model of Crash Recovery in a Distributed System," *IEEE Transactions on Software Engineering*, vol. 9, no. 3, May 1983, pp. 219–228.

45. Tang, J., and N. Natarajan, "A Scheme for Maintaining Consistency and Availability of Replicated Files in a Partitioned Distributed System," *Proceedings of the 5th International Conference on Data Engineering*, Feb. 1989, pp. 530–537.

46. Tong, Z., and R. Y. Kain, "Vote Assignments in Weighted Voting Mechanisms," *Proceedings of the 7th Symposium on Reliable Distributed Systems*, Oct. 1988, pp. 138–143.

47. Walter, B., "A Robust and Efficient Protocol for Checking the Availability of Remote Sites," *Proceedings of the 6th Workshop on Distributed Data Management and Computer Networks*, Feb. 1982, pp. 45–68.

PART
V

PROTECTION AND SECURITY

14

RESOURCE SECURITY AND PROTECTION: ACCESS AND FLOW CONTROL

14.1 INTRODUCTION

Security and protection deal with the control of unauthorized use and the access to hardware and software resources of a computer system. Business organizations and government agencies heavily use computers to store information to which unauthorized access must be prevented. For example, in business organizations, this information includes financial or personnel records, monetary transactions, legal contracts, payrolls, product information, future planning and strategies, etc. With the prevalent use of electronic fund transfers, the banking industry has become highly susceptible to malicious access and use. Examples in government agencies include strategic military information, CIA files, FBI files, blueprints of military hardware, information about military installations, etc.

Clearly, an unauthorized use of a company's confidential information can have catastrophic financial consequences and the unauthorized use of secret information of a government can have serious implications for the security of that nation. Therefore, with the widespread use of computers in business and government organizations, the security and protection of computer systems have become extremely important factors.

Note that not only should the misuse of secret information be prevented, but the destruction of such information should be prevented as well. For example, the destruction of information about customer account balances and bank transactions can have serious socioeconomic ramifications.

In this chapter, we study models of protection and techniques to enforce security and protection in computer systems.

14.2 PRELIMINARIES

14.2.1 Potential Security Violations

Anderson [2] has classified the potential security violations into three categories:

Unauthorized information release. This occurs when an unauthorized person is able to read and take advantage of the information stored in a computer system. This also includes the unauthorized use of a computer program.

Unauthorized information modification. This occurs when an unauthorized person is able to alter the information stored in a computer. Examples include changing student grades in a university database and changing account balances in a bank database. Note that an unauthorized person need not read the information before changing it. Blind writes can be performed.

Unauthorized denial of service. An unauthorized person should not succeed in preventing an authorized user from accessing the information stored in a computer. Note that services can be denied to authorized users by some internal actions (like crashing the system by some means, overloading the system, changing the scheduling algorithm) and by external actions (such as setting fire or disrupting electrical supply).

14.2.2 External vs. Internal Security

Computer systems security can be divided into two parts: external security and internal security. External security, also called physical security, deals with regulating access to the premises of computer systems, which include the physical machine (hardware, disks, tapes, power supply, air conditioning), terminals, computer console, etc. External security can be enforced by placing a guard at the door, by giving a key or secret code to authorized persons, etc.

Internal security deals with the access and use of computer hardware and software information stored in the computer system. Aside from external and internal securities, there is an issue of *authentication* by which a user "logs into" the computer system to access the hardware and the software resources.

Clearly, issues involved in external security are simple and administrative in nature. In this chapter, we will mainly be concerned with the internal security in computer systems, which is more challenging and subtle.

14.2.3 Policies and Mechanisms

Recall from Chap. 1 that policies refer to what should be done and mechanisms refer to how it should be done. A protection mechanism provides a set of tools that can be used to design or specify a wide array of protection policies, whereas a policy gives assignment of the access rights of users to various resources. The separation of policies and mechanisms enhances design flexibility.

Protection in an operating system refers to mechanisms that control user access to system resources, whereas policies decide which user can have access to what resources. Policies can change with time and applications. Thus, a protection scheme must be amenable to a wide variety of policies to enforce security in computer systems. In this chapter, we will mainly be concerned with the design of protection mechanisms in operating systems.

PROTECTION VS. SECURITY. Hydra [39] designers make a distinction between protection and security. According to them, *protection is a mechanism and security is a policy.* Protection deals with mechanisms to build secure systems and security deals with policy issues that use protection mechanisms to build secure systems.

14.2.4 Protection Domain

The protection domain of a process specifies the resources that it can access and the types of operations that the process can perform on the resources. In a typical computation, the control moves through a series of processes. To enforce security in the system, it is good policy to allow a process to access only those resources that it requires to complete its task. This eliminates the possibility of a process breaching security maliciously or unintentionally (such as by a software bug) and increases accountability.

The concept of protection domain of a process enables us to achieve the policy of limiting a process's access to only needed resources. Every process executes in its protection domain and protection domain is switched appropriately whenever control jumps from a process to another process.

14.2.5 Design Principles for Secure Systems

Saltzer and Schroeder [34] gave the following principles for designing a secure computer system:

Economy. A protection mechanism should be economical to develop and use. Its inclusion in a system should not result in substantial cost or overhead to the system. One easy way to achieve economy is to keep the design as simple and small as possible [34].

Complete Mediation. The design of a completely secure system requires that every request to access an object be checked for the authority to do so.

Open Design. A protection mechanism should not stake its integrity on the ignorance of potential attackers concerning the protection mechanism itself (i.e., the underlying principle used to achieve the security). A protection mechanism should work even if its underlying principles are known to an attacker.

Separation of Privileges. A protection mechanism that requires two keys to unlock a lock (or gain access to a protected object) is more robust and flexible than one that allows only a single key to unlock a lock. In computer systems, the presence of two keys may mean satisfying two independent conditions before an access is allowed.

Least Privilege. A subject should be given the bare minimum access rights that are sufficient for it to complete its task. If the requirement of a subject changes, the subject should acquire it by switching the domain. (Recall that a domain defines access rights of a subject to various objects.)

Least Common Mechanism. According to this principle, the portion of a mechanism that is common to more than one user should be minimized, as any coupling among users (through shared mechanisms and variables) represents a potential information path between users and is thus a potential threat to their security.

Acceptability. A protection mechanism must be simple to use. A complex and obscure protection mechanism will deter users from using it.

Fail-Safe Defaults. Default case should mean lack of access (because it is safer this way). If a design or implementation mistake is responsible for denial of an access, it will eventually be discovered and be fixed. However, the opposite is not true.

14.3 THE ACCESS MATRIX MODEL

A model of protection abstracts the essential features of a protection system so that various properties of it can be proven. A protection system consists of mechanisms to control user access to system resources or to control information flow in the system. In this section, we study the most fundamental model of protection—the access matrix model—in computer systems. Advanced models of protection are covered in Sec. 14.6. A survey of models for protection in computer systems can be found in a paper by Landwehr [23].

The access matrix model was first proposed by Lampson [21]. It was further enhanced and refined by Graham and Denning [18] and Harrison et al. [19]. The description of the access matrix model in this section is based on the work of Harrison et al. [19]. This model consists of the following three components:

Current Objects. Current objects are a finite set of entities to which access is to be controlled. The set is denoted by 'O'. A typical example of an object is a file.

Current Subjects. Current subjects are a finite set of entities that access current objects. The set is denoted by 'S'. A typical example of a subject is a process. Note that $S \subseteq O$. That is, subjects can be treated as objects and can be accessed like an object by other subjects.

Generic Rights. A finite set of generic rights, $R = \{r_1, r_2, r_3, ..., r_m\}$, gives various access rights that subjects can have to objects. Typical examples of such rights are read, write, execute, own, delete, etc.

THE PROTECTION STATE OF A SYSTEM. The *protection state* of a system is represented by a triplet (S, O, P), where S is the set of current subjects, O is the set of current objects, and P is a matrix, called the *access matrix*, with a row for every current subject and a column for every current object. A schematic diagram of an access matrix

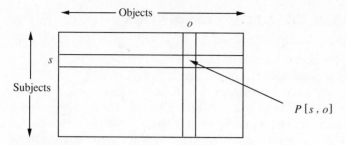

FIGURE 14.1
A schematic of an access matrix.

is shown in Fig. 14.1. Note that the access matrix P itself is a protected object. Let variables s and o denote a subject and an object, respectively. Entry $P[s, o]$ is a subset of R, the generic rights, and denotes the access rights which subject s has to object o.

ENFORCING A SECURITY POLICY. A security policy is enforced by validating every user access for appropriate access rights. Every object has a monitor that validates all accesses to that object in the following manner.

1. A subject s requests an access α to object o.
2. The protection system presents triplet (s, α, o) to the monitor of o.
3. The monitor looks into the access rights of s to o. If $\alpha \in P[s, o]$, then the access is permitted; Else it is denied.

> **Example 14.1.** Figure 14.2 illustrates an access matrix that represents the protection state of a system with three subjects, s_1, s_2, s_3, and five objects, o_1, o_2, s_1, s_2, s_3. In this protection state, subject s_1 can read and write object o_1, delete o_2, send mail to s_2, and receive mail from s_3. Subject s_3 owns o_1 and can read and write o_2.

The access matrix model of a protection system is very popular because of its simplicity, elegant structure, and amenability to various implementations. We next discuss implementations of the access matrix model.

	o_1	o_2	s_1	s_2	s_3
s_1	*read, write*	*own, delete*	*own*	*sendmail*	*recmail*
s_2	*execute*	*copy*	*recmail*	*own*	*block, wakeup*
s_3	*own*	*read, write*	*sendmail*	*block, wakeup*	*own*

FIGURE 14.2
An access matrix representing a protection state.

14.4 IMPLEMENTATIONS OF THE ACCESS MATRIX

Note that the access matrix is likely to be very sparse. Therefore, any direct implementation of the access matrix for access control is likely to be very storage inefficient. In this section, we study three implementations of the access matrix model.

The efficiency can be improved by decomposing the access matrix into rows and assigning the access rights contained in rows to their respective subjects. Note that a row denotes access rights that the corresponding subject has to objects. A row can be collapsed by deleting null entries for efficiency. This approach is called the *capability-based* method. An orthogonal approach is to decompose the access control matrix by columns and assign the columns to their respective objects. Note that a column denotes access rights of various subjects to the object. A column can be collapsed by deleting null entries for higher efficiency. This technique is called the *access control list* method. The third approach, called the *lock-key* method, is a combination of the first two approaches.

14.4.1 Capabilities

The capability based method corresponds to the row-wise decomposition of the access matrix. Each subject s is assigned a list of tuples $(o, P[s, o])$ for all objects o that it is allowed to access. The tuples are referred to as *capabilities*. If subject s possesses a capability $(o, P[s, o])$, then it is authorized to access object o in manners specified in $P[s, o]$. Possession of a capability by a user is treated as prima facie evidence that the user has authority to access the object in the ways specified in the capability. The list of capabilities assigned to subject s corresponds to access rights contained in the row for subject s in the access matrix. At any time, a subject is authorized to access only those objects for which it has capabilities. Clearly, one must not be able to forge capabilities.

A schematic view of a capability is shown in Fig. 14.3. A capability has two fields. First, an object descriptor, which is an identifier for the object and second, access rights, which indicate the allowed access rights to the object. The object descriptor can very well be the address of the corresponding objects and therefore, aside from providing protection, capabilities can also be used as an addressing mechanism by the system. The main advantage of using a capability as an addressing mechanism is that it provides an address that is context independent. That is, it provides an absolute address [14]. However, when a capability is used as an addressing mechanism, the system must allow the embedding of capabilities in user programs and data structures, as a capability will be a part of the address.

CAPABILITY-BASED ADDRESSING. Capability-based addressing is illustrated in Fig. 14.4. A user program issues a request to access a word within an object. The

Object descriptor	Access rights
	read, write, execute, etc.

FIGURE 14.3
A schematic view of a capability.

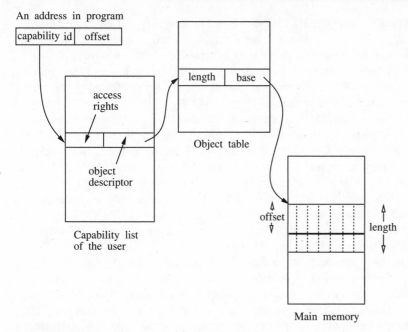

FIGURE 14.4
An illustration of capability-based addressing.

address of the request contains the capability ID of the object (which tells what object in the main memory is to be accessed) and an offset within the object (which gives the relative location of the word in the object to be accessed). The system uses the capability ID to search the capability list of the user to locate the capability that contains the allowed access rights and an object descriptor. The system checks if the requested access is permitted by checking the access rights in the capability. The object descriptor is used to search the object table to locate the entry for the object. The entry consists of the base address of the object in main memory and the length of the object. The system adds the base address to the offset in the request to determine the exact memory location of the accessed word.

Capability-based addressing has two salient features, relocatability and sharing. An object can be relocated anywhere in the main memory without making any change to the capabilities that refer to it. (For every relocation, only the base field of the object needs be changed in the object table.) Sharing is made easy as several programs can share the same object (program or data) with different names (object descriptors) for the object. Note that this type of sharing and relocatability is achieved by introducing a level of indirection (via the object table) in addressing the objects—the object descriptor in a capability contains the address of the address of the object.

If there is a separate object table for each process or subject, then the resolution of an object descriptor is done in the context of a process. If there is a global object table, then the resolution of an object descriptor is done in a single global context.

IMPLEMENTATION CONSIDERATIONS. Since a capability is used as an address, a typical address in a program consists of a capability and word number (i.e., offset) pair, and the capability can be embedded in the user programs and data structures. However, to maintain forgery-free capabilities, a user should not be able to access (read, modify, or construct) a capability. There are two ways to implement capabilities [14]: the *tagged* approach and the *partitioned* approach.

In the tagged approach, one or more bits are attached to each memory location and to every processor register. The tag is used to indicate whether the memory word or a register contains a capability. Generally, if the tag is ON, the information is a capability; otherwise, it is ordinary data (user data or instruction). A user cannot manipulate words with their tag bits ON. There are separate sets of instructions to manipulate the words with their tag bits ON, which cannot be executed by users. Whenever a user presents the system a capability to access the corresponding object, the system checks if the tag bit of the capability is ON. Examples of systems with tagged approach are the Burrough's B6700 and the Rice Research Computer [15].

In the partitioned approach, capabilities and ordinary data are partitioned, i.e., stored separately. Corresponding to every object are two segments, one segment storing only the ordinary data and the other storing only the capabilities of the object. Also, the processor has two sets of registers, one for ordinary data and the other for capabilities. Users cannot manipulate segments and registers storing capabilities. Examples of systems with the partitioned approach are the Chicago Magic Number Machine [13] and Plessey System 250 [12].

ADVANTAGES OF CAPABILITIES. The capability-based protection system has three main advantages [34]: efficiency, simplicity, and flexibility. It is efficient because the validity of an access can be easily tested; an access by a subject is implicitly valid if it has the capability. It is simple due to the natural correspondence between the structural properties of capabilities and the semantic properties of addressing variables. It is flexible because a capability system allows users to define certain parameters. For example, a users can decide which of his addresses contain capabilities. Also, a user can define any data structure with an arbitrary pattern of access authorization.

DRAWBACK OF CAPABILITIES

Control of propagation. When a subject passes a copy of a capability for an object to another subject, the second subject can pass copies of the capability to many other subjects without the first subject's knowledge. In some applications, it may be desirable (to induce unrestricted sharing), while in other applications, it may be necessary to control the propagation of capabilities for the purpose of accountability as well as security.

The propagation of a capability can be controlled by adding a bit, called the *copy* bit, in a capability that indicates whether the holder of the capability has permission to copy (and distribute) the capability. The propagation of a capability can be prevented by setting this bit to OFF when providing a copy of the capability to other users. Another way to limit the propagation is to use a depth counter [34]. A depth counter is attached to each capability (whose initial value is one). Every time a copy of a capability is made, the depth counter of the copied capability is one higher than that of the original capability. There is a limit on how large the depth counter can grow (say, four). Any attempt to generate a copy of a capability whose depth counter has reached the limit results into an error, thus, limiting the length of the chain a capability can propagate.

Review. Another fundamental problem with capabilities is that the determination of all subjects who have access to an object (called the *review* of access) is difficult. This is because the determination of who all have access to an object involves searching all the programs and data structures for copies of the corresponding capabilities. This requires a substantial amount of processing. Note, however, that the review of access becomes simpler in the systems with the partitioned approach because now one needs to search only the segments that store capabilities (search space may be substantially reduced).

Revocation of access rights. Revocation of access rights is difficult because once a subject X has given a capability for an object to some other subject Y, subject Y can store the capability in a place not known to X, or Y itself may make copies of the capabilities and pass it to its friends without any knowledge of X. To revoke access rights from some subjects, either X must review all the accesses to that object and delete the undesired ones or delete the object and create another copy of the object and give permissions to only desired subjects. The simplest way to revoke access is to destroy the object, which will prevent all the undesired subjects from accessing it. (Of course, the accesses by other users will also be denied).

Garbage collection. When all the capabilities for an object disappear from the system, the object is left inaccessible to users and becomes garbage. This is called the *garbage collection* or the *lost object* problem. One solution to this problem is to have the creator of an object or the system keep a count of the number of copies of each capability and recover the space taken by an object when its capability count becomes zero.

14.4.2   The Access Control List Method

The access control list method corresponds to the column-wise decomposition of the access matrix. Each object o is assigned a list of pairs $(s, P[s, o])$ for all subjects s that are allowed to access the object. Note that the set $P[s, o]$ denotes the access rights that subject s has to object o. The access list assigned to object o corresponds to all access rights contained in the column for object o in the access matrix. A schematic diagram of an access control list is shown in Figure 14.5.

When a subject s requests access α to object o, it is executed in the following manner:

- The system searches the access control list of o to find out if an entry (s, Φ) exists for subject s.
- If an entry (s, Φ) exists for subject s, then the system checks to see if the requested access is permitted (i.e., $\alpha \in \Phi$).
- If the requested access is permitted, then the request is executed. Otherwise, an appropriate exception is raised.

Subjects	Access rights
Smith	read, write, execute
Jones	read
Lee	write
Grant	execute
White	read, write

FIGURE 14.5
A schematic of an access control list.

Clearly, the execution efficiency of the access control list method is poor because an access control list must be searched for every access to a protected object.

Major features of the access control list method include:

Easy Revocation. Revocation of access rights from a subject is very simple, fast, and efficient. It can be achieved by simply removing the subject's entry from the object's access control list.

Easy Review of an Access. It can be easily determined what subjects have access rights to an object by directly examining the access control list of that object. However, it is difficult to determine what objects a subject has access to.

IMPLEMENTATION CONSIDERATIONS. There are two main issues in the implementation of the access control list method:

Efficiency of execution. Since the access control list need be searched for every access to a protected object, it can be very slow.

Efficiency of storage. Since an access control list contains the names and access rights of all the subjects that can access the corresponding protected object, a list can require huge amounts of storage. However, note that the aggregate storage requirement is about the same as that required for capabilities. In an access control list, the total is taken across objects and in capabilities, the total is taken across users.

The first problem can be solved in the following way. When a subject makes its first access to an object, the access rights of the subject are fetched from the access control list of the object and stored in a place, called the *shadow register*, with the subject. This fetched information in the shadow register acts like a capability. Consequently, the subject can use that capability for all subsequent accesses to that object, dispensing with the need to search the access control list for every access. However, this method has negative implications for the revocability of access rights in the access control list method in that, merely revoking access rights from the access control lists will not revoke the access rights loaded in the shadow registers of processes. Of course, a simple way to get around this problem is to clear all shadow registers whenever an access right is revoked from an access control list. Obviously, this will be followed by a large number of access control list searches to rebuild the shadow registers.

The second problem, large storage requirement, is caused by a large number of users as well as the numerous types of access rights. The large storage requirement due to a large number of users can be solved using the *protection group* technique discussed below. This technique limits the number of entries in an access control list by lumping users into groups.

Note that each entry in an access control list contains allowed access rights. If there are a large number of access rights, their coding and inclusion in an entry will be cumbersome. It will require large space and complex memory management. This problem can be solved by limiting the access rights to only a small number and assigning a bit in a vector for every access type.

PROTECTION GROUPS. The concept of protection group was introduced to reduce the overheads of storing (and searching) lengthy access control lists [34]. Subjects (users) are divided into protection groups and the access control list consists of the names of groups along with their access rights. Thus, the number of entries in an access control list is limited by the number of protection groups, and therefore, high efficiency is achieved. However, the granularity at which access rights can be assigned becomes coarse—all subjects in a protection group have identical access rights to the object. To access an object, a subject gives its protection group and requested access to the system.

AUTHORITY TO CHANGE AN ACCESS CONTROL LIST. The authority to change the access control list raises the question of who can modify the access control information (contained in an access control list). Note that in a capability-based system, this issue is rather vague—any process which has a capability may make a copy and give it to any other process. The access control list method, however, provides a more precise and structured control over the propagation of access rights.

The access control list method provides two ways to control propagation of access rights [34]: *self control* and *hierarchical control*. In the self control policy, the owner process of an object has a special access right by which it can modify the access control list of the object (i.e., can revoke or grant access rights to the object). Generally, the owner is the creator process of an object. A drawback of the self control method is that the control is centralized to one process.

In the hierarchical control, when a new object is created, its owner specifies a set of other processes which have the right to modify the access control list of the new object. Processes are arranged in a hierarchy and a process can modify the access control list associated with all the processes below it in the hierarchy.

14.4.3 The Lock-Key Method

The lock-key method is a hybrid of the capability-based method and the access control list method [7], [25]. This method has features of both these methods.

In the lock-key method, every subject has a capability list that contains tuples of the form (O, k), indicating that the subject can access object O using key k. Every object has an access control list that contains tuples of the form (l, Ψ), called a *lock entry*, indicating that any subject which can open the lock l can access this object in modes contained in the set Ψ.

When a subject makes the request to access object o in mode α, the system executes it in the following manner:

- The system locates the tuple (o, k) in the capability list of the subject. If no such tuple is found, the access is not permitted.
- Otherwise, the access is permitted only if there exists a lock entry (l, Ψ) in the access control list of the object o such that $k = l$ and $\alpha \in \Psi$.

Similar to the access control list, the revocation of access rights is easy. To revoke the access rights of a subject to an object, simply delete the lock entry corresponding to the key of the subject. There is no major advantage obtained from the use of capabilities except that capability-based addressing can be used. The access control list of the object must still be searched for every access. For the revocation of access rights of a subject to an object, the lock corresponding to the subject must be known. Thus, the correspondence between locks and subjects must be known.

The IBM/360's *storage keys* protection method is similar to the lock-key method. The ASAP file system uses the lock-key method for protection [6]. Gifford suggested the lock-key method for protecting data using encryption [16]. Encrypting a data block is similar to placing a lock on it and decrypting a data block is similar to doing an unlock operation with the corresponding key.

14.5 SAFETY IN THE ACCESS MATRIX MODEL

In this section, we study transitions in the protection state and safety in the access matrix model.

14.5.1 Changing the Protection State

A finite set of commands, C, is defined in the access matrix model to change the protection state. A change in the protection state may be necessitated by a change in security policies. The set of commands, C, is defined in terms of the following *primitive operations*:

> **enter** r *into* $P[s, o]$
> **delete** r *from* $P[s, o]$
> **create subject** s
> **create object** o
> **destroy subject** s
> **destroy object** o

These primitive operations define changes to be made to the access matrix P. For example, the primitive operation *delete r from* $P[s, o]$ deletes access right r from the position $P[s, o]$ in the access matrix. Consequently, access right r of subject s

to object o is withdrawn. However, before such a *delete* operation is performed, it should be checked whether the process that is performing this operation has a right to perform this operation on the access matrix. (That is, whether that process has a right to revoke right r from subject s for object o.) Similarly, to destroy an object, the process must have the right to destroy that object and that object must currently exist. Therefore, several checks may need to be performed before these primitive operations are performed. Thus, a command assumes the following syntax:

> **command** <command id>(<formal parameters>)
>   **if** <conditions>
>   **then**
>   <list of primitive operations>
>   **end.**

The <conditions> part consists of checks of the form "r in $P[s, o]$". A command is executed in the following manner. First, all the checks in the condition part are evaluated. If all the checks pass, all the primitive operations listed in <list of operations> are executed. Note that a command need not have any check. If this is the case, the condition part is trivially satisfied. All accesses to objects are validated by a mechanism called a *reference monitor*. The reference monitor rejects accesses that are not currently allowed by the access matrix.

An object need not be owned by a subject. However, an object is usually owned by a subject, called the *owner* of the object. If s is a owner of o, then $own \in P[s, o]$. The owner of an object may confer any right to the object to any other subject.

Example 14.2. The following command creates a file and assigns *own* and *read* rights to it:

> **command** create-read(process, file)
>   **create object** file
>   **enter** *own* **into** P[process, file]
>   **enter** *read* **into** P[process, file]
>   **end.**

Example 14.3. In the following command, the owner of a file confers *write* access to a file to a process:

> **command** confer-write(owner, process, file)
>   **if** $own \in P$[owner, file]
>   **then**
>   **enter** *write* **into** P[process, file]
>   **end.**

There can be a separate command to confer each access right to other processes or there can be just one command and the intended access right is passed as a parameter. The effect of the command in Example 14.2 is to create a column in the access matrix for object 'file' and fill in an entry in this column. Commands of the type in Example 14.3 can be used to fill in entries (i.e., access rights) in the matrix.

PROTECTION STATE TRANSITIONS. Recall that the protection state of a system is denoted by a triplet (S, O, P). Primitive operations change the protection state of the system because they change the contents of the access matrix P. For example, creating a new object adds a new column to the access matrix and revoking an access right from a subject amounts to the deletion of that right from an appropriate matrix entry. Thus, the execution of a primitive operation causes a transition in the protection state of a system.

14.5.2   Safety in the Access Matrix Model

The notion of safety in a protection system was raised and examined for the access matrix model by Harrison et al. [19]. The general connotation of a *safe* protection system is that a process cannot acquire an access right to a file without the consent of its owner. Since the owner of an object must confer its access rights to other processes (to enable sharing, etc.), it is impossible to make a protection system safe and we must be satisfied with a weaker condition [19]: "A process should be able to tell whether its actions (e.g., conferring an access right) can lead to the leakage of an access right to unauthorized subjects." It turns out that even this property is too strong because given an initial access matrix, it is undecidable whether there is a sequence of commands that adds a particular access right into a cell in the access matrix where it did not exist before [19].

> **Definition 14.1. [19]** Given a protection system, we say command c *leaks generic right r from configuration* $Q=(S, O, P)$ if c when run on Q can execute a primitive operation which enters r into a cell of the access matrix that did not initially contain r.

Discussions so far have implied that leaks are bad. A protection system should have commands so that a process can confer access rights to other (trusted) processes to facilitate sharing. What is undesired, however, is that an untrusted process acquires certain access rights to an object.

> **Definition 14.2. [19]** If the execution of a command α in a protection state Q takes the system to a state Q', notationally denoted by $Q \vdash_\alpha Q'$, then
>
> - If all the conditions of α are not satisfied in state Q, then $Q = Q'$.
> - Otherwise, state Q' will be reached by a sequential execution of all the primitive operations, with actual parameters, of the command α.

We say $Q \vdash Q'$, i.e., Q' can be reached from Q, if there exists a command α such that $Q \vdash_\alpha Q'$. Notation $\vdash_*$ denotes the reflexive and transitive closure of $\vdash$.

> **Definition 14.3. [19]** Given a protection system and a generic right r, we say that an initial configuration Q_0 is *unsafe* for r (or *leaks r*) if there is a configuration Q and a command c such that

- $Q_0 \vdash_* Q$, and
- c leaks r from Q.

Q_0 is *safe* for r if Q_0 is not unsafe for r.

Definition 14.4. [19] A protection system is *mono-operational* if each command's interpretation is a single primitive operation.

Thus, commands in a mono-operational protection system contains only one primitive operation.

Theorem 14.1. [19] There exists an algorithm that decides whether or not a given mono-operational protection system and the initial configuration are unsafe for a given generic right r.

Thus, as far as the issue of safety in the access matrix model is concerned, there exists no algorithm that can decide the safety of an *arbitrary* configuration of an *arbitrary* protection system [19]. However, the safety issue can be decided for a *specific* system (because all the rules and their consequences are well defined and known).

14.6 ADVANCED MODELS OF PROTECTION

14.6.1 The Take-Grant Model

The take-grant model uses directed graphs to model access control. The take-grant model has its roots in the access matrix model because a matrix can be represented as a directed graph (values in the matrix can be tagged with the corresponding edges of the directed graph). Nevertheless, a directed graph provides an efficient way to implement an access matrix that is likely to be highly sparse. The take-grant model was first proposed by Jones [20] and has been successively refined by others (e.g., [5], [24]).

THE MODEL. In the take-grant model, the protection state of a system is described by a directed graph. Nodes of the graph are of two types: subjects and objects. An edge from node x to node y denotes that the subject or object corresponding to node x has some access rights to the subject or object corresponding to node y. Edges are tagged with the corresponding access rights.

Besides **read (r), write (w),** and **execute (e)**, two special access rights in the take-grant model are **take (t)** and **grant (g)**. The access rights **take** and **grant** specify how the access rights can be propagated to other nodes.

Take. If node x has the access right **take** to node y, then the entity corresponding to node x can *take* access rights of the entity corresponding to y to any other node.

Grant. If node x has the access right **grant** to node y, then the entity corresponding to node y can be granted any access right that the entity corresponding to node x possesses.

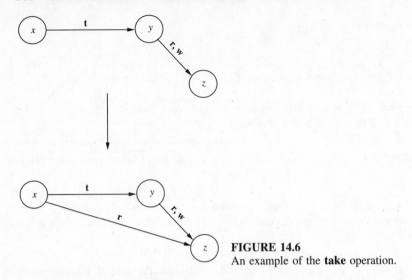

FIGURE 14.6
An example of the **take** operation.

Example 14.4. An illustration of the **take** operation is shown in Fig. 14.6. Node x has **take** access to node y and node y has **read** and **write** access to node z. Thus, node x can take access right **read** from node y and can have this access right for object z. This is done by adding a directed edge labeled **r** from node x to node z in the graph.

Example 14.5. An illustration of the **grant** operation is shown in Fig. 14.7. Node x has **grant** access to node y and also has **read** and **write** access to node z. Thus, node y can take access right **read** from node x and can have this access right for object z (or node x can grant **read** access for z to node y.) This is done by adding a directed edge labeled **r** from node y to node z in the graph.

STATE AND STATE TRANSITIONS. The protection state of a system is denoted by a directed graph. Note that the execution of the **take** and **grant** access rights change the system state because execution of these access rights change the directed graph. Thus, the system undergoes a state transition whenever **take** or **grant** operations are executed. The following operations also change the directed graph and thus cause a system state transition:

Create. The **create** operation allows a new node to be added to the graph.

If a node x creates a new node y, then a node y and a directed edge $x \rightarrow y$ are added to the graph. The edge $x \rightarrow y$ can initially have any nonempty subset of possible access rights.

Remove. The **remove** operation allows a node to delete some of its access rights to another node.

SAFETY. The notion of safety in the graph model is as follows [20]: "Given an initial protection graph, does there exists a sequence of rule applications which will convert

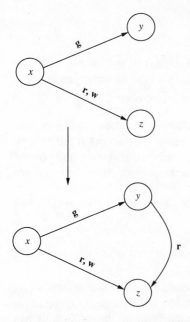

FIGURE 14.7
An example of the **grant** operation.

the initial graph to a graph containing a specific edge." Note that when the results of Harrison et al. [19] are interpreted in the context of graph model, it states that given an arbitrary set of application rules and an initial graph, it is undecidable whether there will ever be an edge in the graph from a node x to a node y with certain access rights [24].

Since the safety issue is undecidable when the set of rules is arbitrary and because operating systems usually have only one fixed set of protection rules, Lipton and Snyder [24] examined safety conditions for a particular take-grant system. They showed that node x can acquire access right **r** to node y if and only if there is an undirected path between x and y and there also exists a node z which has an edge to node y with access right **r**. For the take-grant model with specific application rules, safety can be decided in linear time (proportional to the size of the graph [20]).

14.6.2 Bell-LaPadula Model

The previous two models deal with *access control*, while the Bell-LaPadula model deals with the control of *information flow*. The description of the Bell-LaPadula model in this section is based on a paper by Landwehr [23].

THE MODEL. The Bell-LaPadula model of protection systems consists of the following components:

- Like the access control matrix model, it consists of a set of subjects, a set of objects, and an access matrix.
- It has several ordered security levels. Each subject has a *clearance* and each object has a *classification* (i.e., belongs to a security level). Each subject also has a *current clearance level* which may not exceed the clearance of the subject.

Subjects can have the following accesses to objects:

Read-only. The subject can only read the object.

Append. The subject can only write to the object. (No read permitted.)

Execute. The subject can only execute the object. (No read or write permitted.)

Read-write. The subject can read as well as write to the object.

In addition to these accesses, the subject that creates an object has a *control attribute* to that object. A subject can pass any of the above four access rights of any object for which it has the control attributes to any other subject. However, the control attributes cannot be passed. The *controller* of an object is the subject that has the control attribute to that object.

The Bell-LaPadula [4] model imposes the following two restrictions on information flow and access control:

1. *The simple security property.* A subject cannot have a read access to an object whose classification is higher than the clearance level of the subject.

2. *The ∗-property* (called the *star property*). At any time, a subject has append (i.e., write) access to only those objects whose classification (i.e., the security level) is higher than or equal to the current security clearance level of the subject. It has read access to only those objects whose classification is lower than or equal to the current security clearance level of the subject. It has read-write access to only those objects whose classification is equal to the current security clearance level of the subject.

Figure 14.8 illustrates the allowed accesses of a subject with clearance level i. Note that the ∗-property subsumes the simple security property because the current clearance level of a subject can never exceed its clearance level. These two properties are also referred to as *reading down* and *writing up* properties, respectively. These properties are quite intuitive. The reading down property prevents a subject from getting access to the information contained in security levels higher than its clearance level. The writing up property prevents a subject from disclosing information to entities in security levels below its own level.

An interesting part of the Bell-LaPadula model is that over and above the access matrix, information flow and access to objects are controlled by the above two rules. For example, a subject may acquire the read access rights to an object in the access matrix, but it may not be able to actually exercise this right because the clearance level of the object is higher than the clearance level of the subject. The ∗-property supports mandatory access controls, whereas the access matrix tends to support discretionary access control. For example, **give access** and **rescind access** (defined below) are discretionary rights, whereas level and compartment restrictions are mandatory.

STATE TRANSITIONS. The protection state of a system is defined by the access matrix and the current security levels of subjects. The Bell-LaPadula model allows the following operations (rules) to change the state of a protection system:

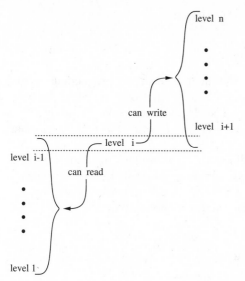

FIGURE 14.8
Allowed accesses in Bell-LaPadula model.

get access. It is used by a subject to initiate access to an object in the requested mode (i.e., read, append, execute, or read-write).

release access. It is used by a subject to terminate an initiated access to an object.

give access. It allows the controller of an object to grant the designated access (to that object) to a subject.

rescind access. It allows the controller of an object to revoke a designated access (to that object) from a subject.

create object. It allows a subject to activate an inactive object.

delete object. It allows a subject to deactivate an active object.

change security level. It allows a subject to change its current security level.

Before a rule can be applied, a set of conditions must hold. For example, a subject must have the control attribute of an object before it can give or rescind an access to it. A subject must have the read access to an object and must have its current security level higher than or equal to the clearance of the object before the subject can read the object.

Bell and LaPadula modeled the behavior of a protection system as a finite state machine. They defined the concept of a secure state and considered the transitions that lead the system to only secure states. Bell showed that the above seven operations maintain the simple security property and the *-property of a protection system [3].

The Bell-LaPadula model has the following drawbacks: the security levels of the objects are static and the *-property may be too restrictive in many applications. For example, the *-property dictates that a subject at one level absolutely does not communicate with the subjects at lower levels, even about the matters outside the context of the protection system. In a computer system, a process (subject) at level i should be able to write some information to processes at a lower level if the information does not depend upon the protected objects at level i or higher.

We next discuss the lattice model of information flow.

14.6.3 Lattice Model of Information Flow

The previously discussed models of protection primarily dealt with regulating access to the objects. The lattice model of information flow, on the other hand, deals with regulating the flow of information among the objects. In addition to controlling subject's access to objects, the control of information flow among objects is an important issue in the security of computer systems.

Although the concept of information flow was first used in the Bell-LaPadula model to secure the access control of objects, it was generalized for controlling the flow of information among objects, called the *lattice model* of information flow, by Denning [8]. The treatment of the lattice model in this section is based on the work of Denning [8], [9].

THE MODEL. The lattice model consists of three entities: a set of objects, a set of processes (so-called subjects), and a set of security classes. Notationally, an object x belongs to the security class denoted by $\underline{x}$.

An information flow policy is modeled by a partially ordered set (SC, $\rightarrow$) where SC is the set of security classes and relation $\rightarrow$ specifies the permissible information flow between classes [8]. For two objects x and y, information flow from x to y is permitted provided $\underline{x} \rightarrow \underline{y}$. Relation $\rightarrow$ is reflexive (that is, information can flow between objects in the same class), antisymmetric (i.e., if information can flow from class sc_1 to class sc_2, then it cannot flow from class sc_2 to class sc_1), and transitive (i.e., if information can flow from class sc_1 to class sc_2 and from class sc_2 to class sc_3, then it can also flow from class sc_1 to class sc_3).

An information flow policy (SC, $\rightarrow$) forms a lattice if it is a partially ordered set and if the *least upper bound* and *greatest lower bound* operators exist on the set of security classes, SC. The symbol $\oplus$ and $\otimes$, are used to denote the least upper bound and greatest lower bound operators of the lattice (SC, $\rightarrow$), respectively. These operators are commutative and associative.

The least upper bound operator is defined in the following manner [7]: $(\forall a)(\forall b)$ such that $a, b \in SC$ there exists a unique class $c = a \oplus b$, $c \in SC$, such that

- $a \rightarrow c \wedge b \rightarrow c$, and
- $\forall d: d \in SC :: (a \rightarrow d \wedge b \rightarrow d) \Rightarrow c \rightarrow d$.

The greatest lower bound operator is defined as follows [7]: $(\forall a)(\forall b)$ such that a, $b \in SC$ there exists a unique class $c = a \otimes b$, $c \in SC$, such that

- $c \rightarrow a \wedge c \rightarrow b$, and
- $\forall d: d \in SC :: (d \rightarrow a \wedge d \rightarrow b) \Rightarrow d \rightarrow c$.

Given a lattice (SC, $\rightarrow$), there exists a highest class **H** that is the least upper bound of all classes and there exists a least class **L** which is the greatest lower bound of all classes.

FIGURE 14.9

A linear lattice.

The lattice model of protection is very powerful because by choosing any ordering between security classes, we can model a wide range of information flow policies. In the lattice model, a system is *secure* if the execution of a process does not result in an information flow from object x to object y unless $\underline{x} \rightarrow \underline{y}$.

Example 14.6. Figure 14.9 shows perhaps the simplest lattice, a linear lattice, with n classes (1, 2, ..., n). This lattice corresponds to the security classification of the Bell-LaPadula model. (However, note that in the Bell-LaPadula model, a linear lattice is not used to restrict information flow, but rather to control access to objects.) In this lattice:

$$SC = \{1, 2, \ldots, n\}$$
$$x \rightarrow y \text{ iff } x \leq y$$
$$x \oplus y = \max(x, y)$$
$$x \otimes y = \min(x, y)$$
$$\mathbf{H} = n \text{ and } \mathbf{L} = 1.$$

Example 14.7. The property lattice in Fig. 14.10 is due to Denning [9]. This is a nonlinear lattice because all the nodes (i.e., classes) of the lattice cannot be linearly ordered. Each class is defined by a three bit vector whose bits represent three properties. (A bit =1 means that the class contains the property corresponding to that bit.) The lattice is defined such that $x \rightarrow y$ iff all the properties of class x are included in class y. The operators $\oplus$ and $\otimes$ now correspond to logical OR and AND operations, respectively. Note that $\mathbf{L} = (000)$ and $\mathbf{H} = (111)$.

MILITARY SECURITY MODEL. In the military security model, objects (i.e., the information to be protected) are ranked in four categories, viz., (1) *unclassified*, (2) *confidential*, (3) *secret*, and (4) *top secret*, based on their sensitivity. These categories satisfy the following rank order: *unclassified* ≤ *confidential* ≤ *secret* ≤ *top secret*; that is, an *unclassified* object is the least sensitive and a *top secret* object is the most sensitive. Based on the subject matter, an object is associated with one or more departments, called

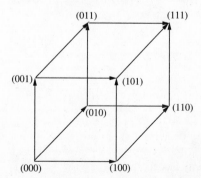

FIGURE 14.10
A property lattice.

compartments. The compartments are used to enforce the need-to-know rule—a subject can access only the object that is essential to perform its job. Examples of compartments are *personnel* (p) and *strategic* (s). A subject with access to only *personnel* compartment must not be able to access an object in *strategic* compartment and vice-versa.

> **Definition 14.5.** The *class* of an object is a tuple (r, c) where r is the rank that indicates the security level of the object and c is a set of compartments to which the object belongs.

> **Definition 14.6.** The *clearance* of a subject is a tuple (r, c) where r indicates the rank that indicates the clearance level of the subject (i.e., the highest rank object the subject is permitted to access) and c is a set of compartments the subject is allowed to access.

> **Definition 14.7.** We define a relation "$\preceq$", called *dominates*, on an object O with class (r_O, c_O) and a subject S with clearance (r_S, c_S) in the following way:

$$O \preceq S \text{ if and only if}$$
$$r_O \leq r_S \text{ and } c_O \subseteq c_S$$

A subject S can access an object O only if $O \preceq S$. Therefore, a subject can access an object only if

- The clearance level of the subject is equal or greater than the security level of the object, and
- The subject has access permissions to all the compartments of the object.

Note that the $\preceq$ relation defines a partial order on the set of *classes* (or the set of *clearances*). It defines a lattice on the set of classes. A lattice for the military security model with two ranks, viz., *unclassified* (1) and *confidential* (2), is shown in Fig. 14.11. The largest element of the lattice is the class $(2, \{p, s\})$ and the smallest element is $(1, \{\})$.

MODES OF INFORMATION FLOW. Information is said to flow from object x to object y, denoted by $x \Rightarrow y$, whenever information stored in x is used to derive information transferred to y. Information flows can be explicit or implicit. In an *explicit*

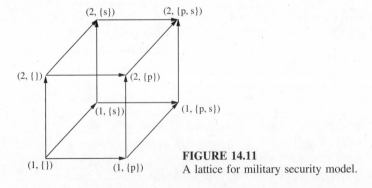

FIGURE 14.11
A lattice for military security model.

flow $x \Rightarrow y$, the value assigned to y directly depends upon the value of x. In explicit flow, assignment statements are of the type

$$y = f(x1, x2, ..., x_m) \tag{14.1}$$

where information explicitly flows from objects x_1, x_2, ..., x_m to object y. Clearly, such flow is permitted only when

$$\underline{x_1} \oplus ... \oplus \underline{x_m} \rightarrow \underline{y}. \tag{14.2}$$

Note that $\underline{x_1} \oplus ... \oplus \underline{x_m} \rightarrow \underline{y}$ is equivalent to $\forall i: 1 \leq i \leq m :: \underline{x_i} \rightarrow \underline{y}$.

An *implicit* flow $x \Rightarrow y$ occurs when the value assigned to y is conditioned on the value of object x. This is because by testing the results of the execution of a conditional statement, we can infer the value of the variables used in the condition of the statement. For example, consider the following statements:

$y:=x+1$;

if $z=0$ then $y:=x$;

In these statements, information implicitly flows from z to y because the value of y depends upon the value of z. One can infer that the value of object z is 0 if the value of object y is equal to the value object x.

Note that an unauthorized (implicit) information flow will occur when an object used in the condition part of a conditional statement belongs to a class with higher security than the class of one of the objects modified in the then part of the statement.

14.7 CASE STUDIES

14.7.1 The UNIX Operating System

In the UNIX operating system, files (and directories) are the main protected entities [33]. Every user in UNIX is identified by a *userid*. A user may also belong to a user group identified by *groupid*. The userid and groupid of a user are available in the process descriptor of the process that is executing on behalf of the user. Thus, an access right check can easily be performed when a process makes an access to a file. For each UNIX file, there is a unique owner (which is generally the user who creates it). A UNIX file has two fields: (1) A userid field that contains the userid of its owner and (2) A groupid field that contains the groupid of the group to which the file belongs.

The protection mechanism of the UNIX operating system uses an access control list in conjunction with protection groups for efficiency. The protection mechanism in UNIX allows one to specify three protection groups, namely, *owner, group,* and *others* separately for each file. Users in each group can have three access rights, viz., read, write, and execute, to a file. Access rights of the three groups to a file are denoted by three fields associated with the file. Each field consists of three bits—one bit for each access right— denoting the access rights of the corresponding group to the file (see Fig. 14.12). Only the owner of a file and the *super user* have the authority to change these bits (for all three groups) for a file. Using *chmod* command, a user can selectively

owner			group			others		
r	w	x	r	w	x	r	w	x

FIGURE 14.12
Protection fields of a file in UNIX.

revoke or assign any access right—read, write, and execute—for a file to any of the three groups.

A protection domain is associated with every user. (A protection domain defines the access rights of a user with regard to various resources/files.) When a user logs into an account, the user starts in a protection domain. Any command issued by the user can access all files allowed by the protection domain. To access files in some other domain, a user must switch to the corresponding domain using the *su* (set userid) command. Switching to a domain requires the password of the corresponding user.

14.7.2 The Hydra Kernel

Hydra is the kernel of a multiprocessor operating system that was developed at Carnegie-Mellon University [39]. The Hydra Kernel provides a rich set of mechanisms on which a wide array of operating systems can be built. The kernel only supports protection mechanisms; policy issues are left to higher layers. Hydra supports a capability-based protection mechanism on which any security policy can be implemented. Description of the Hydra protection mechanism in this section is based on Wulf et al. [39].

HYDRA ENVIRONMENT. In Hydra, the unit of protection is an *object*, which is an abstraction of a resource. *Procedure* is an abstraction of an operation on the objects. The protection mechanism of Hydra regulates the invocation of procedures to instances of objects (i.e., resources). Each object has a unique name, type, and representation. The representation portion of an object consists of *data* and *capability* parts. The data part can be accessed by programs that have appropriate access rights for the object. The capability part of an object may contain capabilities referencing other objects and can be directly manipulated only by the kernel. Primary elements of the Hydra protection mechanism are objects (abstraction of resources) and capabilities (references to objects). A capability includes information about all the operations that its holder can perform on the object referenced by the capability. To perform an operation on an object, a program/user supplies a capability for that object. The kernel examines the access rights in the capability and allows the operation only if the capability contains the appropriate rights.

SALIENT FEATURES

Auxiliary rights. For every object, the Hydra kernel supports basic access rights (such as read, write, execute, copy, etc.) for the controlled manipulation of objects and capabilities. These rights are referred to as *kernel* rights. A very interesting and powerful feature of the Hydra kernel is that it also supports protection of user defined operations (called *auxiliary* rights). When a user defines a new object type and its associated operations, the Hydra kernel automatically treats these operations as the auxiliary access rights for the object. If a user wants to perform these operations on an object, its capability must contain the corresponding auxiliary rights. The kernel only provides mechanisms for enforcing auxiliary rights; it does not interpret those operations. The kernel uses a 24-bit mask to encode access rights. Kernel rights have fixed positions in the mask and the positions of auxiliary right bits depend upon the objects. The kernel checks a capability for certain rights by checking appropriate bits in the 24-bit mask.

Access right enhancement. In Hydra, a procedure contains a list of capabilities for the objects that must be accessed during the execution of the procedure's code. In addition, a procedure may also receive a set of capabilities as *actual* parameters when it is called. The former are called *caller-independent* capabilities (because a procedure always possesses them) and the latter are called *caller-dependent* capabilities (because they may vary from caller to caller).

A procedure contains parameter *templates* for capabilities that are expected to be received as actual parameters when the procedure is called. When a procedure is called, the kernel checks to see if types of the actual and template capabilities match. The kernel also checks if the capabilities supplied as actual parameters contain adequate access rights. If these checks pass, the kernel constructs a capability for the object (procedure) that contains access rights specified by its template, which may be higher than those contained in the capability passed as an actual parameter. Therefore, a callee may have more access rights to an object than the caller that passed the corresponding capability as an actual parameter. However, the caller cannot obtain those access rights because additional rights are present only in the callee's domain. This is called right expansion (or enhancement) across protection domains and is a key factor in achieving flexibility in Hydra [39]. A simple example of access right enhancement is the invocation of a compiler. A compiler has (permanent) access rights to certain files. When a compiler is invoked by a user, the compiler's access rights are enhanced so that it can access the file to be compiled and has the right to create an object code file in the user's directory.

14.7.3 Amoeba

Amoeba [27] is a distributed operating system developed by Tanenbaum's group at the Free University and the Center for Mathematics and Computer Science in Netherlands. Amoeba is an object-based system and is based on the client-server model. Client processes carry out operations on objects by sending requests to server processes via remote procedure calls. Every object is managed by a server process.

Amoeba uses capabilities to protect objects against unauthorized access. A capability contains the object identifier and thus also serves as the address of the object. The structure of a capability in Amoeba is shown in Fig. 14.13. The server port field in a capability gives the identity of the server process that manages the corresponding object. The object field is used by the server process to identify the specific object. The rights field denotes the operations that the holder of the capability is allowed to perform on the object. The check field provides protection against users tampering or forging capabilities. Amoeba uses a cryptographic technique to protect a capability from

48 bits	24 bits	8 bits	48 bits
Server Port	Object number	Rights	Check

FIGURE 14.13
A capability in amoeba.

being tempered or forged. (Readers may like to read Public-Key Encryption in the next chapter before reading the rest of this subsection.)

PROTECTING CAPABILITIES. The check field is the key to providing protection to capabilities. When an object is created, the object's server process selects a random check field and stores it in the capability of the object as well as in its table. All the right bits in this capability are on. This initial capability is called the *owner capability* and is returned to the client that requested creation of the object. When the capability is sent back by the client to the server to perform an operation, the check field is verified. The crux of the technique here is that the check field is chosen from such a huge, sparse address space that it is impossible to correctly guess the check field of an object's capability.

In a restricted capability, not all access right bits are on. A client creates a restricted capability by sending the owner capability and a bit mask for new rights to the server process. The server fetches the original check field from the table and performs an Ex-OR operation on the check field and the bit mask for new rights and then applies a one-way function on the result to obtain the new check field. (A one-way function f is a function such that, given x, it is easy to find y, where $y = f(x)$, but given y it is practically impossible to find x.) The server creates a restricted capability from the owner capability by replacing the check field with the result of the one-way function and the right field with the bit mask received from the client. It then sends this capability to the client process. The client can pass a restricted capability to any other process.

When a restricted capability is presented to the server along with a request, the server fetches the original check field from its table, performs an Ex-OR operation on the check field and the rightfield in the received capability, and applies the same one-way function on the result. The received capability is valid only if the result of this one-way function matches with the check field in the capability. Clearly, if a process is fabricating a restricted capability or is tampering with the rightfield of a restricted capability, it will fail this test. However, capabilities are not protected against eavesdropping—An attacker that observes a capability being passed on the network can steal it.

14.7.4 Andrew

Andrew is a distributed computing environment that was developed at Carnegie Mellon University. Andrew combines powerful workstations and advanced networking technology to provide a large distributed time sharing environment. In this section, we discuss the protection mechanisms of Andrew. Discussion in this section is based on a paper by Satyanarayanan [36].

BASIC ARCHITECTURE. Andrew architecture consists of two components (see Fig. 14.14). First, a set of workstations known as *Virtue*. Second, a local area network and a collection of file servers, collectively called *Vice*. The local area network consists of Ethernets and IBM Token Rings, interconnected by optic fiber links. The distributed file server spans all workstations and provides the primary data sharing mechanism. As Vice maintains shared files in Andrew, it is also responsible for enforing protection policies.

The protection domain in Andrew consists of *users* and *groups*. Users in this context are those who can authenticate themselves to Vice and be held responsible for their actions. A group is a collection of other groups and users. The *Is_a_member_of* relation holds between a user or a group U and a group G if and only if U is a member of G. The reflexive and transitive closure of this relation for U defines a subset of the protection domain called U's *Current Protection Subdomain* (CPS). Thus, the CPS of a user denotes all the groups that he or she is a member of, directly or indirectly.

The total rights possessed by a user at any time are the union of the rights possessed by all the members of his CPS. Therefore, Andrew allows the inheritance of membership (and thus inheritance of rights). Inheritance of membership conceptually simplifies the maintenance and administration of the protection domain.

PROTECTION MECHANISM. Andrew uses the access control list mechanism for the protection of shared information and this choice was motivated by the following factors:

- The user community in a university demands a protection mechanism that is simple to use yet allows complex policies to be expressed.
- The revocation of access privileges is an important and common operation in a university environment.

In Vice, an entry in an access control list (henceforth, called an access list) maps a user or a group into a set of rights, which are bit positions in a 32-bit mask. An access list consists of two lists: a list of *positive rights* and a list of *negative rights*. An entry in a positive right list denotes the possession of rights for the corresponding user. An entry in a negative right list denotes the denial of those rights to the corresponding user. In the case of a conflict, denial overrides possession. Negative rights are an effective

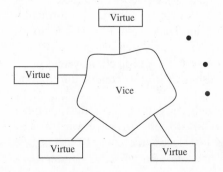

FIGURE 14.14
Basic architecture of Andrew.

means to rapidly and selectively revoke user access rights. A user may be a direct or indirect member of a large number of groups, so in order to revoke the access of a user to an object, the user's entry from all those groups that bestow rights on that object must be deleted. In a large distributed system, the search for such groups and the deletion of the user from those groups may take a significant amount of time. Negative rights can reduce the vulnerability during the update time because changes to the access list are effective immediately. In addition, negative rights provide the capability to grant access rights at finer granularity (than the protection group mechanism provides). For example, one can specify a protection policy of the following form: "Grant a right r to all members of group G except user U."

The following algorithm is executed for the access list check. Suppose C is an access list, CPS_U is the CPS of U, and M and N are right masks whose bits are initially reset. The entries in C and CPS_U are sorted.

1. For each element of CPS_U, if there is an entry in the positive right list of C, inclusive-OR M with the rights part of the entry.
2. For each element of CPS_U, if there is an entry in the negative right list of C, inclusive-OR N with the rights part of the entry.
3. Bitwise subtract N fron M.

After the execution of the algorithm is over, M specifies the rights possessed by U.

GRANULARITY OF PROTECTION.   The granularity of protection in Vice is a directory. Vice associates an access list with each directory and the protection enforced by that access list uniformly applies to all the files in the directory. The motivations for this design decision are conceptual simplicity and reduced storage overhead. Experiences with Andrew showed that this is an excellent compromise between fine granularity of protection and conceptual simplicity. (However, some other users of the Andrew file system have found this tradeoff limiting.) If a file needs to have a protection different from other files in its directory, it can be achieved by placing the file in a separate directory (with appropriate protection) and putting a symbolic link to in the original directory.

14.8   SUMMARY

Security and protection deal with the control of unauthorized access to the resources of a computer system. Potential security violations include unauthorized information release, unauthorized information modification, unauthorized denial of service, etc. In this chapter, we discussed several models of protection in computer systems. A protection model extracts essential features of a protection system. A protection system gives mechanisms to control user access to the system resources and to control information flow in the system.

The access matrix model of a protection system consists of the following three components. (1) Current objects, a finite set of entities to which access is to be controlled, (2) current subjects, a finite set of entities that access the current objects, and (3) generic rights, a finite set of generic rights. The state of a protection system is a triplet (S, O, P), where S is the set of current subjects, O is the set of current objects, and P is a matrix, called the *access matrix*, with a row for every current subject and a column for every current object. Entry $P[s, o]$ denotes the access rights that subject s has to object o.

Two popular access control techniques were studied, viz., capabilities and the access control list, both based on the access matrix model. The capability-based method corresponds to the row-wise decomposition of the access matrix. Each subject s is assigned a list of tuples $(o, P[s, o])$ for all objects o that it is allowed to access. The tuples are referred to as *capabilities*. If subject s possesses a capability $(o, P[s, o])$, then it is authorized to access object o in a manner specified in $P[s, o]$. At any time, a subject is authorized to access only those objects for which it has capabilities. The object identifier in a capability can be the address of the corresponding objects and therefore, besides providing protection, capabilities can also be used as an addressing mechanism by the system. There are two ways to implement capabilities, the tagged approach and the partitioned approach. The main advantages of a capability-based protection system are efficiency, simplicity, and flexibility. The drawbacks of this approach include difficult control of the propagation of capabilities, difficult revocation of access rights, and difficult garbage collection.

The access control list method corresponds to the column-wise decomposition of the access matrix. Each object o is assigned a list of pairs $(s, P[s, o])$ for all subjects s that are allowed to access the object. Note that the set $P[s, o]$ denotes the access rights that subject s has to object o. The access list assigned to object o corresponds to all access rights contained in the column for object o in the access matrix. When a subject s requests access α to object o, the requested access is executed only if an entry (s, Φ) exists for subject s in the access control list of o such that $\alpha \in \Phi$. Major features of the access control list method include: the easy revocation of access rights from a subject and the easy review of an access. The main issues in the implementation of the access control list method are the efficiency of execution and the efficiency of storage.

Transitions in the protection state and safety in the access matrix model were studied in this chapter. A finite set of commands is available in the access matrix model to change the protection state. A finite set of commands was defined to change the contents of the access matrix. A change in the protection state may be due to a change in the security policy.

In the advanced models, we studied take-grant model, the Bell-LaPadula model, and the lattice model. In the take-grant model, the protection state of a system is described by a directed graph. Nodes of the graph are of two types, subjects and objects. An edge from node x to node y denotes that the subject or object corresponding to node x has some access rights to the subject or object corresponding to node y. Edges are tagged with the corresponding access rights. Besides read, write, and execute, two special access rights in the take-grant model are take and grant. The access rights take and grant specify how the access rights can be propagated to other nodes. If node x has the access right take to node y, the entity corresponding to node x can take access rights of the entity corresponding to y to any other node. If node x has the access right *grant* to node y, the entity corresponding to node y can be granted any access right which the entity corresponding to node x has.

The Bell-LaPadula model deals with the control of information flow. This model consists of several security levels, which are ordered. Each subject has a *clearance* and each object has a *classification* (i.e., belongs to a security level). Each subject also has a *current clearance level*, which may not exceed the clearance of the subject. In the Bell-LaPadula model, a subject has append (i.e., write) access to only those objects whose classification (i.e., security level) is higher than or equal to the current security clearance level of the subject. It has read access to only those objects whose classification is lower than or equal to the current security clearance level of the subject.

The lattice model of information flow deals with regulating the flow of information among the objects. The lattice model consists of three entities: a set of objects, a set of processes (so-called subjects), and a set of security classes. An information flow policy is modeled by a lattice (SC, $\rightarrow$) where SC is the set of security classes and the relation $\rightarrow$ specifies permissible information flow between classes. For two objects x and y, information flow from x to y is permitted provided $\underline{x} \rightarrow \underline{y}$. ($\underline{x}$ denotes the security class to which an object x belongs.) The lattice model of security is very powerful because by choosing any ordering between security classes, a wide range of information flow policies can be modeled.

The protection mechanisms in four real-life systems, namely, UNIX, Hydra, Amoeba, and Andrew, were described. Hydra and Amoeba use capabilities for protection, whereas UNIX and Andrew make use of access control list techniques.

14.9 FURTHER READING

Early fundamental papers on protection include Lampson's papers on the access matrix model [21] and the confinement problem [22] and the Graham and Denning paper on the access matrix model [18].

For a comprehensive reading on the subject, readers are referred to two excellent books on the subject, by Denning [7] and by Pfleeger [31]. Popek provides a good survey of protection [32]. The July 1983 issue of *IEEE Computer* is devoted to computer security technology. Landwehr's article [23] in the September 1981 issue of *ACM Computing Surveys* provides a good overview of models for protection in computer systems. Clifford Neuman [29] reviews protection and security issues in the future systems.

Fabry discusses the use of capability as an addressing mechanism in [14]. Techniques for review and revocation of access rights in capability-based systems can be found in a paper by Gligor [17]. Ekanadham and Bernstein have extended the idea of capabilities to conditional capabilities where a capability has a set of conditions associated with it [11].

An article by McLean addresses limitations of the Bell-LaPadula model [26]. A recent book edited by Denning [10] contains a comprehensive treatment of the various security threats in computer systems and their social, legal, and ethical implications. Sandhu [35], Ammann and Sandhu [1] have developed a schematic protection model for security in computer systems. The Computer Security Evaluation Center of the U.S. Department of Defense has developed a set of criteria [37] to evaluate the degree of confidence in the security provided by a computer system.

Wong [38] discusses issues in the design of secure distributed operating systems. Mullender and Tanenbaum [28] describe the application of capabilities for protection in distributed systems. Clifford Neuman [30] discusses an infrastructure for authorization and accounting in distributed systems. For more details of the protection mechanism in Andrew, reader should refer to Satyanarayanan [36].

Readers can also find articles on this topic in the Proceedings of an annual symposium, *IEEE Symposium on Security and Privacy*. Moreover, the *Journal of Computer Security* is devoted to this topic.

PROBLEMS

14.1. A password can be stolen by trial and error (by trying several passwords). Suggest a safeguard against such security violations.

14.2. Consider a protection system where three access rights x, y, and z are defined on the objects. The objects are divided into 8 classes and the access rights of the classes are respectively the 2^3 elements of the powerset of the set $\{x, y, z\}$; that is, elements of $\{\Phi\}$, $\{x\}$, $\{y\}$, $\{z\}$, ..., $\{x, y, z\}$. Information flow is permitted from a class sc_1 to another class sc_2 if the access rights of class sc_1 are contained in the access rights of class sc_2. Show that the set of classes and the flow relation form a lattice. Draw a schematic diagram for the lattice.

14.3. Discuss the pros and cons of the tagged and partitioned approaches to implement a capability-based protection system.

14.4. Suppose a routine is shared by many users. The routine accesses a datum via a capability. The datum is private to each user. (For example, a routine can be a compiler that accesses a user program as the data.) Explain how we can implement this using capability-based addressing. Can we implement this when the object table is global? Why or why not?

14.5. Show that the lock-key method of access control is identical to the access list control method with protection groups.

REFERENCES

1. Ammann, P. E., and R. S. Sandhu,"The Extended Schematic Protection Model," *Journal of Computer Security*, vol. 1, nos. 3 and 4, 1992, pp. 335–383.
2. Anderson, J., "Information Security in a Multi-User Computer Environment. *Advances in Computers*, vol. 12, Academic Press, New York, 1973.
3. Bell, D. E., *Secure Computer Systems: A Refinement of a Mathematical Model,* ESD-TR-73-278, vol. 3, Hanscom AFB, Bedford, MA, Apr. 1974.
4. Bell, D. E., and L. J. LaPadula, *Secure Computer Systems: Mathematical Foundations,* ESD-TR-73-278, vol. 1, Hanscom AFB, Bedford, MA, Nov. 1973.
5. Bishop, M., and L. Snyder, "The Transfer of Information and Authority in a Protection System," *Proceedings of 7th Symposium on Operating Systems Principles*, Dec. 1979.
6. Conway, R. W., W. L. Maxwell, and H. L. Morgan, "On the Implementation of Security Measures in Information Systems," *Communications of the ACM*, Apr. 1972.
7. Denning, D. E., *Cryptography and Data Security*, Addison-Wesley, Reading, MA, 1982.
8. Denning, D. E., "A Lattice Model of Secure Information Flow," *Communications of the ACM*, May 1976.
9. Denning, D. E., and P. J. Denning, "Certification of Programs for Secure Information Flow," *Communications of the ACM*, July 1977.

10. Denning, P. J., *Computers under Attack: Intruders, Worms, and Viruses,* Addison-Wesley, Reading, MA, 1990.

11. Ekanadham, K., and A. J. Bernstein, "Conditional Capability," *IEEE Transactions on Software Engineering*, May 1979.

12. England, D. M., "Operating System of System 250," Paper presented at International Switching Symposium, Cambridge, MA, June 1972.

13. Fabry, R. S., "Preliminary Description of a Supervisor for a Machine Oriented Around Capabilities," *ICR Quarterly Report,* vol. 18, U. of Chicago, Aug. 1968.

14. Fabry, R. S., "Capability-Based Addressing," *Communications of the ACM*, July 1974.

15. Feustal, E. A., "The Rice Research Computer—A Tagged Architecture," *Proceedings of the AFIPS*, 1972.

16. Gifford, D. K., "Cryptographic Sealing for Information Security and Authentication," *Communications of the ACM*, Apr. 1982.

17. Gligor, V. D., "Review and Revocation of Access Privileges Distributed through Capabilities," *IEEE Transactions on Software Engineering*, May 1979.

18. Graham, G. S., and P. J. Denning, "Protection—Principles and Practice," *Proceedings of the AFIPS Spring Joint Computer Conference*, 1972.

19. Harrison, M. A., W. L. Ruzzo, and J. D. Ullman, "Protection in Operating Systems," *Communications of the ACM*, Aug. 1976.

20. Jones, A. K., R. J. Lipton, and L. Snyder, "A Linear Time Algorithm for Deciding Subject-Object Security," *Proceedings of the 17th Annual Foundations of Computer Science*, 1976.

21. Lampson, B., "Protection," *Proceedings of the 5th Princeton Symposium on Information Sciences and Systems*, March 1971.

22. Lampson, B., "A Note on the Confinement Problem," *Communications of the ACM*, Oct. 1973.

23. Landwehr, C. E., "Formal Models of Computer Security," *ACM Computing Surveys*, Sept. 1981.

24. Lipton, R. J., and L. Snyder, "A Linear Time Algorithm for Deciding Subject Security," *Journal of the ACM*, July 1977.

25. Maekawa, M., A. Oldehoeft, and R. Oldehoeft, *Operating Systems: Advanced Concepts*, Benjamin-Cummings, Redwood City, Ca, 1987.

26. McLean, J., "The Specification and Modeling of Computer Security," *IEEE Computer*, Jan. 1990.

27. Mullender, S. P., G. van Rossum, A. S. Tanenbaum, R. van Renesse, and H. van Staveren, "Amoeba: A Distributed Operating System for the 1990s," *IEEE Computer*, May 1990.

28. Mullender, S. P., and A. Tanenbaum, "The Design of a Capability-Based Distributed Operating Systems," *The Computer Journal*, vol. 29, no. 4, 1986.

29. Neuman, B. Clifford, "Protection and Security Issues for Future Systems," *Proceedings of the Workshop on Operating Systems of the 90s and Beyond*, Springer-Verlag, New York, (LNCS 563), July 1991.

30. Neuman, B. Clifford, "Proxy-Based Authorization and Accounting for Distributed Systems," *Proceedings of the 13th International Conference on Distributed Computing Systems,* May 1993, pp. 283–291.

31. Pfleeger, C. P., *Security in Computing*, Prentice-Hall, Englewood Cliffs, N.J., 1989.

32. Popek, G. J., "Protection Structures," *IEEE Computer*, June 1974.

33. Ritchie, D. M., and K. Thompson, "The UNIX Time-Sharing System," *Communications of the ACM*, July 1974.

34. Saltzer, J. R., and M. D. Schroeder, "The Protection of Information in Computer Systems," *Proceedings of the IEEE*, Sept. 1975.

35. Sandhu, R. S., "The Schematic Protection Model: Its Definition and Analysis for Acyclic Attenuating Schemes," *Journal of the ACM*, Apr. 1988.

36. Satyanarayanan, M., "Integrating Security in Large Computer Systems," *ACM Transactions on Computer Systems*, Aug. 1989.
37. U.S. Department of Defense, *Trusted Computer System Evaluation Criteria*, Computer Security Evaluation Center, Ft. Mead, MD 5D, Dec. 1985.
38. Wong, R. M., "Issues in Secure Distributed Operating Systems," *Digest of Papers, IEEE CompCon*, Spring 1989.
39. Wulf, W., E. Cohen, W. Corwin, A. Jones, R. Levin, C. Pierson, and F. Pollack, "HYDRA: The Kernel of a Multiprocessor Operating System," *Communications of the ACM*, June 1974.

CHAPTER
15

DATA SECURITY: CRYPTOGRAPHY

15.1 INTRODUCTION

The techniques for security and protection discussed in the previous chapter help to prevent the unauthorized use and access to resources of a computer system. Nevertheless, there remains the possibility that an unauthorized user can gain access to confidential information. For example, a user can bypass the protection mechanism of a system or tap a physical channel (in a communication network) to steal information being transmitted over the channel. A user, not authorized to access information is called an *intruder*. Note that intruder is relative to the information.

To add extra protection to confidential information, techniques are needed to ensure that an intruder is unable to understand or make use of any information obtained by wrongful access. Cryptography is a technique that provides added protection to the system in the event of such unauthorized information disclosures. Cryptography allows a piece of information to be converted into a cryptic form before being stored in a computer system or before being transmitted over a physical channel. The cryptic form is such that this information is unintelligible unless it is decrypted using secret information (such as a key) known only to persons authorized to read and use this information.

Clearly, cryptography can be used to protect the confidentiality of both stored information and information transmitted over a physical channel. For information transmitted over a physical channel, this is the basic form of protection (besides guarding the physical channel against illegal taps). For information stored in a computer system,

404

it is an added protection in the event that an intruder succeeds in accessing protected information. In addition to the confidentiality of information, cryptography is also used for establishing the authenticity of a user to another user or entity. Establishing authenticity requires the use of a mechanism that enables the system to verify the identity of a user—to verify whether a user is indeed what he claims to be.

In this chapter, various cryptographic techniques used to protect the confidentiality and the integrity of information and authentication techniques are discussed.

15.2 A MODEL OF CRYPTOGRAPHY

15.2.1 Terms and Definitions

A *plaintext* (or a *cleartext*) is an intelligible message that is to be converted into an unintelligible (i.e., encrypted) form. A *ciphertext* is a message in encrypted form. *Encryption*, the process of converting a plaintext to a ciphertext, generally involves a set of transformations that uses a set of algorithms and a set of input parameters. *Decryption* is the process of converting a ciphertext to a plaintext. This also requires a set of algorithms and a set of input parameters. Generally, both encryption and decryption require a key parameter whose secrecy is absolutely essential to the functioning of the entire process. This parameter is referred to as the *key*. (Breaking a cryptographic system essentially involves acquiring the knowledge of the key.) If the key is the same for both encryption and decryption, the system is referred to as the *symmetric*. Otherwise, it is *asymmetric*.

A *cryptosystem* is a system for encryption and decryption of information. *Cryptology* is the science of designing and breaking cryptosystems. *Cryptography* refers to the practice of using cryptosystems to maintain confidentiality of information. The study of breaking cryptosystems is referred to as *cryptoanalysis*.

15.2.2 A Model of Cryptographic Systems

The model of a cryptographic system presented in this section is taken from [14]. Figure 15.1 illustrates the general structure of a cryptographic system.

Block E performs the intended encryption. It takes plaintext M and an encryption key K_e as the input and produces ciphertext C. E_{K_e} denotes the functional notation for the encryption operation using K_e as the key; that is, $C = E_{K_e}(M)$. The ciphertext C is transmitted over an insecure channel to a destination where it is deciphered. (An *insecure* channel is one that can be tapped by an intruder.) The decryption operation is denoted by a box D, which takes ciphertext C and a decryption key K_d as input and produces the original plaintext M as the output. D_{K_d} denotes the functional notation for the decryption operation using K_d as the key; that is, $M = D_{K_d}(C)$.

Block CA denotes a cryptanalyst (i.e., an intruder) whose task is to decipher information transmitted over the channel. The cryptoanalyst has full knowledge of the encryption (E) and decryption (D) techniques in use. The cryptoanalyst can listen to the channel (i.e., knows C) and has access to a variety of side information (SI). Examples of side information include language statistics (i.e., the frequency of letters and words), the context of the ongoing communication, and some portion of plaintext. However,

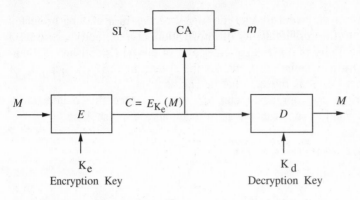

FIGURE 15.1
A schematic of a cryptographic system.

the cryptoanalyst does not have knowledge of the decryption key K_d. To break the system, a cryptoanalyst must find a scheme to determine the decryption key K_d, given the information at his disposal. In some cases, it may be possible to decipher portions of a ciphertext without having any knowledge of K_d.

The protection provided by a cryptographic system is measured by the difficulty in finding the (value of the) decryption key used in the system.

POTENTIAL THREATS. A cryptographic system is subject to various kinds of threats [14]. The threat depends upon how much and what kind of side information (SI) is available to an intruder (i.e., a cryptoanalyst). The threat to a cryptographic system increases as the amount of side information increases. Clearly, a system that can be broken in the absence of side information (or with only very trivial side information) is highly insecure and is therefore useless. To be secure and robust, a system should be able to withstand the most severe threat: it should remain secure even if the most desired side information (except the key) is available. Next, potential threats to cryptographic systems when various degrees of the side information are available to an intruder are discussed.

A threat to a system in which an intruder can have access to only the ciphertext is called a *ciphertext-only* attack. A cryptographic system vulnerable to ciphertext-only attacks has very little utility because it is very easy to get hold of ciphertext (for example, by tapping an insecure channel). In a ciphertext-only attack, an intruder generally uses probabilistic characteristics or the context of the ciphertext to break the cipher. A good cryptographic system should be able to withstand ciphertext-only attacks.

A system in which an intruder can have access to both ciphertext and a considerable amount of corresponding plaintext is said to be subject to a *known-plaintext* attack. Systems that can withstand known-plain text attacks are more secure because an intruder could obtain a considerable amount of plaintext corresponding to a ciphertext. The threat to a system where an intruder can obtain ciphertext corresponding to plaintext of his choice is referred to as a *chosen-plaintext* attack. For example, this happens when an intruder succeeds in breaking into a system to the extent where the system encrypts a plaintext of the intruder's choice.

DESIGN PRINCIPLES. There are two basic principles underlying the design of cryptographic systems: First, Shannon's principles of diffusion and confusion [23] which calls for breaking dependencies and introducing as much randomness in the ciphertext as possible. Second, the exhaustive search principle, which calls for an exhaustive search of a space to determine the key needed to break the system.

Shannon's principles. Shannon's principle of *diffusion* calls for spreading the correlation and dependencies among key-string variables over substrings as much as possible so as to maximize the length of plaintext needed to break the system. Shannon's principle of *confusion* advocates changing a piece of information so that the output has no obvious relation to the input. It calls for making the functional dependencies among related variables as complex as possible so as to maximize the time required for breaking the system.

Exhaustive search principle. The determination of the key—needed to break a cryptographic system—requires an exhaustive search of a space, which is extremely computationally intensive and takes a prohibitively long time. Note that given a sufficiently long time, it may be possible to determine the key uniquely.

Shannon's principles formed the basis for early methods (i.e., conventional cryptography) while the exhaustive search principle forms the basis for modern cryptography.

15.2.3 A Classification of Cryptographic Systems

Figure 15.2 depicts a simple classification of cryptographic systems. These systems can be roughly divided into conventional and modern systems.

Conventional systems were used primarily for ciphering a script written in a language. The basic principle underlying these systems is the mapping of a letter of the alphabet of a language by another letter in the alphabet, derived through a secret

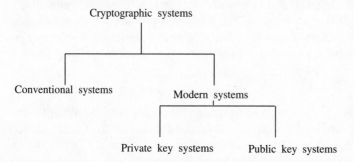

FIGURE 15.2
A classification of cryptographic systems.

mapping procedure. The crux of these systems is the secrecy of the mapping procedure, which can be viewed as a key.

Modern systems, on the other hand, are primarily used for ciphering information that is in binary form. These systems follow the principle of *open design* in the sense that underlying encryption and decryption techniques (algorithms) are not kept secret. Instead, only the values of some parameters (called keys) used in encryption and decryption are kept secret. Here also, there are two types of systems: private key systems and public key systems. In private key systems, keys used for both the encryption and decryption are kept secret. In public key systems, on the other hand, the key used for encryption is known publicly, but the key used in decryption is still kept secret. The crux of the public key system is that even though the procedure to compute the decryption key is known, the procedure is so computationally intensive that it takes a prohibitively long time to compute the key. Private key systems use Shannon's principles of diffusion and confusion for added security [14].

15.3 CONVENTIONAL CRYPTOGRAPHY

Conventional cryptography is based on substitution ciphers. In a substitution cipher, each alphabet in a plaintext is substituted by another alphabet. In this section, we present a series of techniques for conventional cryptography such that each technique presented is a refinement over the previous one. We will use the English language for illustration purposes and we will use the numeral correspondence of the 26 letters whenever arithmetic operations are involved. (That is, A $\Leftrightarrow$ 0, B $\Leftrightarrow$ 1, , ... , Z $\Leftrightarrow$ 25.)

THE CAESAR CIPHER. In the Caesar cipher, a letter is transformed into the third letter following it in the alphabetical sequence (with wrap around). Mathematically, it corresponds to the following mapping, E (M denotes an alphabet):

$$E : M \rightarrow (M + 3) \text{ modulo } 26, \qquad \text{where } 0 \leq M \leq 25.$$

For example, plaintext "*Julius loves Cleopatra*" is transformed into "*mxolxv oryhv fohrsdwud*". In the Caesar cipher, the shift is fixed at 3 letters. It can be generalized to have any degree of shift (between 1 and 25). The main problems with the Caesar cipher are that (1) since the transformation is linear, a search to determine the key is very simple and (2) the number of keys (i.e., the number of possible shifts in letters) is very small (only 25).

SIMPLE SUBSTITUTION. In the simple substitution cipher, any permutation of letters can be mapped to English letters. Thus, the positional correlation of the Caesar cipher has been eliminated. Since each permutation of letters is a key, there are 26! ($> 10^{26}$) keys in this cipher, making an exhaustive search very expensive.

However, the simple substitution cipher preserves the frequency distribution of the letters of an alphabet because the same substitution is performed at all the occurrences of a letter. Therefore, a statistical analysis of the underlying language can be used to break the cipher. For example, in the English language, the frequency of different letters is highly nonuniform and this knowledge can be used to break the simple substitution cipher.

POLYALPHABETIC CIPHERS. Polyalphabetic ciphers use a periodic sequence of n substitution alphabet ciphers. That is, the system switches among n substitution alphabet ciphers periodically. A major impact of this is that the statistical characteristics of the language can be smoothened out by appropriately choosing the mapping (substitution). Also, the effective number of keys is increased to $(26!)^n$.

A popular version of polyalphabetic ciphers is the *vigenere* cipher, which employs a periodic sequence of Caesar ciphers with different keys. For example, if the periodic sequence of integers is 11, 19, 4, 22, 9, 25, then the ciphertext is obtained by adding these integers (in "modulo 26" arithmetic) in this sequence repeatedly to the integers of the plaintext. (Note that each letter of the text is denoted by an integer between 0 and 25.) For this periodic sequence, the first, seventh, thirteenth, ..., letters of the plaintext are shifted by 11 letters; the second, eighth, fourteenth, ... letters are shifted 19 places; the third, ninth, fifteenth, ... letters are shifted 4 places; and so on.

The *vigenere* cipher is vulnerable, however, because if the period is known, the various shifts in the period can be determined by an exhaustive search. Security can be increased by making $n \rightarrow \infty$; that is, by making the period as big as the number of letters in the message. However, the key, which is now as long as the message, must be transmitted securely over the unsecure channel. Such a key is called a *one-time pad*. Substitution ciphers that use a one-time pad are unbreakable because, given a ciphertext, it is impossible for an intruder to guess the key. Ciphertext provides no clue about the key. Shannon has shown that this scheme is provably secure in the information-theoretic sense.

15.4 MODERN CRYPTOGRAPHY

Due to the widespread use of digital computers in information processing, storage, and transmission, modern cryptographic systems are geared toward ciphering information that is in binary form. Plaintext and ciphertext are both in binary form. In modern cryptography, underlying encryption and decryption techniques are generally publicly known. However, the values of keys needed to decrypt a ciphertext are kept secret. Modern cryptographic schemes are based on the principle of exhaustive search—even though the procedure to compute the decryption key is known, the procedure is so computationally intensive that it takes a prohibitively long time to compute the key.

We next present two techniques of modern cryptography, namely, private key systems and public key systems. Recall that in private key systems, keys used for both encryption and decryption are kept secret. Private key systems use the same key for encryption as well as decryption, whereas public key systems use different keys for encryption and decryption. In public key systems, the key used for encryption is known in the public domain, but the key used for decryption is kept secret.

15.5   PRIVATE KEY CRYPTOGRAPHY: DATA ENCRYPTION STANDARD

In private key cryptography, the Data Encryption Standard (DES), developed by IBM, has been the official standard for use by the U.S. federal government [25]. We describe the basic technique of the DES and a more detailed description can be found in [25] and [6].

Two basic operations, permutation and substitution, are used in the DES.

Permutation. A permutation operation permutes the bits of a word. The purpose of a permutation operation is to provide diffusion, as this spreads the correlation and dependencies among the bits of a word.

Substitution. A substitution operation replaces an m-bit input by an n-bit output. There is no simple relation between input and output. Generally, a substitution operation consists of three operations: first, the m-bit input is converted into a decimal form; second, the decimal output is permuted (to give another decimal number); and finally, the decimal output is converted into n-bit output. The purpose of the substitution operation is to provide confusion.

15.5.1   Data Encryption Standard (DES)

The DES is a block cipher that crypts 64-bit data blocks using a 56-bit key, key. For error detection, the key is expanded to 64-bit by adding 8 parity bits. There are three basic steps involved in encryption. First, the plaintext block undergoes an initial permutation IP, in which 64 bits of the block are permuted. Second, the permuted block undergoes a complex transformation. This transformation uses the key and involves 16 iterations (explained later). Third, the output of the second step undergoes a final permutation, IP^{-1}, which is the inverse of the permutation in the first step. The output of the third step is the ciphertext block. The decryption of a ciphertext block requires that exactly these three steps are performed with reverse functionality.

We next discuss the iterative transformation of the second step, which is the heart of this technique. The iterative transformation consists of 16 functionally identical iterations. Every iteration uses a key for transformation that is derived from key and the iteration number.

Let L_i and R_i respectively denote the left and right 32-bit halves of the crypted 64-bit block after the ith iteration ($1 \leq i \leq 16$). Inputs to the ith iteration are L_{i-1}, R_{i-1}, and K_i, where K_i is a 48-bit key used in the ith iteration and is derived from key and the iteration number i, $K_i = \Phi(key, i)$. For the first iteration, L_0 and R_0 are respectively the left and right 32-bit halves of the 64-bit block after the initial permutation IP.

A schematic of the operations performed in the ith iteration is shown in Fig. 15.3. The transformation done at the ith iteration is given by the following equations:

$$L_i = R_{i-1}$$
$$R_i = L_i \oplus f(R_{i-1}, K_i)$$

where $\oplus$ denotes the exclusive-OR operation. Function f produces a 32-bit output that is computed in the following manner:

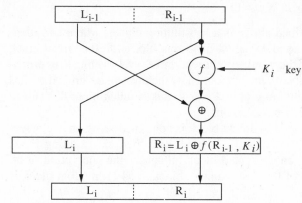

FIGURE 15.3
A schematic of the operations performed in ith iteration.

1. The 32-bit R_{i-1} is expanded into 48-bit $E(R_{i-1})$. (This is done by permuting the bits of R_{i-1} and also by duplicating some bits of R_{i-1}.)

2. The exclusive-OR operation is performed between 48-bit key K_i and $E(R_{i-1})$ and the 48-bit output is partitioned into eight partitions, $Q_1, Q_2, \ldots, Q_8$, of 6 bits each. ($E(R_{i-1}) \oplus K_i = Q_1, Q_2, \ldots, Q_8$.)

3. Each Q_i, $1 \leq i \leq 8$, is fed into a separate 6-to-4 substitution box. (A 6-to-4 substitution box transforms 6 bits into 4 bits such that the input-output relationship is secret.)

4. The 32-bit output of the eight substitution boxes is fed to a permutation box whose 32-bit output is f.

Details of the initial and the final permutations, the computation of the expanded 48-bit $E(R_{i-1})$, the computation of keys K_i, and the eight 6-to-4 substitution boxes can be found in [25] and [6].

DECRYPTION. The decryption of a crypted block requires the execution of the three previously described steps in reverse order, with the reverse function performed at each step. The first decryption step will undo the permutation IP^{-1}, performed in the last encryption step. The second step will undo the transformation performed in the 16 iterations. The iterations are executed in reverse order—starting from key K_{16} and ending at key K_1—using the following formula:

$$R_{i-1} = R_i$$
$$L_{i-1} = R_i \oplus f(L_i, K_i)$$

The keys $K_1, K_2, \ldots, K_{16}$ used in decryption are the same keys used in encryption. The third decryption step undoes the permutation IP performed in the first encryption step, yielding the original plaintext block.

The crux of this method is that the key key is very long (56 bits) and thus determining the key requires an exhaustive search over 2^{56} values. Permutation (in the first and third steps) and substitution (in the second step) provide extra security by adding diffusion and confusion.

15.5.2 Cipher Block Chaining

The mode of DES operation described above is a substitution cipher, where two identical 64-bit blocks are encrypted into identical 64-bit output blocks. In the cipher block chain mode of operation of DES, the result of encryption of a 64-bit block is propagated through the encryption of subsequent blocks. Thus, the encryption procedure has memory and is not a simple substitution cipher. Clearly, this is much more difficult to break than the DES without cipher block chaining.

In the cipher block chain mode, a plaintext block is combined using an exclusive-OR operation with the ciphertext of the previous block and then the resulting block is encrypted using the DES. Thus, an encrypted block influences the encryption of all subsequent blocks. For encryption of the first plaintext block, a 64-bit random block is used.

15.6 PUBLIC KEY CRYPTOGRAPHY

Private key cryptography (as well as conventional cryptographic techniques) requires the distribution of secret keys over the insecure communication network before secure communication can take place. This is called the *key distribution problem*. It is a bootstrap problem: a small secret communication (over an insecure communication network) is required before any further secret communication over the network can take place. A private courier or a secure communication channel is used for the distribution of keys over the network.

Public key cryptography solves this problem by announcing the encryption procedure E (and the associated key) in the public domain. However, decryption procedure D (and the associated key) is still kept secret. The crux of public key cryptography is the fact that it is impractical to derive the decryption procedure from the knowledge of the encryption procedure. This revolutionary concept was advocated by Diffie and Hellman [10]. Encryption procedure E and decryption procedure D must satisfy the following properties:

1. For every message M, $D(E(M)) = M$.

2. E and D can be efficiently applied to any message M.

3. Knowledge of E does not compromise security. In other words, it is impossible to derive D from E.

Public key cryptography allows two users to have a secure communication even if these users have not communicated before, because the encryption procedure used to encrypt messages for every user is available in the public domain. If a user X wants to send a message M to another user Y, X simply uses Y's encryption procedure E_Y to encrypt the message. When Y receives the encrypted message $E_Y(M)$, it decrypts it using its decryption procedure D_Y.

15.6.1 Implementation Issues

Diffie and Hellman suggested that one way to implement public key cryptography systems is to exploit the computational intractability of the inversion of *one-way* functions [10]. A function f is one-way if it is invertible and easy to compute. However, for almost all x in the domain of f, it is computationally infeasible to solve equation $y = f(x)$ for x. Thus, it is computationally infeasible to derive f^{-1} even if f is known. Note that given f and output y ($= f(x)$) of the function, what we want is that computation of input x should be impossible.

Diffie and Hellman introduced the concept of a *trapdoor one-way* function [10]. A function f is referred to as a trapdoor one-way function if f^{-1} is easy to compute, provided certain private trapdoor information is available. An example of private trapdoor information is the value of decryption key K_d. Clearly, a trapdoor one-way function f and its inverse f^{-1} can be used as matching encryption and decryption procedures in a public key cryptography. Various implementations of public key cryptography that make use of such one-way functions, have been proposed. We next discuss a popular implementation by Rivest, Shamir, and Adleman [21].

15.6.2 The Rivest-Shamir-Adleman Method

In the Rivest-Shamir-Adleman (RSA) method, a binary plaintext is divided into blocks and a block is represented by an integer between 0 and $n - 1$. This representation is necessary because the RSA method encrypts integers.

The encryption key is a pair (e, n) where e is a positive integer. A message block M (which is between 0 and $n - 1$) is encrypted by raising it to eth power modulo n. That is, the ciphertext C corresponding to a message M is given by

$$C = M^e \text{ modulo } n$$

Note that ciphertext C is an integer between 0 and $n - 1$. Thus, encryption does not increase the length of a plaintext.

The decryption key is a pair (d, n) where d is a positive integer. A ciphertext block C is decrypted by raising it to dth power modulo n. That is, the plaintext M corresponding to a ciphertext C is given by

$$M = C^d \text{ modulo } n$$

A user X possesses an encryption key (e_X, n_X) and a decryption key (d_X, n_X), where the encryption key is available in public domain, but the decryption key is known only to user X. Whenever a user Y wants to send a message M to user X, Y simply uses X's encryption key (e_X, n_X) to encrypt the message. When X receives the encrypted message, it decrypts it using its decryption key (d_Y, n_X). A schematic of the RSA method is shown in Fig. 15.4.

DETERMINATION OF ENCRYPTION AND DECRYPTION KEYS. Rivest, Shamir, and Adleman [21] identify the following method to determine the encryption and decryption keys. First, two large prime numbers, p and q, are chosen and n is defined as

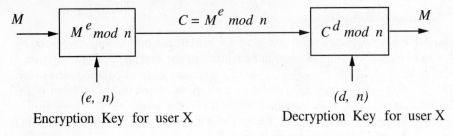

FIGURE 15.4
A schematic of the RSA method.

$$n = p \times q$$

Note that p and q are chosen sufficiently large so that even though n is public, it will be practically impossible to determine p and q by factoring n. After p and q have been decided, a user can choose any large integer as d so long as the chosen d is relatively prime to $(p-1) \times (q-1)$. That is, d should satisfy the condition

$$\text{GCD}(d, (p-1) \times (q-1)) = 1$$

Integer e is computed from p, q, and d such that it is the multiplicative inverse of d in modulo $(p-1) \times (q-1)$. That is,

$$e \times d = 1 \ (\text{modulo } (p-1) \times (q-1))$$

When n, e, and d are computed in this manner, the encryption and decryption process in the RSA method work correctly [21]. Note that every user must compute its own set of n, e, and d.

Even though n and e are public, the determination of d requires that n must be factored into two primes p and q so that the product $(p-1) \times (q-1)$ is known. (Note that this product is needed to compute d.) The main hurdle here is that if n is a sufficiently big number, say of 200 digits, the factorization of n will require an enormously long time, even on the fastest computers.

Example 15.1. Assume $p = 5$ and $q = 11$. Therefore, $n = 55$ and $(p-1) \times (q-1) = 40$. We choose d as 23 because 23 and 40 are relatively prime (GCD(23, 40) = 1). Now we must choose e satisfying the following equation:

$$23 \times e \ (\text{modulo } 40) = 1$$

Note that $e = 7$ satisfies this equation. Below we take some integers between 0 and 54 and show the encryption and decryption process for the RSA method:

M	M^7	$C = M^7 \bmod 55$	C^{23}	$M = C^{23} \bmod 55$
8	2097152	2	8388608	8
9	4782969	4	70368744177664	9
51	897410677851	6	7897302230536028l6	51

15.6.3   Signing Messages

To maintain the confidentiality of a message in public key cryptography, the message is encrypted with the public key and later decrypted with the secret key. However, in public key cryptography, a message can first be encrypted with the secret key and then later be decrypted with the public key. Note that by encrypting a message in this manner, a user is creating a signed message because no one else has the capability of creating such message. The encryption and decryption operations in such situations are referred to as *signing* and *verifying* a message, respectively. However, if public key cryptography is to be used for signing messages, the following condition must hold:

$$(\forall M)(\forall D_{PK})(\forall E_{SK}) :: M = D_{PK}(E_{SK}(M))$$

where M is a message and PK and SK are, respectively, the public and secret keys.

15.7   MULTIPLE ENCRYPTION

The level of security provided by the DES has been hotly debated. It has even been argued that the 56-bit key used in the DES will be too small to escape detection in the event of an exhaustive search on the ultra-fast computers that technology is expected to provide in the near future [9]. However, the security level of the DES can be increased by performing multiple encryption using independent keys [9]. For example, if a plaintext is doubly encrypted by first encrypting it with a 56-bit key and then again encrypting the resulting ciphertext by an independent 56-bit key, an exhaustive search over 2^{112} keys must be performed to break the cipher.

Unfortunately, the level of security provided by double encryption is far less than it appears at first sight [16]. In fact, the level of security provided by double encryption is much less than that of a single encryption with a 112-bit key. Diffie and Hellman [9] have shown that a double encryption with two independent 56-bit keys can be broken under known-plaintext attack with 2^{56} operations and 2^{56} words of memory. Thus, the time complexity of breaking a double encryption is the same as that of breaking an encryption with a 56-bit key. Although an exorbitant amount of memory is required to break a double encryption, this may be feasible in the near future as the cost of main memory decreases.

15.8   AUTHENTICATION IN DISTRIBUTED SYSTEMS

In this section, we discuss the application of encryption in performing authenticated communication between entities (i.e., users, servers, etc.) in distributed systems. In distributed systems, *authentication* means verifying the identity of communicating entities to each other. The description of authentication protocols in this section is based on the seminal work of Needham and Schroeder [18].

The distributed system under consideration consists of a collection of computers (called *machines*) that are connected by a network. There is no shared memory and all the computers communicate solely by passing messages over the network. The network is not secure in the sense that an intruder can copy and play back a message on the network.

AUTHENTICATION SERVICES. We consider the following three authentication services:

1. Establishing authenticated *interactive communication* between two entities on different machines. Interactive communication means that two entities synchronously converse with one another over the network. This service is discussed in Sec. 15.8.2.
2. Performing authenticated one-way communication between two entities on different machines. A typical example of this type of communication is an electronic mail system. This is generally an asynchronous operation because it is impossible to have a sender and a receiver available simultaneously. This service is discussed in Sec. 15.8.3.
3. Performing signed communication where the origin and the contents of a message can be authenticated to a third party. *Digital signature* is a means to achieve such communication between two entities. This service is discussed in Sec. 15.8.4.

We assume that two entities trying to set up an authenticated communication have not necessarily communicated in the past.

POTENTIAL THREATS. The discussion now turns to the various potential threats to achieving a secure authenticated communication. An intruder can gain access to any point in the communication network, and is thereby capable of altering or copying a part of a message. The intruder can replay a message transmitted earlier by an entity as well as transmit erroneous messages on the network. An intruder cannot understand the contents of a message (as they are encrypted), nonetheless, the intruder may have knowledge of the authentication protocol used by the entities. The intruder may know types of messages used in the protocol and their sequencing and purpose, as well as when the protocol has been initiated by an entity. An intruder may not only attempt to break into a communication, but may also prevent two entities from setting up an authenticated communication and interfere with an ongoing communication.

The fundamental goal of maintaining the secrecy of the contents of a message, transmitted over the communication network, is achieved assuming that computers have facilities to encrypt and decrypt messages efficiently. We assume that the keys used in the encryption and decryption of messages are practically impossible to obtain by an intruder and a user has a secure environment to perform computation (that is, to perform encryption, decryption, and message analysis).

Protocols to support the three previously discussed authentication services can use any of the encryption techniques—private key or public key—for encrypting a communication between entities. We will discuss protocols for these services for both types of encryption techniques.

15.8.1 Authentication Servers

Protocols for the three authentication services require the availability of an authoritative service that *securely* distributes *secret conversation* keys, needed for an authenticated communication between two entities. This service is provided by a server called the *authentication server*, AS. Each user X registers a secret key, denoted by KX, with AS, which is known only to X and AS. AS uses this key to securely communicate a secret communication key to the user. If the system is small, one authentication server is usually sufficient. In large systems, the responsibility can be distributed over many authentication servers.

Since the main database of an authentication server is indexed by user names, there is a striking similarity between an authentication server and a name server in a distributed system. Therefore, the implementation of authentication servers need not have additional overhead as the authentication servers can be merged with the name servers in a system [18]. However, merging authentication and naming services is not always appropriate because doing so may make it more difficult to analyze and verify the correctness of the authentication service.

15.8.2 Establishing Interactive Connections

If user A wants to set a secure interactive connection with user B, user A must generate a message with the following properties:

1. The message must be comprehensible only to user B.
2. It must be evident to B that the message originated at A and is not a replay of an earlier message by an intruder.

We assume that users A and B are in the purview of the same authentication server (AS).

A PROTOCOL FOR PRIVATE KEY SYSTEMS. Private key systems are symmetric— the same key is used for both the encryption and decryption of a message. Each user has a secret key that is used for the decryption of received messages and is also employed by other users to encrypt messages destined to this user. We assume that the authentication server AS knows the secret keys of all the users in its purview.

Issues Involved.

Obtaining a Conversation Key. Every secure communication between two entities requires a secret key known only to those two entities. Two communicating entities cannot use each others secret keys for encrypting messages, as this will require these entities to have the knowledge of each others secret key. Thus, a different secret key, called a *conversation* key, is needed for communication between two entities. This raises the question: how does A obtain a secret key, which will be used by both A and B, for interactive communication? (Note that A and B may have never interacted before and it is infeasible to assign a secret key for every pair of users a priori.)

Communicating the Conversation Key. After A obtains a conversation key for secure communication, how does it safely communicate that key to user B? (Note that both A and B don't know the other's encryption-decryption key.)

Obtaining a Conversation Key. A obtains a conversation key from AS in the following manner. A communicates to AS its own identity, the identity of the desired correspondent, B, and A's *nonce* identifier for this transaction, I_A. (The *nonce* identifier must be different from others used by A in previous transactions with AS. Its significance is discussed later.) This communication is syntactically denoted as:

$$A \to AS: \qquad A, B, I_A \qquad\qquad (15.1)$$

Note that the above message is not encrypted. On the receipt of this message, AS looks up secret keys KA and KB for A and B, respectively, and computes a new key CK, which will be used for interactive communication between A and B. AS communicates this new key to A in the following encrypted message:[†]

$$AS \to A: \qquad E_{KA}(I_A, B, CK, E_{KB}(CK, A)) \qquad\qquad (15.2)$$

Since the message from AS is encrypted using A's key, only A can decrypt it and know the conversation key CK. Having decrypted the above message, A checks the intended receiver's name B and identifier I_A in the message to verify if the message is indeed a reply to A's current inquiry to AS. If the recipient's name is left out in the message of Eq. 15.2, then an intruder can change the recipient's name in the message of Eq. 15.1 to some other user, say X, before AS receives the message. This will result in A unknowingly communicating with X instead of B. If the identifier I_A is left out in the message of Eq. 15.2, then an intruder can replay a previously recorded message from AS to A (with B as the intended recipient) forcing A to reuse a previous conversation key. A schematic diagram of the actions needed for A to acquire the conversation key is shown in Fig. 15.5.

Communicating the Conversation Key. Note that the part $E_{KB}(CK, A)$ in the message that A receives from AS is encrypted with the secret key of B. Thus, A can securely communicate the conversation key CK to B by simply communicating this part of the message of Eq. 15.2 to B without having to know the secret key of B.

$$A \to B: \qquad E_{KB}(CK, A) \qquad\qquad (15.3)$$

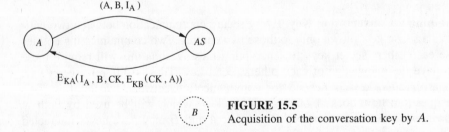

FIGURE 15.5
Acquisition of the conversation key by A.

[†]Recall that $E_k(\text{m})$ denotes message m encrypted using key k.

Only B can decrypt this message. Thus, the conversation key CK and the identity of the intended correspondent, A, is securely conveyed to B.

At this point, A knows that any message it sends with CK encryption can only be understood by B, and any message it receives encrypted with CK must have originated from B. However, as will be shown, such a claim cannot be made about B.

A Small Hitch. A problem arises in communication of the conversation key, CK, from A to B because an intruder can playback a previously recorded message of Eq. 15.3. Unless B keeps a history of all the previously received messages from A (of Eq. 15.3), there is no way for B to distinguish a playback from a legitimate communication from A.

To guard against such threats, B generates a *nonce* identifier, I_B, for this transaction and sends it to A under CK encryption.

$$B \to A: \qquad E_{CK}(I_B) \qquad\qquad (15.4)$$

In response to this message, A sends the following message to B:

$$A \to B: \qquad E_{CK}(I_B - 1) \qquad\qquad (15.5)$$

After having received the above message, B is sure that the message in Eq. 15.3 it received from A is legitimate (i.e., not a playback). This is because A will send the message of Eq. 15.5 only when it receives the message of Eq. 15.4 from B that is encrypted with the current conversation key. A schematic diagram of the actions needed for A to convey the conversation key to B are shown in Fig. 15.6.

COMPROMISE OF A CONVERSATION KEY. This protocol works as long as secret keys or the conversation key has not been compromised by an intruder. Denning and Sacco [8] show that the above protocol breaks if an intruder is able to steal the conversation key. A intruder may succeed in stealing a conversation key due to negligence or flaw in the system.

For example, if an intruder C has intercepted and recorded all messages Eqs. 15.3–15.5 and has obtained a copy of the conversation key, CK, it can impersonate A and start a conversation with B in the following manner:

C first replays the message of Eq. 15.3 to B:

$$C \to B: \qquad E_{KB}(CK, A) \qquad\qquad (15.6)$$

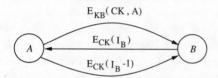

FIGURE 15.6
Communication of the conversation key by A to B.

On receipt of this message, B thinks that A is trying to initiate a conversation and requests a handshake from A by sending it the message.

$$B \rightarrow A: \qquad E_{CK}(I_B) \qquad\qquad (15.7)$$

C intercepts this message and impersonates A's response:

$$A \rightarrow B: \qquad E_{CK}(I_B - 1) \qquad\qquad (15.8)$$

Henceforth, C can impersonate A in a conversation with B and can decipher replies of B.

DENNING-SACCO'S REMEDY. Denning and Sacco suggest a remedy to this problem by adding a timestamp to the messages of Eqs. 15.2 and 15.3. This also eliminates handshaking between A and B (i.e., messages in Eqs. 15.4 and 15.5).

The new protocol is given below:

$$
\begin{aligned}
A \rightarrow AS: & \qquad A, B \\
AS \rightarrow A: & \qquad E_{KA}(B, CK, T, E_{KB}(CK, T, A)) \\
A \rightarrow B: & \qquad E_{KB}(CK, T, A)
\end{aligned}
$$

T is the timestamp assigned by AS to the conversation. B can verify that its messages are not replays by an impostor by checking if the following condition holds:

$$|Clock - T| < \Delta t1 + \Delta t2 \qquad\qquad (15.9)$$

where $Clock$ gives the local time, $\Delta t1$ is an interval denoting the maximum discrepancy between the server's clock and the local clock, and $\Delta t2$ is the expected network delay. This method protects against replays as long as $\Delta t1 + \Delta t2$ is less than the interval since the last use of protocol. However, now old conversation keys cannot be cached at user sites to reduce the number of steps required to initiate a conversation.

A PROTOCOL FOR PUBLIC KEY SYSTEMS. Public key systems are asymmetric in that different keys are used for encryption and decryption. Each user has a public key that other users employ to encrypt messages to be sent to this user and each user has a secret key that it uses for decryption. Let SKX and PKX, respectively, denote the secret and public keys of user X. We assume that the authentication server AS knows the public keys of all users in its purview.

The main issue here is not to acquire a secret key for communication. This is because two communicating entities can use each other's encryption keys (which are publicly known) to encrypt messages. The main issue now is to perform a handshake between two communicating entities so that they can confirm each other's identity (authentication) and start an interactive communication (synchronization). Initially, we discuss a protocol under the assumption that both A and B know the public key of one another. Later we discuss how public keys can be obtained from the AS.

Performing a Handshake. To perform a handshake, A sends the following message to B. The message is encrypted with B's public key.

$$A \to B: \qquad E_{PKB}(I_A, A) \qquad\qquad (15.10)$$

I_A is a *nonce* identifier of A for this transaction and A's identity is included so that B can identify the correspondent. Clearly, this message can only be understood by B. After having decrypted this message, B concludes that A wishes to establish an interactive communication with it. Note that such a message can also be fabricated by an intruder (who can also replay a previously recorded message of this type). To ensure that it is indeed A who sent this message, B sends the following message to A in response: (I_B is *nonce* identifier for B.)

$$B \to A: \qquad E_{PKA}(I_A, I_B) \qquad\qquad (15.11)$$

When A decrypts this message, it knows that B is trying to confirm the initiation of an interactive communication initiated by it. In response to this message, A sends the following message to B:

$$A \to B: \qquad E_{PKB}(I_B) \qquad\qquad (15.12)$$

After having decrypted the above message, B can be assured that it is indeed A who is trying to set up an interactive communication with it. A schematic diagram of the handshake between A and B is shown in Fig. 15.7.

This is not the end of problems. Note that since public keys are not secret, an intruder can simply encrypt spurious messages with the public keys of the recipients and inject them into the network. To guard against such situations, A and B can include some secret identifier in messages they send to each other. These identifiers can very well be their *nonce* identifiers, I_A and I_B.

Obtaining a Public Key. If A does not have the public key of B, it can obtain the key from AS by sending the following message to AS:

$$A \to AS: \qquad (A, B) \qquad\qquad (15.13)$$

AS responds to this message by sending A the following message that is encrypted by the private key of AS:

$$AS \to A: \qquad E_{SKAS}(PKB, B) \qquad\qquad (15.14)$$

A knows the public key of AS and can decrypt the above message to find out the public key of B. The encryption of a message of Eq. 15.14 is needed to insure integrity,

FIGURE 15.7
Handshake between A and B to set up an interactive communication.

not to insure privacy of the contents. Note that the message of Eq. 15.14 is a signed message and only AS can create a message of this type. (Clearly, we require that for any message m, $D_{PKAS}(E_{SKAS}(m)) = m$.) Thus, no intruder can fabricate a reply for a message of Eq. 15.13 and send a bogus public key in the reply to A. The name of the intended recipient B is included in the message of Eq. 15.14 so that A knows that the name of the intended correspondent was correctly communicated to AS.

If B does not have the public key of A, it can obtain the key from AS in the same way.

15.8.3 Performing One-Way Communication

In one-way communication, authentication cannot depend upon the simultaneous availability of sender and receiver. The main issue in one-way communication is to ensure that a receiver is able to check the authenticity of a received communication, even if the sender is not available when the receiver gets the communication. An intruder should not be able to impersonate a user. As a mail system is a typical example of one-way communication, we will discuss private key and public key protocols in this context.

A PROTOCOL FOR PRIVATE KEY SYSTEMS.

Issues Involved.

  Obtaining a Secret Key. The sender of the mail message cannot encrypt the message with the receiver's key because this will require the sender to have the knowledge of the receiver's secret key. A secret key is needed for securely communicating the mail. So, now an issue is how a sender A obtains a secret key that can be used to encrypt a mail message for B.

  Communicating the Secret Key. After A obtains a secret key for encrypting the mail message, it must be able to communicate that key to receiver B.

  Authenticating the Sender. When B receives the message, it should have sufficient information to check the authenticity of the sender of a received mail message. An intruder should not be able to impersonate a user.

  A obtains a common secret key from AS in the same way as for setting up an interactive communication between two entities in a private key system. That is, A sends the following message to AS:

$$A \rightarrow AS: \qquad A, B, I_A \qquad\qquad (15.15)$$

On receipt of this message, AS returns the following encrypted message to A: (CK is the secret key that will be used for communication from A to B.)

$$AS \rightarrow A: \qquad E_{KA}(I_A, B, CK, E_{KB}(CK, A)) \qquad (15.16)$$

After receiving the above message, A knows the secret key, CK, and also has template $E_{KB}(CK, A)$, encrypted with B's secret key, which A can use to convey to B the secret key used to encrypt the mail message. Note that template $E_{KB}(CK, A)$ has been used (through the message of Eq. 15.3) to authenticate the identity of an initiator to a correspondent in setting up an interactive communication in a private key system.

Thus, if this template is put at the head of a mail message, M, which is encrypted with CK, the entire message "$E_{KB}(CK, A); E_{CK}(M)$" is self-authenticating to receiver B as well as sender A, even though B did not play any role in sending the mail. This is because only A can send a message containing template $E_{KB}(CK, A)$. Thus, a mail message from A to B has the format

$$A \rightarrow B: \qquad E_{KB}(CK, A); E_{CK}(M) \qquad (15.17)$$

However, a problem is that an intruder can playback a previous mail message from A to B. This presents a problem similar to that of duplicate or outdated message suppression. Techniques to safeguard against playbacks of previous mail messages are suggested by Needham and Schroeder [18].

A PROTOCOL FOR PUBLIC KEY SYSTEMS. We assume that public keys of A and B are known to each other. If not, these keys can be obtained from AS by exchanging the messages of Eqs. 15.13 and 15.14 with AS.

The protocol for one-way communication proceeds as follows. A sends the following header message to B to identify itself to B:

$$A \rightarrow B: \qquad E_{PKB}(A, I, E_{SKA}(B)) \qquad (15.18)$$

In this message, A denotes the sender and $E_{SKA}(B)$ enables B to authenticate the identity of the sender. Note that an intruder can pretend to be A and send such a message to B. However, this possibility is eliminated because only A can create $E_{SKA}(B)$. Note that this part of the message is signed by A. (Clearly, it is required that for any message m, $D_{PKA}(E_{SKA}(m)) = m$.) I is a *nonce* identifier that is used to connect the header with the corresponding mail message that is encrypted with PKB.

15.8.4 Digital Signatures

With the ever increasing use of electronic mail, automated teller machines, and other electronic business and financial transactions, the concept of digital signature has gained great importance. Digital signature is a way to code an electronic message such that the recipient of the message can certify which sender actually sent the message. A scheme for digital signature must satisfy the following properties:

- A user must not be able to forge the signature of any other user and a digital signature must be unique to a user.
- The sender of a signed message should not be able to deny the validity of his signature on the message. That is, a user should not be able to provably deny sending a message which contains his signature.
- A recipient of a signed message must not be able to modify the signature contained in the message.

- A user must not be able to (electronically) cut and paste the signature from one message to another message.

DIGITAL SIGNATURE IN PRIVATE KEY SYSTEMS. To prevent the cut-and-paste of a signature to any message, the signature should be a (unique) characteristic of the message. Thus, a characteristic function of a plaintext message, which provides a unique characteristic value for every plaintext message, is required. We assume that such a characteristic function of a plaintext message can be computed.

When A wants to send a signed message to B, A first computes the characteristic value, CS, of the message and then requests a *signature block* from AS by sending it the message:

$$A \rightarrow AS: \qquad A, E_{KA}(CS) \tag{15.19}$$

AS responds to A's message by sending it a *signature block* in the message:

$$AS \rightarrow A: \qquad E_{KAS}(A, CS) \tag{15.20}$$

The signature block $E_{KAS}(A, CS)$, contained in the above message, is created by a collaboration between A and AS. Its value CS is supplied by A, but it is encrypted with the secret key of AS. A includes this signature block along with message text to be sent to B. Since A can include any signature block with a message text, B must confirm the validity of the signature in a received signed message. That is, B must confirm that the characteristic value of the message text is the same as the one contained in the signature block. To do this, B decrypts a received signed message and extracts the message text from it, computes the characteristic value CS' of the message text, and sends the signature block in the signed message to AS for deciphering.

$$B \rightarrow AS: \qquad B, E_{KAS}(A, CS) \tag{15.21}$$

AS decrypts the signature block and returns it to B in the message:

$$AS \rightarrow B: \qquad E_{KB}(A, CS) \tag{15.22}$$

B checks if CS matches CS'. If they do match, the signature on the signed message is valid and the user named in the message of Eq. 15.22 is the sender of the signed message.

If B wishes to retain evidence that the received text was signed by A, all B must do is save the signature block along with the text. At any time, B can assert the authenticity of a received signed message to a third party by supplying it with the text and the corresponding signature block. The third party can check the authenticity of the signed message by taking the steps indicated in Eqs. 15.21 and 15.22.

Note that a signature block is encrypted with the secret key of the authentication server, AS. This has two advantages. First, the receiver of a signed message, B, cannot forge the sender's signature in a received signed message. Second, a receiver of a signed message can confirm the validity of the signature by having the signature block deciphered by an independent trusted server, AS. A repudiation by a sender of a signed message is impossible because (1) there is a unique correspondence between message text and the characteristic value in the signature and (2) a signature block contains the identifier of the sender. (Note that only A can send a signature block of type $E_{KAS}(A, CS)$). The cut-and-paste of a signature by a receiver is prevented as a unique correspondence exists between message text and its characteristic value.

DIGITAL SIGNATURE IN PUBLIC KEY SYSTEMS. Public key cryptography can be used to implement digital signatures in the following way. Let A and B be two users with their public and secret keys as PKA, PKB and SKA, SKB, respectively. A sends a signed message M to B in the following manner. A first encrypts the message M using its secret key, SKA:

$$S = E_{SKA}(M)$$

where S is referred to as the signature of message M. (Recall that in public key cryptography, a message can be encrypted with the secret key and then can be decrypted with the public key. This is done when a user wants to sign a message.) Then A encrypts the signature S using B's public key, PKB:

$$C = E_{PKB}(S)$$

and sends the crypted message C to user B. When B receives this message, it decrypts the message using its secret key, SKB:

$$S = D_{SKB}(C)$$

to obtain the message in the signature form S. Now B obtains the plaintext message M by encrypting S with A's public key, PKA, which is publicly available. Note that a recipient of a signed message must know the identity of the sender so that the appropriate encryption procedure can be applied. This can be achieved by having a sender attach its identifier in plaintext to S before producing the corresponding C.

However, it is required that,

$$(\forall M)(\forall D_{PKA})(\forall E_{SKA}):: M = D_{PKA}(E_{SKA}(M))$$

Note that tuple (M, S) acts like a signed message sent from A to B. User B can always prove that this message is sent by user A because no one else knows the secret key SKA of A and thus, nobody else can create S $(=E_{SKA}(M))$. User A cannot deny that it sent this message to B.

15.9 CASE STUDY: THE KERBEROS SYSTEM

Kerberos [24] is an authentication system implemented on Project Athena at MIT. Project Athena [5] provides an open network computing environment where users have complete control of their workstations and a workstation cannot be trusted to identify its users correctly to the network services. Therefore, a third-party authentication must be used, which provides a user with an authenticated means to prove his identity to various network services and vice-versa. Kerberos provides this third-party authentication service to Athena and is based in part on the authentication model of Needham and Schroeder.

Kerberos is based on private key encryption and uses the Data Encryption Standard (DES). Every user has a private key that is also known to Kerberos. Kerberos maintains a database of its users and their private keys. For a user U, U's private key can be obtained by applying a one-way function f to U's password, *password*, e.g., $K_U = f(password)$. Kerberos uses the private key of a user to create encrypted messages for the user that can convince the user of the Kerberos' authenticity. If a user receives a message that is encrypted using that user's private key, the message must be from Kerberos, because aside from the user itself, only Kerberos knows the user's private key. Kerberos also creates temporary private keys, called *session keys*, which can be used for a private encrypted conversation between two parties (i.e, a user and a server).

Kerberos requires the computers of the network to have loosely synchronized clocks. A timestamp, which is the current clock value of the sender, is added to the information exchanged between two parties to aid in the detection of message replay. (A message replay occurs when an intruder copies a message from the network and replays it later.) The receiver of a message checks for its timeliness by comparing its own clock value to that of the message timestamp. A message is *timely* if the message timestamp is approximately equal to the receiver's clock value.

The term *client* refers to a program that runs on the host computer of the user and requests remote services on behalf of the user. In Kerberos, a client must present both a ticket and an authenticator to a server to request a service. A ticket proves the authenticity of the client to the server. A client requests a ticket from a Kerberos authentication server (or a ticket-granting server). A ticket securely passes the identity of the client to whom it was issued from the Kerberos authentication server to the end server. A ticket contains the name of the server, the name of the client, a timestamp, a session key, etc. and is encrypted using the key of the server from which the client will subsequently request service. The session key is used for a private encrypted conversation between the user and the server.

To request a service, a user goes through three phases of authentication through Kerberos:

1. In the first phase, referred to as "getting the initial ticket," the user obtains credentials, i.e., a ticket, from the Kerberos authentication server. This ticket is later used to request other tickets for various services in the network.
2. In the second phase, referred to as "getting the server ticket," the user requests authentication, i.e., a ticket, from the ticket-granting server for a specific service.
3. In the third phase, referred to as "requesting the service," the user presents the ticket to the server for service.

A schematic of these three phases is shown in Fig. 15.8. The ticket-granting server, tgs, and the Kerberos server, K, are usually co-located and implemented as a single Kerberos server. Message 6 is optional and is needed only if the client requires mutual authentication.

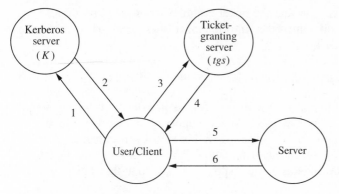

1. Request for *tgs* ticket
2. Ticket for *tgs*
3. Request for server ticket
4. Ticket for Server
5. Request for service
6. Response from Server

FIGURE 15.8
A schematic of the Kerberos authentication protocol.

Kerberos achieves these three phases of authentication with the help of two authentication protocols. (1) The user-authentication protocol, which verifies the authenticity of a user and obtains a session key and an initial ticket for the user. This protocol makes up the first phase of a service request. (2) The client-server authentication protocol, which achieves mutual authentication of a client and a server. The mutual authentication means that the client and the server should be able to verify the authenticity of each other. This protocol makes up the last two phases of a service request.

15.9.1 Phase I: Getting the Initial Ticket

To log into a workstation, a user supplies his userid U to the client C:

$$U \rightarrow C : \qquad U \qquad (15.23)$$

The client then sends the userid and the name of a special service known as the *ticket granting service*, tgs, to the Kerberos server, K:

$$C \rightarrow K : \qquad U, tgs \qquad (15.24)$$

On receipt of this information, the Kerberos server retrieves user key K_U and tgs key K_{tgs} from the database and generates a session key, $K_{U,tgs}$, to be used between the user and the ticket granting server. It then creates a ticket, $T_{U,tgs} = E_{K_{tgs}}\{U, tgs, K_{U,tgs}, timestamp, life\}$, which consists of the userid, the name of the ticket granting server, the current time, lifetime of the ticket, and the session key just created. (The $lifetime$ of a ticket gives the duration for which the ticket is valid.) The ticket is encrypted in a key, K_{tgs}, known only to Kerberos and the ticket-granting server. Kerberos then sends the ticket, the session key, and some other information to the client. This response is encrypted in the user's private key, K_U:

$$K \rightarrow C : \qquad E_{K_U}\{T_{U,tgs}, K_{U,tgs}, tgs, timestamp, life\} \qquad (15.25)$$

On receipt of this response, the client asks the user for his *password*. It then generates the user's private key, K'_U from the *password* by applying a one-way function f, $K'_U = f(password)$ and decrypts the response using this key. User authentication fails if the decryption fails. Otherwise, the authentication is successful and the ticket, the session key, and the other information in the response are stored at the client for future use.

This completes the user-authentication phase and the client now possesses information that it can use to prove the identity of the user for the lifetime of the ticket. The ticket $T_{U,tgs}$ can be used to request a ticket for any server from the ticket-granting server. Therefore, this ticket will henceforth be referred to as the *ticket-granting ticket*.

15.9.2 Phase II: Getting Server Tickets

A user must obtain a ticket for each service that he wants to use. After a user has obtained a ticket from Kerberos (Phase I), the user can use this ticket to obtain a ticket for any service from the ticket-granting server in the following way. The client sends a request to the ticket-granting server. The request contains the name of the server, S, for which the ticket is requested, the ticket-granting ticket, and an authenticator $A_U = E_{K_{U,tgs}}\{C, timestamp\}$. Since a ticket-granting ticket is susceptible to copying and replay, it does not constitute sufficient proof that the client presenting it is the same client to which the ticket was issued by Kerberos. The authenticator serves this purpose because the construction of the authenticator requires the knowledge of the session key, $K_{U,tgs}$.

$$C \rightarrow TGS : \qquad S, T_{U,tgs}, A_U \qquad (15.26)$$

On receipt of this information, the ticket-granting server decrypts the ticket $T_{U,tgs}$, obtains the session key $K_{U,tgs}$ from it, and then decrypts the authenticator using the session key. If the decryption is successful and the authenticator is timely, the ticket-granting server creates a new session key, $K_{C,S}$, to be used between the client and the intended servers. It then builds a ticket, $T_{C,S} = E_{K_S}\{C, S, K_{C,S}, timestamp, life\}$ that is encrypted with the server key K_S. The ticket-granting server then sends the ticket, the new session key, and other information to the client. This information is encrypted in the session key $K_{U,tgs}$ that was a part of the ticket-granting ticket.

$$TGS \rightarrow C : \qquad E_{K_{U,tgs}}\{T_{C,S}, K_{C,S}, S, timestamp, life\} \qquad (15.27)$$

On receipt of this response, the client decrypts it and obtains the new session key $K_{C,S}$ and the ticket $T_{C,S}$, which can be used to request service from the server.

15.9.3 Phase III: Requesting the Service

After having obtained a new session key $K_{C,S}$ and a ticket $T_{C,S}$ for a server S, client C can request the service from the server in the following manner.

The client builds an authenticator $A_C = E_{K_{C,S}}\{C, timestamp\}$ and sends it along with the ticket to the server.

$$C \to S: \qquad T_{C,S}, A_C \qquad\qquad (15.28)$$

On receipt of this request, the server decrypts the ticket $T_{C,S}$. (Note that the ticket $T_{C,S}$ is encrypted using server S's private key.) The server then uses the session key in the ticket to decrypt the authenticator. If the decryption is successful and the authenticator is timely, the requested service is performed.

If the client wants the server to prove its identity as well, the server adds one to the timestamp received from the client, encrypts it with the session key $K_{C,S}$, and sends it to the client.

$$S \to C: \qquad E_{K_{C,S}}\{timestamp + 1\} \qquad\qquad (15.29)$$

This last step corresponds to message 6 in Fig. 15.8 and is optional. It is only used if the client requires mutual authentication. The timestamp is incremented in the response to C to guard against replays of previous responses.

15.10 SUMMARY

Cryptography deals with the maintenance of the confidentiality of data rather than with access control to data. The confidentiality of a text is achieved by converting the text into a cryptic form before it is stored into a computer system or before it is transmitted over a communication channel. The cryptic form is such that the information is unintelligible unless it is decrypted using some secret key known only to persons authorized to read and use the information.

In this chapter, we studied various techniques for cryptography. Cryptography systems are roughly divided into the conventional and the modern systems. The conventional systems were primarily used for ciphering a script written in a language. The basic principle underlying these systems is the mapping of a letter of an alphabet of a language by another letter in the alphabet, derived through a secret procedure. The crux of these systems is the secrecy of the mapping procedure.

Modern systems are primarily used for ciphering binary information. These systems usually follow the principle of *open design* in the sense that the underlying encryption and decryption techniques (algorithms) are not kept secret. Instead, the values of some of the parameters (called keys) used in encryption and decryption are kept secret. There are two types of modern cryptography systems, private key systems and public key systems. In private key systems, keys used for both encryption and decryption are kept secret. In the public key systems, on the other hand, the key used for encryption is known in the public domain, but the key used for decryption is kept secret. The crux of the public key systems is that even though the procedure to compute the decryption key is known, the procedure is so computationally intensive that it takes a prohibitively long time to compute the key. In private key cryptography, we discussed the Data Encryption Standard (DES), developed by IBM, which is the official standard used by the U.S. federal government. In public key cryptography, the Rivest-Shamir-Adleman (RSA) method was discussed.

As a case study, we discussed the Kerberos system, a third-party authentication service implemented in MIT's Project Athena. Since Project Athena provides an open network computing environment, a third-party authentication must be used to prove the users' identity to various network services. Kerberos is in part based on the authentication model of Needham and Schroeder. It makes use of private key encryption and uses the Data Encryption Standard (DES).

15.11 FURTHER READINGS

For a comprehensive reading on the subject, readers are referred to several excellent text books on cryptography and data security, namely, Denning [6], Meyer and Matyas [17], Seberry and Pieprzyk [22], Pfleeger [19], and Hsiao et al. [13]. The December 1979 issue of *ACM Computing Surveys* is completely devoted to data security. Lempel's article in the December 1979 issue of *ACM Computing Surveys* provides a good overview of conventional and modern cryptographic techniques [14]. Readers can refer to an article by Denning and Denning [7] for a good overview on data security. The February 1983 issue of *IEEE Computer* magazine is devoted to "data security in computer networks," which includes a survey article on digital signatures by Akl [1]. A landmark article by Diffie and Hellman [10] provides a development of public key systems. Goldwasser and Micali [12] propose the idea of probabilistic encryption. Feige et al. [11] propose a 0-knowledge protocol for verification of identities (i.e., for authentication).

The application of cryptography in the design of secure computer networks and more details on digital signatures can be found in a paper by Popek and Kline [20]. Anderson et al. [2] present a protocol for end-to-end secure communication in very large distributed systems by providing authentication at the level of a host-to-host datagram. Burrows et al. discuss [4] a logic of authenication. An up-to-date discussion of authentication in distributed systems can be found in a paper by Woo and Lam [26]. A comprehensive overview of cryptography and cryptoanalysis can be found in a paper by Massey [15]. A survey of cryptoanalysis can be found in a paper by Brickell and Odlyzko [3].

The *Journal of Cryptology* is devoted to articles on this topic. Readers can also find articles on this topic in the Proceedings of an annual symposium, *IEEE Symposium on Security and Privacy*.

PROBLEMS

15.1. Compute the number of different keys in a *vigenere* cipher with a period of n.

15.2. Discuss how a public key scheme can be used to solve the key distribution problem in a private key cryptographic scheme.

15.3. Show that in the RSA method to implement the public key cryptography, when $p = 5$ and $q = 7$, both e and d are 11, and this is the only possible value for e and d.

REFERENCES

1. Akl, S. G., "Digital Signatures: A Tutorial Survey," *IEEE Computer*, Feb. 1983.
2. Anderson, D. P., D. Ferrari, P. V. Rangan, and B. Sartirana, "A Protocol for Secure Communication and Its Performance," *Proceedings of the 7th International Conference on Distributed Computing Systems*, Sept. 1987.
3. Brickell, E. F., and A. M. Odlyzko, "Cryptoanalysis: A Survey of Recent Results," *Proceedings of the IEEE*, May 1988.
4. Burrows, M., M. Abadi, and R. M. Needham, "A Logic of Authentication," *ACM Trans. on Computer Systems*, Feb. 1990.
5. Champine,G. A., D. E. Geer, and W. N. Ruh, "Project Athena as a Distributed Computer System," *IEEE Computer*, Sept. 1990.
6. Denning, D. E., *Cryptography and Data Security*, Addison-Wesley, Reading, MA, 1982.
7. Denning, D. E., and P. J. Denning, "Data security," *ACM Computing Surveys*, Sept. 1979.
8. Denning, D. E., and G. M. Sacco, "Timestamps in Key Distribution Protocols," *Communications of the ACM*, Aug. 1981.
9. Diffie, W., and M. E. Hellman, "Exhaustive Cryptoanalysis of the NBS Data Encryption Standards," *IEEE Computer*, June 1977.
10. Diffie, W., and M. E. Hellman, "New Directions in Cryptography," *IEEE Trans. on Information Theory*, Nov. 1976.
11. Feige, U., A. Fiat, and A. Shamir, "Zero-Knowledge Proofs of Identity," *ACM Symposium on Theory of Computing*, 1987.
12. Goldwasser, S., and S. Micali, "Probabilistic Encryption," *Journal of Computer and System Sciences*, Apr. 1984.
13. Hsiao, D., D. S. Kerr, and S. E. Madnick, *"Computer Security,"* Academic Press, San Diego, CA, 1979.
14. Lempel, A., "Cryptology in Transition," *ACM Computing Surveys*, Dec. 1979.
15. Massey, J. L., "An Introduction to Contemporary Cryptology," *Proceedings of the IEEE*, May 1988.
16. Merkle, R. C., and M. E. Hellman, "On the Security of Multiple Encryption," *Communications of the ACM*, July 1981.
17. Meyer, C. H., and S. M. Matyas, "Cryptography: A New Dimension in Computer Data Security," John Wiley and Sons, New York, 1982.
18. Needham, R. M. and M. D. Schroeder, "Using Encryption for Authentication in Large Network of Computers," *Communications of the ACM*, Dec. 1978.
19. Pfleeger, C. P., *"Security in Computing,"* Prentice-Hall, Englewood Cliffs, N.J., 1989.
20. Popek, G. J. and C. S. Kline, "Encryption and Secure Computer Networks," *ACM Computing Surveys*, Dec. 1979.
21. Rivest, R. L., A. Shamir, and L. Adleman, "A Method for Obtaining Digital Signatures and Public Key Cryptosystems," *Communications of the ACM*, Feb. 1978.
22. Seberry, J. and J. Pieprzyk, "Cryptography: An Introduction to Computer Security," Prentice-Hall, Englewood Cliffs, N.J., 1989.
23. Shannon, C. E., "Communication Theory of Secrecy Systems," *Bell Systems Journal*, Oct. 1949.
24. Steiner, J. G., C. Neuman, and J. I. Schiller, "Kerberos: An Authentication Service for Open Network System," *Proceedings of the Winter USENIX Conf.*, Feb. 1988.
25. U. S. National Bureau of Standards, *"Federal Information Processing Standards, Publication 46,* Jan. 1977.
26. Woo, T. Y. C., and S. S. Lam, "Authentication for Distributed Systems," *IEEE Computer*, Jan. 1992.

PART
VI

MULTIPROCESSOR OPERATING SYSTEMS

CHAPTER

16

MULTIPROCESSOR SYSTEM ARCHITECTURES

16.1 INTRODUCTION

Historically, higher computing power was achieved by employing faster processors that used high-speed semiconductor technology. With hardware technology approaching its physical limit, multiprocessor systems have emerged as a viable alternative to achieve higher computing power and speed. Typically, a multiprocessor system consists of several processors that share a common physical memory. All the processors operate under the control of a single operating system. Users of a multiprocessor system see a single powerful computer system. Multiplicity of the processors in a multiprocessor system and the way processors act together to perform a computation are transparent to the users. This chapter discusses various architectures of multiprocessor systems and serves as a background to the next chapter on multiprocessor operating systems.

16.2 MOTIVATIONS FOR MULTIPROCESSOR SYSTEMS

The main motivations for a multiprocessor system are to achieve enhanced performance and fault tolerance.

Enhanced Performance. Multiprocessor systems increase system performance in two ways. First, concurrent execution of several tasks by different processors increases the system throughput—the number of tasks completing per time unit—without speeding up the execution of individual tasks. Second, a multiprocessor system can speed up the execution of a single task in the following way: if parallelism exists in a task, it can be divided into many subtasks and these subtasks can be executed in parallel on different processors.

Fault tolerance. A multiprocessor system exhibits graceful performance degradation to processor failures because of the availability of multiple processors.

16.3 BASIC MULTIPROCESSOR SYSTEM ARCHITECTURES

According to the classification of Flynn [6], in MIMD (multiple instruction multiple data) architectures, multiple instruction streams operate on different data streams. In the broadest sense, an MIMD architecture qualifies as a full-fledged multiprocessor system. Thus, a multiprocessor system consists of multiple processors, which execute different programs (or different segments of a program) concurrently. The main memory is typically shared by all the processors. Based on whether a memory location can be directly accessed by a processor or not, there are two types of multiprocessor systems: tightly coupled and loosely coupled [7].

16.3.1 Tightly Coupled vs. Loosely Coupled Systems

In *tightly coupled systems*, all processors share the same memory address space and all processors can directly access a global main memory. Examples of commercially available tightly coupled systems are Multimax of Encore Corporation, Flex/32 of Flexible Corporation, and FX of Sequent Computers.

In *loosely coupled systems*, not only is the main memory partitioned and attached to processors, but each processor has its own address space. Therefore, a processor cannot *directly* access the memory attached to other processors. One example of a loosely coupled system is Intel's Hypercube.

Tightly coupled systems can use the main memory for interprocessor communication and synchronization (see Chap.2). Loosely coupled systems, on the other hand, use only message passing for interprocessor communication and synchronization (see Chap. 4).

We limit our discussion to tightly coupled multiprocessor systems. Figure 16.1 illustrates the schematic diagram of a typical tightly coupled multiprocessor system. A number of processors are connected to the shared memory by an interconnection network. The shared memory is normally divided into several modules and multiple modules can be accessed concurrently by different processors. A *memory contention* occurs when two or more processors simultaneously try to access the same memory module. In case of a memory contention, the request of only one of the requesting processors can be met. The requests of other processors can be queued up for later processing.

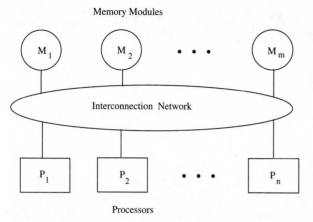

Memory Modules

Interconnection Network

Processors

FIGURE 16.1
A tightly coupled multiprocessor system.

16.3.2 UMA vs. NUMA vs. NORMA Architectures

Based on the vicinity and accessibility of the main memory to the processors, there are three types of multiprocessor system architectures: UMA (uniform memory access), NUMA (nonuniform memory access), and NORMA (no remote memory access).

In UMA architectures, the main memory is located at a central location such that it is equidistant from all the processors in terms of access time (in the absence of conflicts). That is, all the processors have the same access time to the main memory. In addition to this centralized shared memory, processors may also have private memories, where they can cache data for higher performance. Some examples of UMA architectures are Multimax of Encore Corporation, Balance of Sequent, and VAX 8800 of Digital Equipment.

In NUMA architectures, main memory is physically partitioned and the partitions are attached to the processors. All the processors, however, share the same memory address space. A processor can directly access the memory attached to any other processor, but the time to access the memory attached to other processors is much higher than the time to access its own memory partition. Examples of NUMA architectures are Cm* of CMU and Butterfly machine of BBN Laboratories.

In NORMA architectures, main memory is physically partitioned and the partitions are attached to the processors. However, a processor cannot directly access the memory of any other processor. The processors must send messages over the interconnection network to exchange information. An example of NORMA architecture is Intel's Hypercube.

16.4 INTERCONNECTION NETWORKS FOR MULTIPROCESSOR SYSTEMS

The interconnection network in multiprocessor systems provides data transfer facility between processors and memory modules for memory access [5]. The design of the interconnection network is the most crucial hardware issue in the design of multiprocessor systems. Generally, circuit switching is used to establish a connection between processors and memory modules. Thus, during a data transfer, a dedicated path exists between the processor and the memory module. Various types of interconnection networks include:

- Bus
- Cross-bar Switch
- Multistage Interconnection Network

16.4.1   Bus

In bus-based multiprocessor systems, processors are connected to memory modules via a bus (Fig. 16.2). Conceptually, this is the simplest multiprocessor system architecture. It is also easy to implement and is relatively inexpensive. However, aside from the shared memory, the bus is also a source of contention because the bus can support only one processor-memory communication at any time. Moreover, this architecture can support only a limited number of processors because of the limited bandwidth of the bus. These problems can be mitigated by using multiple buses to connect processors and memories. In a b bus system, up to b processor-memory data transfers can take place concurrently. CMU's Cm* and Encore Corporation's Multimax are examples of bus-based multiprocessor systems.

16.4.2   Cross-bar Switch

A cross-bar switch is a matrix (or grid structure) that has a switch at every cross-point. Figure 16.3 shows a multiprocessor system with n processors and m memory modules. A cross-bar is capable of providing an exclusive connection between any processor-memory pair. Thus, all n processors can concurrently access memory modules provided that each processor is accessing a different memory module (and $n \leq m$). A cross-bar switch does not face contention at the interconnection network level. A contention can occur only at the memory module level.

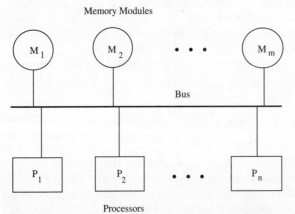

FIGURE 16.2
A multiprocessor system with a bus.

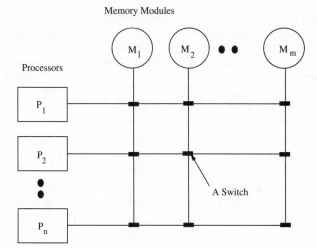

FIGURE 16.3
A multiprocessor system with a cross-bar.

Cross-bar based multiprocessor systems are relatively expensive and have limited scalability because of the quadratic growth of the number of switches with the system size ($n \times n$ if there are n processors and n memory modules). Alliant FX/8 is an example of a commercially available cross-bar architecture.

16.4.3 Multistage Interconnection Network

A multistage interconnection network is a compromise between a bus and a cross-bar switch. A multistage interconnection network permits simultaneous connections between several processor-memory pairs and is more cost-effective than a cross-bar. A typical multistage interconnection network consists of several stages of switches. Each stage consists of an equal number of cross-bar switches of the same size (such as 2×2 or 4×4). The outputs of the switches in a stage is connected to the inputs of the switches in the next stage. These connections are made in such a way that any input to the network can be connected to any output of the network (by making the appropriate connections in the switches at each stage). Depending upon how output-input connections between adjacent stages are made, there are numerous types of interconnection networks [5]. The routing path between a processor and a memory module pair is given by a binary string that is derived from the binary addresses of the processor and the memory module. The ith bit of this binary string determines to which output the input should be connected at the switch at stage i.

An $N \times N$ multistage interconnection network can connect N processors to N memory modules. If $N = 2^k$, it will consist of k ($= \log_2 N$) stages of 2×2 switches with $N/2$ switches in each stage. Thus, an $N \times N$ multistage interconnection network requires only $(N/2) \times \log_2 N$ switches as compared to N^2 switches in an $N \times N$ cross-bar.

Example 16.1. Figure 16.4 shows an 8×8 Omega multistage interconnection network that is constructed from 2×2 cross-bar switches. Note that there exists a *unique* path between a processor-memory pair. In this case, the routing through various stages is completely determined by the binary address of the destination memory module. If the ith bit of the destination address is 0, then at the switch at the ith stage, input should be connected to the upper output. If the ith bit of the destinatin address is one, input should be connected to the lower output. For example, any processor can access memory module M_8 (with address 111) by simply connecting the input to the lower output at every stage. The thick path in Fig. 16.4 shows the connections needed for communication between processor P_2 and memory module M_1.

Note that a contention can arise at a switch in a switching stage even when two processors are trying to access different memory modules. In the previous example, a contention at a switch in the first stage arises when P_2 is trying to access M_1 and P_6 is trying to access M_4 concurrently. In case of a contention at a switch, only one request succeeds and rest of the requests are dropped and subsequently retried by their respective processors. The wastage of multistage interconnection network bandwidth due to the retry of requests can be avoided by providing buffers at each switch and buffering the requests, which cannot be forwarded due to contention at that switch, for later transmission. Clearly such multistage interconnection networks fall under the category of store-and-forward networks. The BBN Butterfly machine is an example of a commercially available multiprocessor system that uses multistage interconnection network.

16.5 CACHING

Multiprocessor systems commonly use caching to reduce memory access time. Under caching, every processor has a private memory, called a *cache*, in addition to the shared global memory. When a processor needs to fetch a word from a data block in the global memory, it fetches the entire block and saves it in its cache for future use. A global memory access through the interconnection network is much slower compared to the cache access time. Also, the global memory access time may not be constant due to contention at the interconnection network. If the locality of data reference is high,

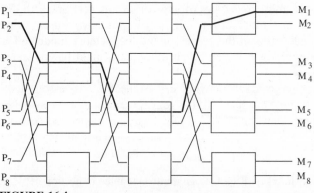

FIGURE 16.4
An 8×8 Omega multistage interconnection network.

caching will substantially reduce the effective memory access time. The cost of fetching the entire data block from the global memory is amortized over several accesses to that block when it is in the cache.

Caching has two other advantages. First, the traffic over the interconnection network is reduced (because most memory accesses can be satisfied by the cache.) Second, contention at memory modules is reduced (because different blocks of a memory module can be fetched by several processors and can be accessed concurrently from their respective caches).

16.5.1 The Cache Coherence Problem

Caching poses a problem when a processor modifies a cached block that is also cached by some other processors currently. Modifying a cached block by a processor invalidates the copies of this block in the cache of other processors because these copies have an outdated value. This is called the *cache coherence* problem in multiprocessor systems [3].

Two basic approaches that address the cache coherence problem are the *write-update* and *write-invalidate* approaches. In the write-update method, a process that is modifying a block also modifies the copies of this block in the cache of other processors. In the write-invalidate method, a process that is modifying a block invalidates the copies of this block in the cache of other processors. There are several variations of both these approaches and their implementation requires hardware support and depends upon the type of interconnection network employed. Readers are referred to Chap. 10 for a discussion of the cache coherence problem in greater detail. In distributed shared memory systems, the cache coherence problem arises at the software level.

16.6 HYPERCUBE ARCHITECTURES

Hypercube based architectures have recently emerged as a viable alternative in the design of multiprocessor systems with a large number of processors. In an n-degree hypercube (called an *n-cube*), 2^n nodes are arranged in an n-dimensional cube, where each node is connected to n other nodes. In hypercube based architectures, the processors are the nodes of a hypercube and a hypercube edge corresponds to a bidirectional communication link between two processors. Each of the 2^n nodes of an n-cube are assigned a unique n-bit address ranging from 0 to $2^n - 1$ such that the addresses assigned to two adjacent nodes differ only in 1 bit position. The address of a node in the ith dimension of a node differs from that node's address only in ith bit. The maximum distance between any two nodes in an n-cube is n hops. Thus, the delay characteristics of hypercube architectures grow logarithmically with the number of nodes and these architectures are highly scalable. Figure 16.5 shows a 3-cube.

Generally, in hypercube based architectures, data transfer from one processor to another processor goes through several other intermediate processors. Consequently, hypercube based architectures are mostly used for store-and-forward communication between processors and are used in loosely coupled multiprocessor systems. The Connection Machine CM-2 of the Thinking Machines Corporation, Intel's iPSC/2, and Ncube's Ncube/10 are examples of commercially available systems in this class.

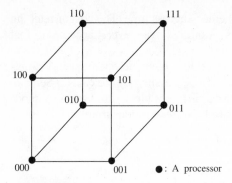

●: A processor

FIGURE 16.5
A 3-cube.

16.7   SUMMARY

Multiprocessor systems have emerged as a viable architecture to provide higher computing power and speed. A multiprocessor system consists of multiple processors that share a main memory. Multiprocessor systems increase system performance by concurrently executing several tasks on different processors or by executing a single task in parallel on different processors. In tightly coupled systems, all processors can directly access a global memory. In loosely coupled systems, each processor has a local memory and a processor cannot directly access the local memory of other processes. In UMA architectures, the main memory is located at a central location such that all the processors have the same access time to the main memory. In NUMA architectures, all the processors share the same memory address space, however, the time it takes processors to access different memory locations varies.

The design of the interconnection network, which provides paths between processors and memory modules, is the most crucial hardware issue in the design of multiprocessor systems. Typical interconnection networks include the bus, the cross-bar switch, and the multistage interconnection network. Bus-based systems can support only a limited number of processors because the bandwidth of the bus is limited. A cross-bar switch does not have contention at the interconnection network level. However, cross-bar based multiprocessor systems are relatively expensive and have limited scalability because of the quadratic growth of the number of switches relative to system size. Multistage interconnection networks are a compromise between a bus and a cross-bar switch. They permit simultaneous connections between several processor-memory pairs and are more cost-effective than a cross-bar.

Multiprocessor systems commonly employ caching to reduce memory access time. In caching, data blocks are fetched from the main memory and saved into their cache memories by the processors for future use. Caching reduces both the traffic on the interconnection network and contention at the memory modules. Caching, however, poses the cache coherence problem, which occurs when a processor modifies a cached block that currently exists in the cache memory of other processors. Modifying a cached block by a processor invalidates the copies of this block in the cache of other processors because these copies now have an outdated value. Two basic methods that address the cache coherence problem are write-update and write-invalidate. In the write-update method, a process that modifies a block also modifies the copies of this block in the cache of other processors. In the write-invalidate method, a process that modifies a block invalidates the copies of this block in the cache of other processors.

In hypercube based architectures, the processors are the nodes of a hypercube and a hypercube edge corresponds to a bidirectional communication link between two processors. The communication diameter of hypercube architectures grows logarithmically with the number of nodes and thus, these architectures are highly scalable and offer a viable alternative to connect a large number of processors.

16.8   FURTHER READING

There are several excellent books that cover parallel architectures and multiprocessors systems; e.g., Hwang and Briggs [7], Stone [9] and Almasi and Gottlieb [1]. Duncan [4] provides a comprehensive taxonomy and tutorial review of parallel architectures. Feng [5] provides a survey of interconnection networks. The June 1990 issue of IEEE Computer [3] is devoted to the problem of cache coherence in multiprocessor systems. Seitz [8] proposes the idea of hypercube architectures. Bhuyan and Agrawal [2] discuss generalized hypercube structures.

REFERENCES

1. Almasi, G.S. and A. Gottlieb, *Highly Parallel Computing*, Benjamin-Cummings, Redwood City, CA, 1988.
2. Bhuyan, L.N. and D.P. Agrawal, "Generalized Hypercube and Hypercube Structures for a Computer Network", *IEEE Trans. on Computers*, Apr. 1984.
3. Dubois, M., and S. Thakkar, "Guest Editors' Introduction: Cache Architectures in Tightly Coupled Multiprocessors," *IEEE Computer*, June 1990.
4. Duncan, R., "A Survey of Parallel Computer Architectures," *IEEE Computer*, Feb. 1990.
5. Feng, T., "A Survey of Interconnection Networks," *IEEE Computer*, Dec. 1981.
6. Flynn, M.J., "Very High-Speed Computing Systems," *Proceedings of the IEEE*, 1966.
7. Hwang, K., and F. Briggs, *Multiprocessor Systems Architectures*, McGraw-Hill, New York, 1984.
8. Seitz, C.L., "The Cosmic Cube," *Communications of the ACM*, Jan. 1985.
9. Stone, H.S., *High-Performance Computer Architectures*, Addison-Wesley, Reading, MA, 1987.

CHAPTER
17

MULTIPROCESSOR OPERATING SYSTEMS

17.1 INTRODUCTION

Multiprocessor operating systems are similar to multiprogrammed uniprocessor operating systems in many respects and they perform resource management and hide unpleasant idiosyncracies of the hardware to provide a high-level machine abstraction to the users. However, multiprocessor operating systems are more complex because multiple processors execute tasks concurrently (with *physical* as opposed to *virtual* concurrency in multiprogrammed uniprocessors.) Thus, a multiprocessor operating system must be able to support the concurrent execution of multiple tasks and must prudently exploit the power of multiple processors to increase performance.

17.2 STRUCTURES OF MULTIPROCESSOR OPERATING SYSTEMS

Based upon the nature of the control structure and its organization, there are three basic classes of multiprocessor operating systems: separate supervisor, master-slave, and symmetric [13].

THE SEPARATE SUPERVISOR CONFIGURATION. In the separate supervisor configuration, all processors have their own copy of the kernel, supervisor, and data structures. There are some common data structures for the interaction among processors, the access to which is protected by using some synchronization mechanism (such as semaphores). Each processor has its own I/O devices and file system. There is very little coupling among processors and each processor acts as an autonomous, independent system. Therefore, it is difficult to perform parallel execution of a single task (that is, to break up a task and schedule the subtasks on multiple processors concurrently). Also, this configuration is inefficient because the supervisor/kernel/data structure code is replicated for each processor. This configuration, however, degrades gracefully in the face of processor failures because there is very little coupling among processors.

THE MASTER-SLAVE CONFIGURATION. In the master-slave configuration, one processor, called the *master*, monitors the status and assigns work to all other processors, the *slaves*. Slaves are treated as a schedulable pool of resources by the master. Such an operating system is simple because it runs only on the master processor. (The slave processors essentially execute application programs.) Since the operating system is executed by a single processor, it is efficient and its implementation (synchronization of access to shared variables, etc.) is easy. The master-slave configuration permits the parallel execution of a single task, where a task can be broken into several subtasks and the subtasks can be scheduled on multiple processors concurrently.

However, an operating system based on the master-slave configuration is highly susceptible to the failure of the master processor. Also, the master can become a bottleneck and will consequently fail to fully utilize slave processors. Examples of such operating systems are Cyber 170 and DEC-10.

THE SYMMETRIC CONFIGURATION. In the symmetric configuration, all processors are autonomous and are treated equally. There is one copy of the supervisor or kernel that can be executed by all processors concurrently. However, concurrent access to the shared data structures of the supervisor needs to be controlled in order to maintain their integrity. The simplest way to achieve this is to treat the entire operating system as a critical section and allow only one processor to execute the operating system at one time. This method is called the *floating master* method because it can be viewed as a master-slave configuration where the master "floats" from one processor to another. Note that the execution of the operating system by processors can become a bottleneck in this method. This problem can be mitigated by dividing the operating system into segments that normally have very little interaction (i.e., the sharing of variables, communication, etc.) such that the segments can be executed concurrently by the processors (although each segment is still executed serially). This method requires a serialization mechanism that controls concurrent access to the shared data structures of the supervisor.

The symmetric configuration is the most flexible and versatile of all the configurations. It permits the parallel execution of a single task. It degrades gracefully under failures and makes very efficient use of resources. However, it is the most difficult configuration to design and implement. Examples of such an operating system include Hydra on C.mmp.

17.3   OPERATING SYSTEM DESIGN ISSUES

A multiprocessor operating system encompasses all the functional capabilities of the operating system of a multiprogrammed uniprocessor system. However, the design of a multiprocessor operating system is complicated because it must fulfill the following requirements. A multiprocessor operating system must be able to support concurrent task execution, it should be able to exploit the power of multiple processors, it should fail gracefully, and it should work correctly despite physical concurrency in the execution of processes. The design of multiprocessor operating systems involves the following major issues:

Threads. The effectiveness of parallel computing depends greatly on the performance of the primitives that are used to express and control parallelism within an application. It has been recognized that traditional processes impose too much overhead for context switching. In light of this, threads have been widely utilized in recent systems to run applications concurrently on many processors.

Process Synchronization. In a multiprocessor operating system, disabling interrupts is not sufficient to synchronize concurrent access to shared data. A more elaborate mechanism that is based on shared variables is needed. Moreover, a synchronization mechanism must be carefully designed so that it is efficient, otherwise, it could result in significant performance penalty.

Processor Scheduling. To ensure the efficient use of its hardware, a multiprocessor operating system must be able to utilize the processors effectively in executing the tasks. A multiprocessor operating system, in cooperation with the compiler, should be able to detect and exploit the parallelism in the tasks being executed.

Memory Management. The design of virtual memory is complicated because the main memory is shared by many processors. The operating system must maintain a separate map table for each processor for address translation. When several processors share a page or segment, the operating system must enforce the consistency of their entries in respective map tables. Moreover, efficient page replacement becomes a complex issue.

Reliability and Fault Tolerance. The performance of a multiprocessor system must be able to degrade gracefully in the event of failures. Thus, a multiprocessor operating system must provide reconfiguration schemes to restructure the system in the face of failures to ensure graceful degradation.

Next, these issues in the design of multiprocessor operating systems are discussed in detail. Other issues include protection and interprocess communication. Protection deals with the design of mechanisms that prevent unauthorized access to resources. Interprocess communication in an operating system calls for a support of a variety of models for communication between processes.

17.4   THREADS

Traditionally, a process has a single address space and a single thread of control to execute a program within that address space. To execute a program, a process has to initialize and maintain state information. The state information typically comprises page tables, swap images, file descriptors, outstanding I/O requests, saved register values, etc. This information is maintained on a per program basis, and thus, a per process basis. The volume of this state information makes it expensive to create and maintain processes as well as switch between them.

With the advent of shared memory multiprocessor machines, it became imperative to create and switch between processes to take advantage of the concurrency available in many programs. The effectiveness of parallel computing depends to a great extent on the performance of the primitives that are used to express and control the parallelism within the program [2]. In networking systems, servers provide various services to machines connected to the network. For instance, file servers provide file system services to the machines in the network (see Chap. 9). These servers (typically uniprocessor machines) cater to different requests from different users. The design of servers may be simplified if separate processes are maintained at the server to cater to each active user. To provide service to different users, it becomes necessary to switch between processes efficiently.

To handle the situations where creating, maintaining, and switching between processes occur frequently, *threads* or *lightweight processes* have been proposed.

A thread separates the notion of execution from the rest of the definition of a process [3]. A single thread executes a portion of a program, cooperating with other threads concurrently executing within the same address space. Each thread makes use of a separate program counter, a stack of activation records (which describe the state of the execution), and a control block. The control block contains the state information necessary for thread management such as putting a thread into a ready list and synchronizing with other threads. Most of the information that is part of a process is also common to all the threads executing within a single address space and hence can be maintained in common to all the threads. By sharing common information, the overhead incurred in creating and maintaining the information, and the amount of information that needs to be saved when switching between threads of the same program, is reduced significantly.

Threads can be supported either at the user-level or at the kernel-level. We next discuss the advantages, disadvantages, and performance implications of supporting threads at these levels.

17.4.1   User-Level Threads

In user-level threads, a run-time library package provides the routines necessary for thread management operations. These routines are linked at runtime to applications. Kernel intervention is not required for the management of threads. The libraries multiplex a potentially large number of user-defined threads on top of a single kernel-implemented process. Typically, the cost of a user-level thread operation is within an order of magnitude of the cost of a procedure call. Because of their low cost, user-level threads can provide excellent performance compared to kernel-level threads. In addition, user-level threads have the following advantages.

- No modifications in the existing operating system kernel are required to support user-level threads.

- They are flexible. They can be customized to suit the language or needs of the users and libraries can be used to implement different thread packages that are customized differently for various users. Thus, overhead due to providing all the capabilities or facilities in one package can be avoided. An example of customizing is where one set of library routines can provide preemptive priority scheduling, while another set can provide the simpler first-in-first-out scheduling.

While user-level threads have their advantages, they have the following disadvantages.

- The generally excellent performance of user-level threads may be limited to applications such as parallel programs that require little kernel involvement. User-level threads operate within the context of traditional processes. Thread systems treat a process as a virtual processor, and consider it a physical processor executing under its control. In reality, however, the physical processors are controlled by the operating system kernel. The kernel might assign a different physical processor to a virtual processor during each timeslice. In addition, other factors such as I/O, multiprogramming, and page faults can distort the equivalence between the virtual processor and the physical processor assumed by the thread system. In other words, there is a lack of coordination between scheduling and synchronization. For example, a thread executing in a critical section may be preempted by the kernel, making other threads wait longer. Another example is that of an application that assumes that all its runnable threads are served in a finite time. However, timeslicing across a fixed number of kernel threads by the kernel across many applications may make this assumption untrue. Note that when a thread blocks, the underlying kernel process also blocks. Eventually, the application may run out of kernel threads to serve its execution contexts, even when there are runnable threads. This situation may lead to a deadlock [2].
- User-level threads require that system calls be nonblocking. If a thread blocks because of a system call, it will prevent other runnable threads from executing. Note that many frequently performed system calls—file open, file close, read, and write—block under UNIX [16].

17.4.2 Kernel-Level Threads

In kernel-level threads, the kernel directly supports multiple threads per address space [7], [26], [27]. The kernel also provides the operations for thread management. The kernel-level threads have the following advantages.

- Coordination between the synchronization and scheduling of threads is easy to achieve, since the kernel has all the information concerning the status of all the threads.
- They are suitable for multithreaded applications, such as server processes, where interactions with the kernel are frequent due to IPC, page faults, exceptions, etc. [9].
- They incur less overhead compared to traditional processes.

The disadvantages of kernel-level threads are as follows.

- Thread management operations incur higher overhead relative to user-level threads. Every operation involves a kernel trap, even when the processor is multiplexed between the threads in the same address space. On every thread operation, there is overhead due to copying and checking of parameters being passed to the kernel to ensure safety [2].
- Since the kernel is the sole provider of thread managing operations, it has to provide any feature needed by any reasonable application. This generality means that even applications not using a particular feature still have to incur overhead due to unused features provided in the kernel.

In summary: (1) kernel-level threads are too costly to use, and (2) user-level threads can provide excellent performance, but problems such as a lack of coordination between synchronization and scheduling, and blocking system calls, pose serious obstacles to the realization of performance potential.

System developers have favored user-level threads, despite their disadvantages, because of their potential for excellent performance. The cause of the problems with user-level threads are traced to the following facts.

- User-level threads are not recognized or supported by the kernel [16].
- Kernel events, such as processor preemption and I/O blocking and resumption, are handled by the kernel in a manner invisible to the user-level [2].
- Kernel threads are obliviously scheduled with respect to the user-level thread state [2].

The above problems have been addressed in at least two different ways: (1) by granting user-level threads a first-class status so that they can be used as traditional processes, while leaving the details of the implementations to the user-level code [16], and (2) through the explicit vectoring of kernel events to the user-level threads scheduler [2]. We next describe two thread mechanisms based on the above approaches.

17.4.3 First-Class Threads

First-class threads [16] were developed as a part of the Psyche parallel operating system [21]. Kernel processes are used to implement the virtual processor that execute user-level threads. Creating many virtual processors in the same address space and assigning them to different physical processors provides parallelism.

In Psyche, a thread package creates and maintains the state of the threads in user-space. Most of the thread operations, such as creation, destruction, synchronization, and the context switching of threads, are handled by the thread package. However, coarse-grain resource allocation and protection (such as preemptive scheduling) is in the domain of the kernel.

Under first-class threads, to overcome the problems associated with the user-level threads, three mechanisms are provided to communicate (in both directions) between the kernel and the thread package. These communications occur without any kernel traps. Descriptions of these mechanisms follow.

1. The kernel and the thread package share important data structures. The kernel managed data is made available to the thread package through read-only access. For example, thread package can obtain the current processor ID and process ID without making a system call. In the opposite direction, through the shared data structure, the thread package can communicate with the kernel. For instance, the thread package can specify what actions are to be taken when the kernel detects events such as a timer expiration.

2. The kernel provides the thread package with software interrupts (signals, upcalls) whenever a scheduling decision is required. Essentially, on interruption, a user-level interrupt handler is activated. The interrupt handler then takes care of the scheduling decision. Following are instances when the software interrupts are employed. When a thread blocks or resumes after blocking because of a system call, the kernel delivers an interrupt that allows the thread package to schedule an appropriate thread. Timer interrupts support the timeslicing of threads. Warnings prior to imminent preemption allow the thread package to coordinate synchronization with the kernel resource allocation. For example, the thread package may decide to postpone obtaining locks if it is faced with imminent preemption.

3. Scheduler interfaces are provided to enable the sharing of data abstractions between dissimilar thread packages. The interfacing occurs through the thread scheduling routines available in the thread package. These routines are listed in the thread data structure shared between the kernel and the thread package. The typical usage of these interfaces is to block and unblock threads at the user-level. Consider for example, the producer-consumer problem where producer and consumer threads are from different thread packages. When the consumer thread tries to read a buffer and finds it empty, the identity of the thread unblocking routines (available in the thread data structure) can be stored in the shared buffer before blocking the consumer. The producer, on storing data in the buffer, will find the address of the saved routines and can unblock the consumer thread.

17.4.4 Scheduler Activations

A scheme based on scheduler activations to overcome the disadvantages of user-level threads has been developed at the University of Washington [2].

Under this scheme, communication between the kernel and a user-level thread package is structured in terms of scheduler activations. A scheduler activation has three roles. (1) It serves as an execution context for running user-level threads. (2) It notifies the user-level thread system of kernel events. (3) It provides space in the kernel for saving the processor context of the activation's current user-level thread when the thread is stopped by the kernel.

When a program starts, the kernel creates a scheduler activation, assigns it to a processor, and upcalls into the program's address space at a fixed entry point. Once the thread system receives the upcall, it uses the activation's context to initialize itself and then runs a program's thread. This thread may create additional threads and request additional processors. For each processor request, the kernel will create a scheduler activation and assigns a processor to it, and then upcall into the thread system's user-space. Note that once an upcall is started, the activation is similar to a thread. It can be used to run a user-level thread, process an event, or make system calls (which can block).

NOTIFYING KERNEL-LEVEL EVENTS TO THE USER-LEVEL THREAD SYSTEM. To notify the thread system of kernel-level events, the kernel creates a new scheduler activation, assigns it to a processor, and then upcalls into the user-space. We next describe how several common kernel events are handled.

When a user-level thread blocks in the kernel space, the kernel creates a new scheduler activation to inform the thread system that the thread has blocked. The thread system then saves the state of the blocked thread, frees the activation used by the blocked thread, and informs the kernel that the activation is free for reuse. Then the thread system decides which thread to run next using the new activation. Note that the number of scheduler activations assigned to an application is always equal to the number of processors assigned to the application.

When a user-level thread that was stopped in the kernel resumes, it may have to continue in the kernel space. In such a case, the kernel resumes the thread temporarily until it reblocks or is at a point where it will exit the kernel space. In the latter case, the thread system is informed of the unblocking of the thread through an activation.

Sometimes, when the kernel wishes to inform the thread system of an event, a processor may not be available to assign to an activation. In such a case, the kernel stops a thread belonging to the application to which the event has to be informed, uses that processor to upcall into the thread system, and informs the thread system of the event and that a thread has been stopped. Now the thread system is free to handle the event and schedule an appropriate thread.

If the kernel decides to take a processor away from an application, the kernel stops two threads belonging to that application, thus freeing two processors. One processor is assigned to an activation meant for a different address space. The second processor is assigned to a new activation, using which the kernel informs the thread system that two threads of the application are stopped. Now the thread system is free to schedule any one of the threads that it deems appropriate.

Whenever the thread system learns that a thread is preempted, it checks to see whether the thread was executing a critical section. If so, the thread system assigns a processor to the thread through a user-level context switch. Once the thread is out of the critical section, the thread is put back into the ready queue.

It is important to note that under no circumstance does the kernel deal with the scheduling of threads. It is always the thread system that handles this.

NOTIFYING USER-LEVEL EVENTS TO THE KERNEL. The thread system notifies the kernel whenever the thread system enters a state wherein it has more processors than runnable threads or has more runnable threads than the number of assigned processors.

17.5 PROCESS SYNCHRONIZATION

The execution of a concurrent program on a multiprocessor system may require the processors to access shared data structures and thus may cause the processors to concurrently access a location in the shared memory. Clearly, a mechanism is needed to serialize this access to shared data structures to guarantee its correctness. This is the classic mutual exclusion problem. The mechanism should make accesses to a shared data structure appear atomic with respect to each other.

17.5.1 Issues in Process Synchronization

Although numerous solutions exist for process synchronization in uniprocessor systems, these solutions are not suitable for a multiprocessor system. This is because busy-waiting by processors can cause excessive traffic on the interconnection network, thereby degrading system performance. For example, software solutions to the mutual exclusion problem (such as Dekker's solution or, Peterson's method [22]) are impractical for multiprocessor systems because they do busy-waiting and are likely to consume substantial bandwidth of the interconnection network. To overcome this problem, multiprocessor systems provide instructions to atomically read and write a single memory location (in the main memory). If the operation on shared data is very elementary (such as an integer increment), it can be embedded in a single atomic machine language instruction. Thus, mutual exclusion can be implemented completely in hardware provided the operation on the shared data is elementary.

However, if an access to a shared data constitutes several instructions (which is, the critical section consists of several instructions), then primitives such as lock and unlock (or P and V operations) are needed to ensure mutual exclusion. In such cases, the acquisition of a lock itself entails performing an elementary operation on a shared variable (which indicates the status of the lock). Atomic machine language instructions can be used to implement the lock operation, which automatically serialize concurrent attempts to acquire a lock. Next, we discuss several such atomic hardware instructions and describe how they can be used to implement P and V operations [8], [10].

17.5.2 The Test-and-Set Instruction

The test-and-set instruction atomically reads and modifies the contents of a memory location in one memory cycle. It is defined as follows (variable m is a memory location):

```
function Test-and-Set(var m: boolean): boolean;
begin
        Test-and-Set:=m;
        m:=true
end;
```

The test-and-set instruction returns the current value of variable m and sets it to *true*. This instruction can be used to implement P and V operations on a binary semaphore, S, in the following way (S is implemented as a memory location):

P(*S*): while Test-and-Set(*S*) do nothing;
V(*S*): *S*:= false;

Initially, S is set to *false*. When a P(*S*) operation is executed for the first time, Test-and-Set(*S*) returns a *false* value (and sets S to *true*) and the "while" loop of the P(*S*) operation terminates. All subsequent executions of P(*S*) keep looping because S is *true* until a V(*S*) operation is executed.

17.5.3 The Swap Instruction

The swap instruction atomically exchanges the contents of two variables (e.g., memory locations). It is defined as follows (x and y are two variables):

```
procedure swap(var x, y: boolean);
var temp: boolean;
begin
        temp:= x;
        x:= y;
        y:=temp
end;
```

P and V operations can be implemented using the swap instruction in the following way (p is a variable private to the processor and S is a memory location):

P(*S*): *p*:=true;
       repeat swap(*S*, *p*) until *p*=false;
V(*S*): *S*:= false;

Clearly, the above two implementations of the P operation employ busy-waiting and therefore increase the traffic on the interconnection network. Another problem with test-and-set and swap instructions is that if n processors execute any of these operations on the same memory location, the main memory will perform n such operations on the location even though only one of these operations will succeed. Next, we discuss a *fetch-and-add* instruction that eliminates this overhead from the memory.

17.5.4 The Fetch-and-Add Instruction of the Ultracomputer

The fetch-and-add instruction of the NYU Ultracomputer [12] is a multiple operation memory access instruction that atomically adds a constant to a memory location and returns the previous contents of the memory location. This instruction is defined as follows (m is a memory location and c is the constant to be added).

```
Function Fetch-and-Add(m: integer; c: integer);
var temp: integer;
begin
        temp:= m;
        m:= m + c;
        return (temp)
end;
```

An interesting property of this instruction is that it is executed by the hardware placed in the interconnection network (not by the hardware present in the memory modules). When several processors concurrently execute a fetch-and-add instruction on the same memory location, these instructions are combined in the network and are executed by the network in the following way. A single increment, which is the sum of the increments of all these instructions, is added to the memory location. A single value is returned by the network to each of the processors, which is an arbitrary serialization of the execution of the individual instructions. If a number of processors simultaneously perform fetch-and-add instructions on the same memory location, the net result is as if these instructions were executed serially in some unpredictable order.

The fetch-and-add instruction is powerful and it allows the implementation of P and V operations on a general semaphore, S, in the following manner:

P(S): while (Fetch-and-Add(S, -1) < 0) do
  begin
        Fetch-and-Add(S, 1);
        while ($S \leq 0$) do nothing;
  end;

The outer "while-do" statement ensures that only one processor succeeds in decrementing S to 0 when multiple processors try to decrement variable S. All the unsuccessful processors add 1 back to S and again try to decrement it. The second "while-do" statement forces an unsuccessful processor to wait (before retrying) until S is greater than 0.

V(S): Fetch-and-Add(S, 1)

17.5.5   SLIC Chip of the Sequent

The Sequent Balance/21000 multiprocessor system supports a low-level mutual exclusion in hardware using a technique that is totally different from the previously discussed techniques, which use atomic multi-operation machine language instructions. The main component of a Balance/21000 is a SLIC (system link and interrupt controller) chip that supports many other functions in addition to low-level mutual exclusion.

A SLIC chip contains 64 single-bit registers and supports the operations necessary for process synchronization. Each processor has a SLIC chip and all the SLIC chips are connected by a separate SLIC bus. Each bit in the SLIC chip, called a *gate*, acts as a separate lock and stores the status of the corresponding lock. Balance/21000 replicates these 64 status bits over all the processors instead of keeping them at a central place, e.g., the shared main memory (as in the previous techniques). Thus, this method substantially reduces traffic on the network that connects memory modules to the processors and it also expedites lock access time.

To lock a gate in the SLIC chip, a processor executes a lock-gate instruction. A lock-gate instruction is executed in the following manner. If the local copy (i.e., the bit in its SLIC chip) indicates that the gate is closed, the instruction fails. Otherwise, the local SLIC of the processor attempts to close the gate by sending messages to other

SLIC chips over the SLIC bus. If multiple SLIC chips attempt to close the same gate concurrently, only one of them succeeds and the rest of them fail. When the status of a gate changes because of the successful execution of a lock-gate or an unlock-gate instruction, an appropriate message is sent over the SLIC bus, which causes every SLIC chip to update its copy of the gate.

The following code implements P and V operations on a semaphore S:

P(S): while (lock-gate(S) = failed) do nothing;
V(S): unlock-gate(S);

Since busy-waiting is performed by checking the local SLIC, the SLIC bus is not overloaded due to busy-waiting. However, processors still waste CPU cycles because they continuously check the status of their SLIC chips.

17.5.6   Implementation of Process Wait

In all the implementations of a P operation discussed thus far, several processors may *wait* for the semaphore to open by executing the respective atomic machine language instructions concurrently. This wait can be implemented in three ways:

Busy Waiting. In busy-waiting, processors continuously execute the atomic instruction to check for the status of the shared variable. Busy-waiting (also called *spin lock*) wastes processor cycles and consumes the bandwidth of the network connecting memory modules to the processors. Increased traffic on the network due to busy-waiting can interfere with the normal memory accesses and degrade the system performance due to the increased memory access time.

Sleep-Lock. In sleep-lock, instead of continuously spinning the lock, a process is suspended when it fails to obtain the lock and a suspended process relies on interrupts to become reactivated when the lock is freed. When a process fails to obtain a lock, it is suspended. In this suspended state, a process does not relinquish its processor and all interrupts except interprocessor interrupts are disabled. When a process frees the lock, it sends interprocessor interrupts to all the suspended processors. This method substantially reduces network traffic due to busy-waiting, but it still wastes processor cycles.

Queueing. In queueing, a process waiting for a semaphore to open is placed in a global queue. A waiting process is dequeued and activated by a V operation on the semaphore. Although queueing eliminates network traffic and the wastage of processor cycles due to busy-waiting, it introduces other processing overhead because the enqueue and the dequeue operations require the execution of several instructions. Also, the queue forms a shared data structure and must be protected against concurrent access.

17.5.7   The Compare-and-Swap Instruction

The compare-and-swap instruction of IBM 370 is used in the optimistic synchronization of concurrent updates to a memory location. This instruction is defined as follows ($r1$ and $r2$ are two registers of a processor and m is a memory location):

Compare-and-Swap(var $r1$, $r2$, m: integer);
var temp: integer;
begin
    temp:= m;
    if temp = $r1$ then $\{m:= r2; z:=1\}$
    else $\{r1:= \text{temp}; z:= 0\}$
end;

If the contents of $r1$ and m are identical, this instruction assigns the contents of $r2$ to m and sets z to 1. Otherwise, it assigns the contents of m to $r1$ and sets z to 0. Variable z is a flag that indicates the success of the execution of the instruction. An execution of the instruction is successful if $z = 1$ after the execution. The intuitive meaning of "successful" should become clear from the example in the next paragraph.

The compare-and-swap instruction can be used to synchronize concurrent access to a shared variable, say m, in the following manner. A processor first reads the value of m into a register $r1$. It then computes a new value, which is x plus the original value, to be stored in m and stores it in register $r2$. The processor then performs a compare-and-swap($r1$, $r2$, m) operation (see Fig. 17.1). If $z = 1$ after this instruction has been executed, this means no other process has modified location m since it was read by this processor. Thus, mutually exclusive access to m is maintained. If $z = 0$, then some other processor has modified m since this processor read it. In this case, the new value of m is automatically stored in $r1$ by the compare-and-swap instruction so that this processor can retry its update in a loop.

17.6 PROCESSOR SCHEDULING

A parallel program is a task force consisting of several tasks. In processor scheduling, ready tasks are assigned to the processors so that performance is maximized. These tasks may belong to a single program or they may come from different programs. Since tasks often cooperate and communicate through shared variables or message passing, processor scheduling in multiprocessor systems is a difficult problem. Processor scheduling is very critical to the performance of multiprocessor systems because a naive scheduler can degrade performance substantially [28].

17.6.1 Issues in Processor Scheduling

The following are three major causes of performance degradation in multiprocessor systems [28]. These should be given consideration during the design of a processor scheduling scheme.

Preemption inside Spinlock-controlled Critical Sections. This situation occurs when a task is preempted inside a critical section when there are other tasks spinning

      $r1:= m$
label: $r2:= r1+x$
      compare-and-swap($r1$, $r2$, m)
      if $z=0$ then go to label

FIGURE 17.1
An illustration of the compare-and-swap instruction.

the lock to enter the same critical section. These tasks waste CPU cycles because they continue to spin locks until the preempted task is rescheduled and completes the execution of the critical section. Although the probability that a task is preempted while it is inside a critical section is very small (as critical sections are normally small), the time a task waits for a preempted process to be rescheduled is likely to be very long. Thus, the expected wait can be significant. This problem can be serious when a few large critical sections are entered frequently.

Cache Corruption. If tasks executed successively by a processor come from different applications, it is very likely that on every task switch, a big chunk of data needed by the previous tasks must be purged from the cache and new data must be brought into the cache. Initially, this will manifest itself as a very high miss ratio whenever a processor switches to another task. (Tasks from different applications are likely to have different working sets.) This problem, called *cache corruption*, can seriously degrade performance as overhead to handle cache misses can be significant.

Context Switching Overheads. Context switching entails the execution of a large number of instructions to save and store the registers, to initialize the registers, to switch address space, etc. This is a pure overhead as it does not contribute toward the progress of application tasks. (In addition, note that a context switch causes the problem of cache corruption.)

Next, several multiprocessor scheduling strategies that address the above issues in various ways are discussed.

17.6.2   Co-Scheduling of the Medusa OS

Co-scheduling was proposed by Ousterhout [19] for the Medusa operating system for Cm*. In co-scheduling, all runnable tasks of an application are scheduled on the processors simultaneously. Whenever a task of an application needs to be preempted, *all* the tasks of that application are preempted. Effectively, co-scheduling does context switching between applications rather than between tasks of several different applications. That is, all the tasks in an application are run for a timeslice, then all the tasks in another application are run for a timeslice, and so on.

Co-scheduling alleviates the problem of tasks wasting resources in lock-spinning while they wait for a preempted task to release the critical section. However, it does not alleviate the overhead due to context switching nor performance degradation due to cache corruption. The cache corruption problem may even be aggravated by co-scheduling; by the time an application is rescheduled, it is very likely that its working set has been flushed out of all the caches. Note that the designers of the Medusa operating system did not face this problem because the Cm* multiprocessor did not employ caches.

17.6.3   Smart Scheduling

Smart scheduling was proposed by Zahorjan et al. [29]. The smart scheduler has two nice features. First, it avoids preempting a task when the task is inside its critical section.

Second, it avoids the rescheduling of tasks that were busy-waiting at the time of their preemption until the task that is executing the corresponding critical section releases it. When a task enters a critical section, it sets a flag. The scheduler does not preempt a task if its flag is set. On exit from a critical section, a task resets the flag.

The smart scheduler eliminates the resource waste due to a processor spinning a lock that is held by a task preempted inside its critical section. However, it does not make any attempt to reduce the overhead due to context switching nor to reduce the performance degradation due to cache corruption.

17.6.4   Scheduling in the NYU Ultracomputer

Scheduling in the NYU Ultracomputer was proposed by Edler et al. [11] and it combines the strategies of the previous two scheduling techniques. In this technique, tasks can be formed into groups and the tasks in a group can be scheduled in *any* of the following ways:

- A task can be scheduled or preempted in the normal manner.
- All the tasks in a group are scheduled or preempted simultaneously (as in co-scheduling).
- Tasks in a group are never preempted.

In addition, a task can prevent its preemption irrespective of the scheduling policy (one of the above three) of its group. This provision can be used to efficiently implement a spin-lock (as in the smart scheduler).

This scheduling technique is flexible because it allows the selection of a variety of scheduling policies and a different scheduling technique can be used for different task groups. However, this scheduling technique does not reduce the overhead due to context switching nor the performance degradation due to cache corruption.

17.6.5   Affinity Based Scheduling

Affinity based scheduling, proposed by Lazowska and Squillante [15], is the first scheduling policy to address the problem of cache corruption. In this policy, a task is scheduled on the processor where it last executed. This policy alleviates the problem of cache corruption because it is likely that a significant portion of the working set of that task is present in the cache of that processor when the task is rescheduled. Lazowska and Squillante show that in affinity based scheduling, a task can save a significant amount of time that is normally spent in reloading its working set in the cache of its processor. Affinity based scheduling also decreases bus traffic due to cache reloading.

Affinity based scheduling, however, restricts load balancing among processors because a task cannot be scheduled on any processor. (Tasks are tied to specific processors.) Since tasks are always executed on processors for which they have an affinity, the system suffers from load imbalance because a task may wait at a busy processor while other processors are idle. Squillante proposes and mathematically analyzes several threshold-based scheduling policies for task migration for load balancing in systems with affinity based task scheduling [23].

17.6.6 Scheduling in the Mach Operating System

In the Mach operating system, an application or a task consists of several threads. A thread is the smallest independent unit of execution and scheduling in Mach. In the Mach operating system, all the processors of a multiprocessor are grouped in disjoint sets, called *processors sets*. The processors in a processor set are assigned a subset of threads for execution. These processors use priority scheduling to execute the threads assigned to their processor set. Threads can have priority ranging from 0 to 31, where 0 and 31 are the highest and the lowest priorities, respectively. Each processor set has an array of 32 ready queues—one queue to store the ready threads of each priority. When a thread with priority i becomes ready, it is appended to the ith queue. In addition, every processor has a local ready queue that consists of the threads that must be executed only by that processor. Clearly, it is two-level priority scheduling: all the threads in a local queue have priority over all the threads in the global queue and there are also priorities inside each of these two queues.

When a processor becomes idle, it selects a thread for execution in the following manner. If the local ready queue of the processor is nonempty, it selects the highest priority thread for execution. Otherwise, it selects the highest priority thread from the global ready queues for execution. If both the queues (local and global) are empty, the processor executes a special *idle* thread until a thread becomes ready. When a thread runs out of its timeslice at a processor, it is preempted only if an equal or higher priority ready thread is present. Otherwise, the thread receives another timeslice at the processor. The length of the timeslice is variable and depends upon the number of ready threads. The higher the number of ready threads, the shorter the timeslice.

HINTS IN THE MACH OPERATING SYSTEM. The scheduler in the Mach operating system uses the concept of a *hint* to effectively schedule tasks that are believed to communicate with each other [6]. A user may have application-specific information that may help the operating system make intelligent scheduling decisions. A hint is the information in coded form, which is supplied by the user at the time of a task submission to the system. Hints essentially help modulate (elevate as well as suppress) priority and determine the timing of the execution of threads such that communication and synchronization are efficiently made between the threads. Scheduling information specific to an application (such as the senders and receivers of messages, processes synchronizing through a rendezvous, etc.) can be advantageously used to effectively carry out communication and synchronization among threads. Sometimes a hint can be a mere guess and sometimes it can be known accurately, depending on the deterministic nature of the application.

The Mach operating system supports the following two classes of hints:

Discouragement Hints. A discouragement hint allows the scheduler to delay execution of a task. It indicates that the current thread should not be run at present.

Discouragement hints can be mild, strong, or absolute. A mild hint suggests that the thread should relinquish the processor to some other thread if possible. A strong hint suggests that the thread should not only relinquish the processor, but that it should also suppress its priority temporarily. An absolute hint blocks a thread for a specific period.

Discouragement hints can be effectively used to schedule threads in an application. For example, discouragement hints can be used to optimize the performance of applications that perform synchronization through shared variables. When one thread holds the lock on a shared variable, other threads that are competing for the same lock can reduce the wastage of resources by delaying their execution using discouragement hints.

Handsoff Hints. Handsoff scheduling indicates that a specific thread should be run instead of the currently executing thread. A handsoff hint "hands off" the processor to the specified thread, bypassing the scheduler. Handsoff scheduling may designate a thread within the same task or within a different task (on the same host) that should run next.

One excellent application of handsoff hints is the *priority inversion* problem, where a low priority thread holds a resource that is needed by high priority threads. In such situations, a high priority thread can hand the processor off to the low priority thread. For example, a thread that is waiting for a semaphore to open should hand off the processor to the thread that holds the semaphore.

17.7   MEMORY MANAGEMENT: THE MACH OPERATING SYSTEM

In this section, we explain memory management in multiprocessor operating systems by studying the virtual memory management of the Mach operating system, developed at Carnegie Mellon University. We discuss issues in the design of memory management and describe how the Mach operating system addresses these issues. The discussion of the Mach virtual memory system in this section is based on the work of Tevanian [25].

17.7.1   Design Issues

Portability. Portability implies the ability of an operating system to run on several machines with different architectures. The virtual memory system is a component of the operating system that heavily relies on the idiosyncracies of the underlying architecture and can thus be an impediment to the portability of the operating system. For wide spread applicability of an operating system, architecture-independence should be an important consideration in the design of a virtual memory system.

Data Sharing. In multiprocessor systems, an application is typically executed as a collection of processes that run on different processors. These processes generally share data for communication and synchronization. A virtual memory system must provide a facility for flexible data sharing to support the execution of parallel programs.

Protection. When memory is shared among several processes, memory protection becomes an important requirement. The operating system must support mechanisms that a virtual memory system can employ to protect memory objects against unauthorized access.

Efficiency. A virtual memory system can become a bottleneck and limit the performance of the multiprocessor operating system. A virtual memory system must be efficient in performing address translations, page table lookups, page replacements, etc. Moreover, it should run in parallel to take advantage of multiple processors.

The Mach operating system is designed for parallel and distributed environments. It can run on multiprocessor systems and support the execution of parallel applications. In fact, the Mach operating system itself is designed to run in parallel—all algorithms are designed to run in parallel and all the data structures are designed to allow highly parallel access. The implementation of the virtual memory system is fully parallel in Mach to exploit the parallelism in multiprocessor systems. The Mach virtual memory system provides flexible data sharing and protection primitives to support high performance parallel applications.

17.7.2 The Mach Kernel

A key component of the Mach operating system is the Mach kernel, which provides only the basic primitives necessary for building parallel and distributed applications. It provides primitives for process management, memory management, interprocess communication, and I/O services. Other operating system services, which are useful to developers or end users, are built on top of the Mach kernel (Fig. 17.2). Since the Mach kernel provides only a small number of simple services and because only a few decisions are made within the Mach kernel, it is readily adaptable and portable to a wide array of architectures. A number of operating systems can be built on the Mach kernel as user programs.

The Mach kernel supports five abstractions: threads, tasks, ports, messages, and memory objects.

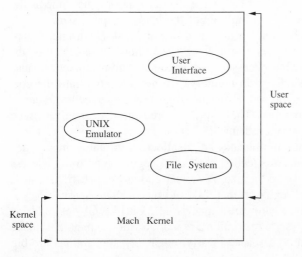

FIGURE 17.2
Mach operating system.

Tasks and Threads. A thread is the smallest independent unit of execution in Mach. A thread has a program counter and a set of registers. A task is an execution environment that may consist of many threads. A task includes a paged virtual address space and protected access to the system resources. A task is the basic unit of resource allocation.

Messages and Ports. A message is a typed collection of data used by threads for communication. Messages may be of an arbitrary size and can contain pointers and capabilities. A port is a unidirectional channel associated with an object (e.g., task, thread) that queues up messages for that object. A port can be viewed as a queue of messages. Tasks and threads communicate with other tasks and threads by performing send and receive operations on their ports. A port is protected in the kernel to ensure that only authorized tasks or threads can read or write to a port.

Memory Objects. A *memory object* is a contiguous repository of data, indexed by byte, upon which various operations, such as read and write, can be performed. Memory objects act as a secondary storage in the Mach operating system. Mach allows several primitives to map a virtual memory object into an address space of a task. Data in a memory object become available for direct access in an address space after the object or its part has been mapped into the address space. In Mach, every task has a separate address space. An address space consists of a collection of memory objects that are mapped into it. The kernel acts as a cache manager for memory objects where the physical memory is treated as the cache memory. A reference to data in a memory object that is not present in the physical memory causes a page fault and is translated into a page request.

17.7.3 Task Address Space

In the Mach operating system, each task is assigned a single paged-address space. The size of the address space is limited by the addressing capabilities of the underlying hardware (e.g., the size of *memory address register* of the processor). Mach treats an address space as a sequence of pages. The Mach page size need not be the same as the underlying hardware page size; it can be a multiple of the hardware page size.

A page in a task address space is either allocated or unallocated. An unallocated page may not be addressed by the threads of a task while an allocated page can be directly accessed. Allocated pages do not necessarily consume system resources because pages in the physical memory (i.e., the main memory) are not allocated until the corresponding virtual addresses are referenced. Even the pages that have been referenced need not be present in the main memory. They can be stored on a secondary storage and are brought into the main memory on demand.

The Mach virtual memory system allocates and deallocates virtual address space in contiguous chunks of virtual addresses, called *regions*. A region in a virtual address space is specified by a base address and a size. A virtual address issued by a task is valid only if it falls in an allocated region in that task's virtual address space.

A typical memory management hardware supports a 32-bit (4.3 Gbytes) address space. However, due to operating system restrictions, few applications are able to make use of the entire 4.3 Gbytes of address space. Clearly, not many applications are big enough to use the entire address space. Nonetheless, there are applications that benefit from using a large address space sparsely; that is, they have a large address space at their disposal but use only a small fraction of it. For example, the extensive use of a mapped file may fragment the address space, creating large holes when a file is deleted. The Mach virtual memory system supports such large, sparse address spaces.

The Mach virtual memory system supports several operations that are often needed in advanced applications. For example, a thread can normally access only the address space of the task in which it executes. However, it is sometimes necessary for a task to read or write the address space of other tasks. For example, a debugger needs to examine and modify the address space of the task being debugged. The Mach virtual memory system provides primitives to perform these operations. In addition, it provides several other primitives, such as primitives to efficiently copy a region within an address space, primitives to query current virtual memory statistics maintained by the kernel, etc.

17.7.4 Memory Protection

Virtual memory protection is enforced at the page level. Each allocated page has the following two protection codes associated with it. (1) The *current* protection code, which corresponds to the protection associated with a page for memory references and (2) the *maximum* protection code, which limits the value of the current protection. A page's protection consists of a combination of read, write, and execute permissions. Each type of permission is mutually exclusive. Mach provides primitives that set the current or maximum protection. The current protection can only include the permissions specified in the maximum protection. The maximum protection can only be lowered. That is, permissions specified in the maximum protection can be deleted, but new permissions cannot be added.

17.7.5 Machine Independence

To support portability across a wide range of architectures, a machine-independent virtual memory system is the paramount goal of the Mach virtual memory system. Mach achieves this goal by splitting the implementation into two parts, namely, a *machine-independent* part and a *machine-dependent* part. This split is based on the assumption that there exists a paged *memory management unit* (MMU) with minimal functionality. No assumption is made about the type of data structure (such as a page table) that is directly manipulated by an MMU.

The machine-independent part is responsible for maintaining high level machine-independent data structures. These data structures represent the state of the virtual memory systemwide. In case of a page fault, entire mapping information can be constructed from the machine-independent data structures. The *pmap module* is the only machine-dependent part in the Mach virtual memory system implementation, and it is responsible for the management of the physical address space. This module consists of a machine-dependent memory mapping data structure, called the *pmap structure*, which is a hardware defined physical map that translates a virtual address to a physical address.

A pmap structure corresponds to a page table. All machine-dependent mapping is performed in the pmap module. The pmap module executes in the kernel and implements page level operations on pmap structures. It ensures that the correct hardware map is in place whenever a context switch takes place. It is reponsible for managing the MMU and setting up hardware page tables. Clearly, the pmap module depends upon MMU architecture and must be recoded for a new multiprocessor system architecture.

The interface of the pmap module assumes the existence of a simple, paged MMU architecture and it has been designed to support a wide variety of MMUs. The pmap module also deals with any discrepancy between operating system page size and the underlying hardware page size. The implementation of pmap module need not know any details of the machine-independent implementation and data structures. The pmap module provides an interface (i.e., a set of primitives) to the machine-independent part that are used by the machine-independent part to notify the machine-dependent part of any changes in the mapping, creation and destruction of address spaces, etc. This information is used by the pmap module to appropriately set up hardware page table registers and other machine specific hardware registers that are related to memory management.

In addition, the Mach virtual memory system provides two types of independence to higher layers: operating system independence and paging-store independence.

OS Independence. The Mach virtual memory system is implemented such that it is almost completely decoupled from the rest of the system. It makes few assumptions about other kernel functions and is easily adaptable to different systems. Also, the virtual memory system implementation has clean interfaces to the rest of the system.

Paging-Store Independence. The Mach virtual memory system assumes no knowledge of secondary storage systems for paging purposes. Instead, the Mach virtual memory implementation defines a simple *pager interface* to which any client may conform. An external pager is responsible for managing the secondary storage. It keeps track of which pages in the virtual address space are in the main memory and where the pages in the virtual address space are located on the secondary storage.

17.7.6 Memory Sharing

The ability to share memory among several tasks is very important for the efficient execution of parallel applications. These applications can use shared memory for efficient process synchronization and interprocess communication. Without these facilities, parallel applications must use expensive synchronization primitives that have high overhead.

In Mach, all the threads of a task automatically share all the memory objects that reside in the address space of the task. Different tasks can share a page (or a memory object) by installing that page in their virtual address spaces and by initializing entries in their page tables so that all references to a virtual address in the shared page are correctly translated into a reference to a physical page. Although a shared page may be mapped at different locations in the virtual address space of the tasks, only one copy of the page is present in the main memory.

The Mach virtual memory system allows the sharing of memory via the *inheritance* mechanism. In Mach, a new address space is created when a task is created. The new address space can either be empty or it can be based on an existing address space. When a new address space (child) is based on an existing address space (parent), a page in the new address space is based on the value of the inheritance attribute of the corresponding page in the existing address space. The inheritance attribute of a page can take three values: *none, copy,* and *share.* If a page is in the none inheritance mode, the child task does not inherit that page. If a page is in the copy mode, the child receives a copy of the page and subsequent modifications to that page only affect the task making the modifications. If a page is in the share mode, the same copy of the page is shared between the parent and the child tasks. Consequently, all subsequent modifications to that page are seen by both the tasks.

In addition to supporting shared memory via the inheritance mechanism, if interfaces provided by a host export primitives that permit more unrestricted memory sharing, Mach will allow this form of memory sharing. Thus, unrestricted memory sharing can be supported within a Mach host.

17.7.7   Efficiency Considerations

The Mach virtual memory system uses the following techniques to increase efficiency:

Parallel Implementation. The implementation of the Mach virtual memory system is fully parallel to exploit the parallelism in multiprocessor systems—all algorithms are designed to run in parallel and all data structures are designed to allow highly parallel access.

Simplicity. The underlying Mach philosophy is to use simple algorithms and data structures because complex algorithms and data structures are likely to waste CPU cycles without much performance improvement.

Lazy Evaluation. In lazy evaluation, the evaluation of a function is postponed as long as possible in the hope that the evaluation will never be needed. The Mach virtual memory system makes extensive use of lazy evaluation to increase time and space efficiency. For example, virtual to physical mapping of a page is postponed until it is actually needed (i.e., a page reference occurs). The Mach virtual memory system does not even allocate space to page tables until they are needed. Thus, Mach postpones the creation of page tables and the lookup of disk addresses until needed.

THE COPY-ON-WRITE OPERATION.   Copy-on-write is a succint example of lazy evaluation in Mach that optimizes memory space and CPU cycles. The copy-on-write operation postpones the actual copying of a data page until the copied page is written. When two tasks, A and B want to share a page, the system allows them to share the same copy of the physical page, but each process has read-only access to the page (See Fig. 17.3). When task B attempts to write into the page, a protection fault is generated and the page is copied into a new physical page and a new virtual mapping is set up for the newly created page. Now B has a separate physical copy of the page.

Copy-on-write optimization improves efficiency in a variety of ways. It reduces memory overhead because several pages that are copied may never be written. No CPU

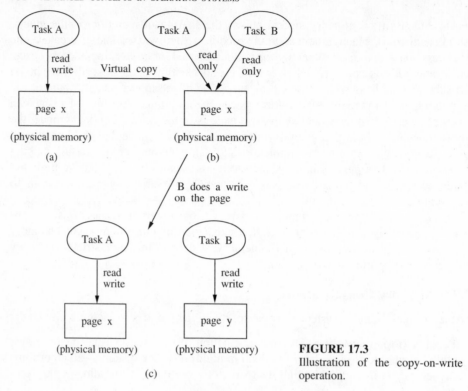

FIGURE 17.3
Illustration of the copy-on-write operation.

time is wasted in copying pages that are never written. If copied pages are never accessed, these pages do not incur mapping overhead because mapping is lazily evaluated.

17.7.8   Implementation: Data Structures and Algorithms

Data Structures

The Mach virtual memory system uses four basic data structures: memory objects, pmap structures, resident page tables, and address maps. Recall that a memory object is a repository of data that can be mapped into the address space of a task and a pmap structure is a hardware defined physical map that translates a virtual address to a physical address. Below we discuss resident page tables and address maps.

Resident Page Tables. The Mach operating system treats the physical memory as a cache for virtual memory objects. Information about physical pages (e.g., whether they are modified, referenced, etc.) is maintained in a page table (called a *resident page table*) whose entries are indexed by physical page number. A page entry in the page table may be linked into the following lists. (1) *Memory object list*: all page entries associated with an object are linked together as a memory object to speed up object deallocation and virtual copy operations. (2) *Memory allocation queues*: queues are maintained for free, reclaimable, and allocated pages and are used by the Mach pager to determine a free page in the case of page fault. (3) *Object/offset hash bucket*: Fast lookup of a physical page associated with an object/offset, at the time of a page fault, is done using a bucket hash table (keyed by the memory object and byte offset). Byte offsets in memory objects are used to avoid binding the implementation to a particular physical page size.

Address Maps. An address map is a data structure that maps contiguous chunks of virtual addresses (i.e., memory regions) in the address space of a task to memory objects. An address map is a doubly linked list of *address map entries*, each of which maps a contiguous range of virtual addresses in the address space of a task onto a contiguous area of a memory object. Each address map entry contains byte offsets of the beginning and end of the region represented by it. The linked list is sorted in the ascending order of virtual addresses. Each address map entry contains information about the inheritance and protection attributes of the memory region it defines. Thus, all addresses (pages) within a memory region mapped by a map entry have the same attributes. The address map data structure permits the efficient implementation of the most frequently performed operations on the address space of a task, namely, page fault lookups, copy/protection operations on a memory region, and the allocation and deallocation of memory regions. An address map allows us to perform operations on memory regions simply and quickly. Also, an address map allows for the efficient maintenance of sparse address spaces.

Algorithms

The Page Replacement Algorithm. A page replacement algorithm decides which page in the physical memory to replace in the event of a page fault. Mach philosophy is to use a simple page replacement algorithm because a complex algorithm is likely to waste CPU cycles without vastly improving performance. The replacement algorithm in Mach is a modified-FIFO algorithm that keeps all the physical memory pages in one of the following three FIFO queues:

The free list. This contains pages that are free to use. These pages are not currently allocated to any task and can be allocated to any task.

The active list. This contains all pages that are *actively* in use by tasks. When a page is allocated, it is removed from the free list and placed at the end of the active list.

The inactive list. This contains pages that are not in use in any address space, but were recently in use. These are the pages that will be freed if they are not referenced soon.

A special kernel thread called a *pageout daemon* performs page replacement and management of these lists. In the event of a page fault, the daemon performs page replacement by taking a page from the inactive list and placing it in the free list. (The same action is taken when the page count is low in the free list.) The pageout daemon always maintains a small number of pages in the inactive list by moving pages from the active list to the inactive list (and then removing mapping to those pages). The page replacement algorithm is a FIFO algorithm except that a page in the inactive list is activated if a task makes a reference to it. Thus, the inactive list serves as a second chance for pages targeted for replacement.

The Page Fault Handler. The page fault handler is invoked when a page is referenced for which there is either an invalid mapping or a protection violation. The page fault handler has the following responsibilities. (1) *Validity and protection:* it determines if the faulting thread has the desired access to the address by performing a lookup in its task's address space. (2) *Page lookup:* it attempts to find an entry for a cached page in the virtual to physical hash table. If the page is not present, the kernel requests the data from the pager. (3) *Hardware validation:* It informs the hardware physical map (i.e., the pmap module) of the new virtual to physical mapping.

Locking Protocols. All algorithms and data structures used in virtual memory implementation are designed to run in a multiprocessor environment and are thus fully parallel. The synchronization of accesses to shared data structures is achieved by the following locks. (1) *Map locks:* map locks provide exclusive access to address map data structures. (2) *Object locks:* object locks guarantee exclusive access to physical memory resources cached within an object. (3) *Hash table bucket locks:* these locks provide proper access to the object/resident page table hash table on a per bucket basis. (4) *Busy page locks:* these locks are used to indicate that some operation is pending on a given physical page. To prevent deadlocks, all algorithms acquire locks in the same order, i.e., map locks, object locks, and then either bucket or busy page locks.

17.7.9 Sharing of Memory Objects

Mach supports copy-on-write operations, which allow the sharing of the same copy of a memory object by several tasks as long as all the tasks only read the memory object. When a task performs a copy-on-write operation on a memory object, its address map starts pointing at the original copy of the memory object; that is, it shares the same copy with the original owner of the memory object.

If one of the tasks writes data in a copied memory object using the copy-on-write operation, a new page for that data is allocated, which is accessible only to the writing task. This new page contains the modifications by the writing task. Note that a separate copy is created only for the pages of a memory object that have been modified. Mach maintains special objects, called *shadow objects*, to hold pages of a memory object that have been modified. A shadow object collects and remembers all the modified pages of a memory object copied/shared using the copy-on-write operation. A shadow object typically does not contain all the pages of the region it defines. It relies on the original object for unmodified pages. A shadow object can itself be shadowed on subsequent copy-on-write operations, thus creating a chain of shadows.

Note that if the address maps of all the tasks that share a memory object using copy-on-write directly point to the shared memory object, then the mapping and remapping of the shared memory objects will require the manipulation of all the address maps. Yet, many tasks may share the same region of memory in read/write mode and may simultaneously share the same region with other tasks in copy-on-write mode. To circumvent these problems, a level of indirection is introduced when accessing shared memory objects. An address map, called a *sharing map*, points to a shared object, which in turn is pointed to by the address map entries of all the tasks sharing that memory object.

17.8 RELIABILITY/FAULT TOLERANCE: THE SEQUOIA SYSTEM

A multiprocessor system has inherent redundancy in processors for reliability and fault tolerance. However, a multiprocessor operating system must provide reconfiguration schemes to restructure the system in the face of failures to ensure graceful degradation. In this section, we first discuss issues in the design of fault-tolerance multiprocessor operating systems and then study fault-tolerant features and techniques of the Sequoia System [5], a loosely-coupled multiprocessor system. This system attains a high level of fault tolerance by performing fault detection in hardware and fault recovery in the operating system.

17.8.1 Design Issues

Fault Detection and Isolation. A multiprocessor operating system must promptly detect a fault and take measures to isolate and contain it. Loosely-coupled multiprocessor systems have the benefit of fault isolation in the event of processor failure, because the failure of a processor does not influence other processors. This is, however, untrue for tightly-coupled multiprocessor systems because the failure of a component (e.g., processor, main memory, etc.) can corrupt the shared memory, causing all processors to fail.

Fault Recovery. After the failure of a system component has been detected, the operating system must be able to recover the processes affected by the failure. The system must be able to restore the states of these processes to consistent states so that these processes can resume processing.

Efficiency. Fault detection and fault recovery mechanisms should have low overhead. A number of functions should be delegated to the hardware and the hardware architecture and the operating system should work together to achieve high performance.

17.8.2 The Sequoia Architecture

The Sequoia architecture consists of processor elements (PEs), memory elements (MEs), and I/O elements (IOEs), which are connected by a system bus (Fig. 17.4).

The system bus consists of two 40-bit 10 Mhz buses that operate independently. The system bus is divided into three segments: processor local segments that connect the PEs; memory local segments that connect the MEs and the IOEs; and global segments that connect the processor and the memory local segments through master interfaces

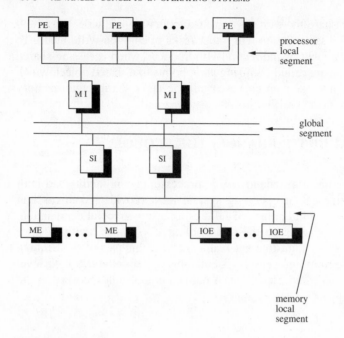

FIGURE 17.4
The Sequoia architecture.

(MIs) and slave interfaces (SIs), respectively. A processor local segment can consist of up to eight PEs and a local memory segment can consists of up to eight elements. An MI arbitrates access to the buses. Up to eight processor local segments and sixteen memory local segments can be connected by global segments.

A PE consists of dual 20 Mhz MC 68020 processors that operate in a lock-step manner with comparators that test for identical operation on each clock cycle. For fault tolerance, each PE has its own clock. Each ME consists of 8 or 16 Mbytes of 4-way interleaved RAM. It also consists of 1024 test-and-set locks that can be used for mutually exclusively access to shared data structures.

17.8.3 Fault Detection

The Sequoia system makes extensive use of hardware fault detection mechanisms to detect faults in different system components. It makes use of three fault detection mechanisms: error-detecting codes, comparison of duplicated operations, and protocol monitoring.

Error Detecting Codes. All data—whether stored in main memory, a processor cache, or being transferred on a bus—are protected by error-detecting codes. The main memory uses an extended Hamming code and all other components use byte parity for error detection. The hardware that implements all data storage and buses is partitioned so that a single component failure can produce only a single error in any byte and all such errors are detectable. In addition, half of each 4-byte address or data word is protected by odd parity and the other half by even parity. Therefore, the faults that leave data paths in a quiescent state—typically all zeros or all ones—produce detectable errors. Thus, extreme attention has been paid to insure that all single component failures are detectable.

Comparison of Duplicated Operations. The cost of logic hardware for the generation and detection of error-detecting codes for some system components may be considerably higher than the cost of the component itself. (In the Sequoia system, examples of such components are microprocessors, address generation units, and cache managers.) For these components, it is cheaper to use hardware duplication and comparison to detect failures. Each component is duplicated and is augmented with a comparator. Both components independently execute all operations and compare their outputs with a comparator to detect any discrepancy.

Protocol Monitoring. Error-detection codes and hardware duplication and comparison together are not adequate to detect all hardware faults, especially when timing is involved. For example, if a PE addresses an ME and the ME cannot respond due to some fault, then the PE (possibly along with the connecting bus) could be waiting for a response that never arrives. *Protocol monitoring* is used to detect such errors, which works by detecting violations in the sequence and timing of the communication between two components.

These faults detection techniques detect all single errors resulting from hardware failures, except those resulting from the faults in the error detection circuitry itself. The Sequoia operating system periodically tests each fault detection circuitry to verify that it can detect and report all the errors it is designed for.

PEs observe hardware faults in various ways. When an ME or IOE experiences a fault, it enters into an error state and does not respond to normal requests until the error is cleared. A PE detects such errors through a watchdog timing error. A fault in a PE is detected using polling. Each PE has a 128-byte status block in main memory and updates that block every 100 milliseconds. A designated PE periodically polls these status blocks to determine if a PE has failed. All other PEs periodically check if the designated PE has failed. When a PE observes a hardware fault, it notifies it to all other PEs using a high-priority interrupt.

When a fault is detected in a component, the component immediately disables its outputs to prevent the fault from affecting other components. The operating system is notified of the faulty component, which takes over and initiates a fault recovery, discussed next.

17.8.4 Fault Recovery

In this section, we discuss the support the Sequoia system provides for recovery from processor, main memory, and IOE failures. For recovery from the failure of these components, it should be possible, irrespective of when and where a fault occurs, to reconstruct a consistent process state of all the processes that are affected by the fault so that they can resume execution.

RECOVERY FROM PROCESSOR FAILURES. A processor can fail when it is flushing a block of its cache to the main memory or can fail when it is not. If a processor fails when it is not flushing its cache, the memory images of its cache blocks are consistent even though they are old (they reflect the state when they were last flushed). To ensure that the complete state of a process is available, the contents of the internal registers of a processor and all dirty blocks in the cache are also flushed along with every cache flush. Thus, in this situation a consistent state of a failed processor exists in the main memory and recovery from a processor failure can be done by simply assigning the process that was running on the failed processor to another processor.

However, if a processor fails while flushing its cache, it may leave the memory image of a process state being flushed in an inconsistent state because a cache flush operation is not atomic. That is, some part of the memory image has the process state before the flush and the other part has the process state after the flush. This problem is handled by having a backup copy (called *a shadow*) of every writable block/page. Every writable block is stored on two different MEs. When a processor flushes a cache block, it flushes it to both copies in the main memory, one by one. Keeping two copies of all blocks guarantees that at least one copy of every block will be consistent even if a processor fails when it is flushing its cache.

RECOVERY FROM MAIN MEMORY FAILURES. The sequoia system handles main memory failures by using hardware redundancy. There is a backup main memory for all writable data blocks/pages. Two MEs are paired as shadows under the kernel control and a writable page is stored on both the MEs. All executable and read-only data pages are backed up on a disk. Thus, if an ME fails, a backup for every page stored in that ME exists in the system. When a main memory element containing a shadowed block fails, it can be recovered from its shadow block. When a main memory element containing an unshadowed page fails, the page tables are updated to reflect that those pages are no longer in the main memory. The next access to these pages causes a page fault, which fetches these pages from the disk and loads them into main memory.

RECOVERY FROM I/O FAILURES. Disk failures are handled using dual-ported mirrored disks on different IOEs. A write is performed to both the disks of a mirrored pair. Reads are load balanced by sending half to each of the mirrored disks. If a disk fails, the other disk in the mirrored pair is used and the failed disk is recovered online. If a disk controller or an IOE fails, an alternative path to the disk is used. If no such path is operational, then the other disk in the mirrored pair is used.

17.9 SUMMARY

The design of multiprocessor operating systems is difficult because such systems must be able to support the parallel execution of multiple tasks to harness the power of multiple processors. A multiprocessor operating system must effectively schedule tasks to various processors, its performance must degrade gracefully in case of failures, and it must be able to run an application in parallel. In addition, it must support primitives for process synchronization and virtual memory management. There are three basic configurations of multiprocessor operating systems: separate supervisor, master-slave, and symmetric.

Software solutions to the critical section problem are impractical for multiprocessor systems because they consume a substantial bandwidth of the communication network. Multiprocessor systems generally provide machine language instructions to atomically read and write a single memory location. Such atomic machine language instructions can be used to implement a lock operation (like a P and V operation) that can be used to enforce mutual exclusion.

Threads are widely used primitives to effectively express, implement, and control parallelism available in parallel applications. User-level threads promise excellent performance potential relative to to kernel-level threads. However, to realize their performance potential, efficient mechanisms to exchange information between the underlying kernel and the thread system must be provided.

In processor scheduling, runnable tasks are assigned to the processors so that system performance is maximized. A scheduler should address three issues. First, it should not preempt a task inside a critical section if some other tasks are spinning the lock to enter the critical section. Likewise, a task should not be scheduled if it is going to spin the lock next. Secondly, when a task is rescheduled after an interruption, it should be scheduled to the process where it last executed. This is because it is quite likely that the processor still has a good amount of data needed by this task in its cache. If it is scheduled to another processor, it is bound to generate a large number of page faults. Third, context switching overhead should be kept small. A variety of schedulers have been developed at several universities and research labs that address these issues.

Memory management in the Mach operating system is a typical example of virtual memory system design in multiprocessor operating systems. The Mach virtual memory system provides flexible data sharing and protection primitives to support high performance parallel applications. Flexible data sharing permits the efficient implementation of process synchronization and interprocess communication. To support portability across a wide range of architectures, machine-independent virtual memory system was a major goal of the Mach virtual memory system. Mach achieved this goal by splitting the implementation in two parts: a machine-independent part and a machine-dependent part. The Mach virtual memory system makes extensive use of lazy evaluation to increase time and space efficiency. For example, the virtual to physical mapping of a page can be postponed until it is actually needed (i.e., when a page reference occurs).

Inherent redundancy in processors in a multiprocessor system provides the basic ingredients for higher reliability and fault tolerance. A multiprocessor operating system, however, must be able to restructure itself in the face of failures for graceful degradation. The Sequoia multiprocessor system attains a high degree of fault tolerance, which performs fault detection in hardware and fault recovery in the operating system. The Sequoia system makes extensive use of hardware fault detection mechanisms (such as error-detecting codes, comparison of duplicated operations, and protocol monitoring) to detect faults in different system components. It uses hardware/software redundancy to achieve fault tolerance and to perform failure recovery.

17.10 FURTHER READING

The literature on multiprocessor system operating systems is scanty. The following books deal with the design of multiprocessor operating systems to a limited extent: Hwang and Briggs [13], Stone [24], and Milenkovic [18]. Papers by Dinning [8] and Dubois et al. [10] describe process synchronization in multiprocessor systems. Case studies on two prototype multiprocessor operating systems can be found in Jones et al. [14] and Scott et al. [21].

Anderson, Lazowska, and Levy [3] present a detailed discussion on thread management in multiprocessor systems. A discussion by Draves et al., on how storage requirements for threads have been reduced in the Mach kernel, can be found in [9]. The implementation of threads in the Synthesis kernel is described by Massalin and Pu [17].

There are several papers on the Mach operating system. Rashid [20] describes the history and evolution of the Mach Operating System. Accetta et al. [1] give a detailed description of the Mach Kernel. Black [6] discusses the scheduling algorithm in Mach and the Ph.D. dissertation of Tevanian [25] contains a detailed description on memory management in Mach.

For more details on the fault-tolerant features of the Sequoia operating system, readers are referred to the original paper [5]. Barlett [4] discusses the kernel of a commercial, fault-tolerant multiprocessor system.

PROBLEMS

17.1. Can the performance of a multiprocessor system with two identical processors be worse than the performance of a uniprocessor (with an identical CPU)? Explain your answer.

17.2. A task consists of several subtasks. If these subtasks communicate (synchronously) with each other frequently, which scheduling policy would you recommend and why?

17.3. If the subtasks of a task have large critical sections, which scheduling policy is most desirable? Explain.

17.4. If nothing about the subtasks of a task is known, which scheduling policy would you recommend and why?

17.5. If several processors try to execute an atomic hardware instruction on the same memory location simultaneously, only one processor succeeds and the rest fail and retry. This is analogous to many sites trying to transmit packets on a shared medium (e.g., Ethernet). Discuss the similarities and differences between the two systems. Decide whether or not the techniques used in Ethernet can be used in multiprocessor systems to increase performance (i.e., to reduce overhead due to wasteful execution of the atomic hardware instruction).

17.6. Compare the process synchronization techniques discussed in Sec. 17.5 with respect to various overheads (e.g., communication overhead, processing overhead).

17.7. Do you think the page replacement algorithm for multiprocessor systems should be different from that of a uniprocessor system? Explain your answer.

17.8. Compare the overhead of various "wait" methods discussed in Sec. 17.5.6. Which method is preferred if the contention to access a memory location is short lived (that is, there are no hot spots).

REFERENCES

1. Accetta, M., R. Baron, D. Golub, R. Rashid, A. Tevanian, and M. Young, "Mach: A New Kernel Foundation for UNIX Development," *Proc. of the Summer 1986 USENIX Conference*, 1986.

2. Anderson, T. E., B. N. Bershad, E. D. Lazowska, and H. M. Levy, "Scheduler Activations: Effective Kernel Support for the User-Level Management of Parallelism," *Proc. of the 13th ACM Symposium on Operating System Principles, in Operating Systems Review*, vol. 25, no. 5, Oct. 1991, pp. 95–109.

3. Anderson, T. E., E. D. Lazowska, and H. M. Levy, "The Performance Implications of Thread Management Alternatives for Shared-Memory Multiprocessors," *IEEE Transactions on Computers*, vol. 38, no. 12, Dec. 1989, pp. 1631–1644.

4. Barlett, J., "A NonStop Kernel," *Proc. of the 8th Symposium on Operating Systems Principles*, 1981.

5. Bernstein, A., "Sequoia: A Fault-Tolerant Tightly Coupled Multiprocessor for Transaction Processing," *IEEE Computer*, Feb. 1988.

6. Black, D. L., "Scheduling Support for Concurrency and Parallelism in the Mach Operating Systems," *IEEE Computer*, May 1990.

7. Cheriton, D. R., "The V Distributed System," *Communications of the ACM*, March 1988.

8. Dinning, A., "A Survey of Synchronization Methods for Parallel Computers," *IEEE Computer*, July 1989.

9. Draves, R. P., B. N. Bershad, R. F. Rashid, and R. W. Dean, "Using Continuations to Implement Thread Management and Communication Operating Systems," *Proceedings of the 13th ACM Symposium on Operating System Principles, in Operating Systems Review*, vol 25, no. 5, Oct. 1991.

10. Dubois, M., C. Scheurich, and F. Briggs, "Synchronization, Coherence, and Event Ordering in Multiprocessors," *IEEE Computer*, Feb. 1988.

11. Edler, J., J. Lipkis, and E. Shonberg, "Process Management for Highly Parallel UNIX Systems," *Technical Report Ultracomputer*, Note 136, New York University, 1988.

12. Gottlieb, A., R. Grishman, C. P. Kruskal, K. P. McAuliffe, R. Rudolph, and M. Snir, "The NYU Ultracomputer—Designing an MIMD Shared Memory Parallel Computer," *IEEE Transactions on Computers*, Feb. 1983.

13. Hwang, K. and F. Briggs, *Multiprocessor Systems Architectures*, McGraw-Hill, New York, 1984.

14. Jones, A. K., R. J. Chansler, I. Durham, K. Schwan, and S. R. Vegdahl, "StarOS: A Multiprocessor Operating System for the Support of Task Forces," *Proc. of the 7th ACM Symposium on Operating Systems Principles*, Dec. 1979.

15. Lazowska, E. and M. Squillante, "Using Processor-Cache Affinity in Shared-Memory Multiprocessor Scheduling," Tech. Report, Dept. of Computer Science, Univ. of Wa., 1989.

16. Marsh, B. D., M. L. Scott, T. J. LeBlanc, and E. P. Markatos, "First-Class User-Level Threads," *Proceedings of the 13th ACM Symposium on Operating System Principles, in Operating Systems Review*, vol 25, no. 5, Oct. 1991.

17. Massalin, H., and C. Pu, "Threads and Input/Output in the Synthesis Kernel," *Proceedings of the 12th ACM Symposium on Operating System Principles, in Operating Systems Review*, vol 23, no. 5, Dec. 1989.

18. Milenkovic, M., *Operating Systems: Concepts and Design*, McGraw-Hill, New York, 1992.

19. Ousterhout, R., "Scheduling Techniques for Concurrent Systems," *in the Proceeding of the 3rd Intl. Conf. on Distributed Computing Systems*, 1982.

20. Rashid, R., "From RIG to Accent to Mach: The Evolution of a Network Operating System," *Fall Joint Computer Conference*, AFIPS, 1986.

21. Scott, M. L., T. J. LeBlanc, and B. D. Marsh, "Design Rationale for Psyche, a General-Purpose Multiprocessor Operating System," *Proceedings of the International Conference on Parallel Processing*, Aug. 1988.

22. Silberschatz, A., J. Peterson, and D. Gavin, *Operating Systems Concepts*, 3rd ed., Addison-Wesley, Reading, MA, 1990.

23. Squillante, M., "Issues in Shared-Memory Multiprocessor Scheduling: A Performance Evaluation," Ph.D. dissertation, Dept. of Computer Science and Engineering, Univ. of Washington, Seattle, WA, Oct. 1990.

24. Stone, H. S., *High-Performance Computer Architectures*, Addison-Wesley, Reading, MA, 1987.

25. Tevanian, A., "Architecture-Independent Virtual Memory Management for Parallel and Distributed Environments: The Mach Approach," Tech. Report CMU-CS-88-106, Dept. of Computer Science, Carnegie Mellon University, Pittsburgh, PA, Dec. 1987.

26. Tevanian, A., R. Rashid, D. Golub, D. Black, E. Cooper, and M. Young, "Mach Threads and the UNIX Kernel: The Battle for Control," In *Proceedings of the USENIX Summer Conf.*, 1987.

27. Thacker, C., L. Stewart, and J. E. Satterthwaite, "Firefly: A Multiprocessor Workstation," *IEEE Transactions on Computers*, vol. 37, no. 8, Aug. 1988.

28. Tucker, A., and A. Gupta, "Process Control and Scheduling Issues for Multiprogrammed Shared Memory Multiprocessors," *ACM Symposium on the Principles of Operating Systems*, 1989.

29. Zahorjan, J., E. Lazowska, and D. Eager, "Spinning Versus Blocking in Parallel Systems with Uncertainty," Technical Report 88-03-01, Dept. of Computer Science, Univ. of WA, Seattle, WA, 1988.

PART
VII

DATABASE OPERATING SYSTEMS

CHAPTER
18

INTRODUCTION TO DATABASE OPERATING SYSTEMS

18.1 INTRODUCTION

Traditionally, database systems have been implemented as an application on top of general purpose operating systems. However, such configurations generally do not yield the best performance because a host operating system may not provide sufficient functionalities needed to implement a database system. Since the requirements of a database system are different from those of a general purpose computer system, the functionality of a general purpose operating system may have to be greatly enhanced to build an efficient database system on top of it (see Fig. 18.1(a)). Moreover, a general purpose operating system may support features to maintain generality—they are all things to all people at a much higher overhead. These features may not be required in a database system or sometimes these features can be specialized for a database system such that they deliver better performance. Sometimes, existing operating system features may not be appropriate and some new features may have to be implemented in the user space.

Another approach is to write a new operating system that efficiently supports only the functions needed by database systems (see Fig. 18.1(b)). Such database systems will have high performance. However, the development of the entire operating system from scratch is very expensive. In addition, the operating system must be modified whenever the interface to the database system changes.

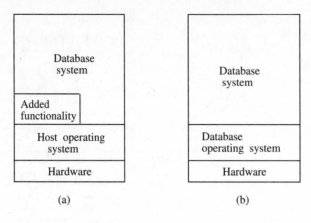

FIGURE 18.1
Two approaches to database systems design.

(a) (b)

18.2 WHAT IS DIFFERENT?

General purpose operating systems are designed to provide the users with facilities for general purpose software development, testing and execution, and file manipulation. They support the concepts of a process (by providing mechanisms for process creation, deletion, synchronization, scheduling, and interprocess communication), a virtual memory system (by providing mechanisms for address translation, buffer management, page replacement, etc.), a file system (by providing mechanisms for file storage, manipulation, and protection), and general purpose library routines. CPU scheduling, buffer management, memory management, I/O services, protection, file system management, etc. are all designed to provide a general purpose computing environment.

In a general purpose operating system, data output or data that a program manipulates are generally shortlived. General purpose operating systems support persistent (i.e., long lived) data in the form of files that have very simple structure (a stream of bytes). Also, in these operating systems, there is little sharing at the data level among the users. In addition, data size is typically much smaller than the user program size in general purpose operating system environments.

We now discuss some typical services provided by a general purpose operating system and explain why they are inadequate for supporting database systems. All operating systems use main memory as a buffer pool to cache the files stored on the secondary storage. To increase the cache hit-ratio, the operating systems generally use the least-recently-used (LRU) page replacement policy and perform prefetching of pages whenever a sequential file access is detected. The LRU policy and the prefetching of pages may not be suitable for database systems. In some cases, they may adversely affect performance [4]. In addition, for the purpose of crash recovery, database systems require that certain pages are flushed from the main memory to disk in a specific order (called the *selected force out*). This service is generally not provided by the operating systems. Database systems have circumvented these deficiencies by maintaining a buffer pool, for caching files, in the user space. This buffer pool is managed by the database system and thus the database system can use any page replacement policy and can perform selected force out.

Operating systems support an abstraction of files, which are variable size arrays of characters. This abstraction is suitable for language processors, text processors, editors, etc., but it is not suitable for database systems. If a database system requires objects with rich, complex structures, it has to build them on top of the file abstraction. Instead, for database systems, it is desirable that the operating system support complex objects on which the database system can create structured files. The operating system should support primitives for creation, manipulation, and navigation through complex objects.

Finally, most operating systems provide support for locking files. However, database systems require support for locking at a finer granularity, such as a page, a record or a byte. Finer, variable size locks are essential in database systems for efficiency reasons (to increase execution concurrency).

18.3 REQUIREMENTS OF A DATABASE OPERATING SYSTEM

We now discuss the requirements that a database system places on an operating system to meet its goals. These requirements primarily arise due to the following features of database systems. (1) A database system must support the concept of a transaction, which is the unit of consistency and reliability [1]. (2) Database systems are characterized by the existence of huge, persistent, complex data that are shared among its users. (3) Nontrivial integrity constraints must be satisfied by the shared data of the database system. A database system is consistent if its data satisfy a set of integrity constraints. We next discuss the requirements of a database system.

TRANSACTION MANAGEMENT. A user accesses a database system by executing a program, called a transaction. Informally, a transaction consists of a sequence of read and write operations on the database and is the unit of user interaction with the database system. Transaction is a unit of consistency in the sense that when a transaction is executed alone in a database system, it maintains database consistency. A database system must ensure that database consistency is maintained even when several transactions are running concurrently (called the problem of concurrency control). The database system should also ensure that a transaction is either executed completely or is not executed at all (called transaction atomicity). Note that a partially executed transaction may leave the database in an inconsistent state. In addition, in the face of a system failure, the database system must guarantee that either the actions of all partially executed transactions are undone or all partially executed transactions are run to completion (called failure recovery).

In database systems, a user runs a transaction by indicating its beginning and end to the system, thereby ignoring the problems associated with concurrent transaction execution and system failures. It is the responsibility of the database system to maintain database system consistency and transaction atomicity in the presence of concurrent transaction execution and system failures. The operating system should support mechanisms to facilitate the implementation of the following properties in transactions: concurrency control, atomic commit, and failure recovery.

Under database operating systems, we will study the problem of concurrency control. This is the issue in database systems that has received the most attention and has been widely studied. The issues of atomic commit, failure recovery, and fault tolerance are studied in Chaps. 12 and 13.

SUPPORT FOR COMPLEX, PERSISTENT DATA. Database systems manage a large volume of complex, persistent data. Traditional operating systems support persistent data in the form of files. As discussed before, files are not suitable for the direct creation and manipulation of complex data.

Database operating systems must support definition, efficient manipulation, and efficient storage on secondary devices of files with complex structures. In database systems, a file is a collection of structured records. An environment to build database systems must provide facilities to define and manipulate files of records of any arbitrary structures. Database systems are dominated by heavy I/O accesses and I/O traffic is usually a bottleneck. I/O efficiency can be improved by judiciously structuring blocks of a file on a disk so that disk-head movement is reduced while accessing blocks of a file. Thus, an operating system should organize a file on secondary storage such that neighboring pages of a file are stored next to each other on the disk.

BUFFER MANAGEMENT. Data of a database system are stored on a secondary storage (e.g., disks) and database systems maintain buffers in the main memory to cache the needed data. Data on secondary storage and the buffer in main memory are divided into equal size pages and data pages are brought into the buffer as and when needed for computation. When a transaction accesses a data page, the database system looks into the buffer to check if the page is present in it. If not, a page fault occurs and the page is brought from the secondary storage into the buffer. If the buffer is full, a page in the buffer must be swapped out to secondary storage.

Therefore, a database system requires mechanisms to perform the following operations efficiently: search the buffer to see if a page is present; select a page for replacement (that optimizes the cache hit ratio); and locate and retrieve the needed data page from secondary storage. In addition, for higher reliability, a database system must be able to flush a selected set of pages in the buffer to secondary storage (stable storage). These pages constitute the "log" [2] of a transaction execution or an "intentions list" and "flags" [3] for recovery purposes.

18.4 FURTHER READING

There are two classical papers on database operating systems: Gray [2] and Stonebraker [4]. Gray primarily concentrates on operating system support for locking and recovery in database systems. Stonebraker examines the applicability of several major operating system services to database systems and suggests alternative services at the operating system level that can provide better support to database systems.

REFERENCES

1. Gray, J., "The Transaction Concept: Virtues and Limitations," *Proceedings of the 7th Intl. Conf. on Very Large Data Bases*, Sept. 1981.
2. Gray, J. N., "Notes on Database Operating Systems," in *Operating Systems: An Advanced Course*, Springer-Verlag, N.Y., 1978, pp. 393–481.
3. Lampson, B., and H. Sturgis, "Crash Recovery in a Distributed Data Storage System," Technical Report, Computer Science Lab., XEROX PARC, Palo Alto, CA, 1976.
4. Stonebraker, M., "Operating System Support for Database Management," *Communications of the ACM*, July 1981.

CHAPTER
19

CONCURRENCY CONTROL:
THEORETICAL ASPECTS

19.1 INTRODUCTION

In database systems, users concurrently access data objects by executing transactions. The concurrent actions of transactions can interfere in unexpected ways to produce undesired results. Concurrency control is the process of controlling concurrent access to a database to ensure that the correctness of the database is maintained. In this chapter, we discuss the theoretical aspects of concurrency control. We introduce terms and definitions, discuss the problem of concurrency control, and describe the correctness criterion for concurrency control algorithms.

19.2 DATABASE SYSTEMS

A database system consists of a set of shared data objects that can be accessed by users. A data object can be a page, a file, a segment or a record. For the purpose of concurrency control, we will view a database as a collection of data objects $(d_1, d_2,..., d_M)$. Each data object takes values from a specified domain. The *state* of a database is given by the values of its data objects. In a database, certain semantic relationships, called *consistency assertions* or *integrity constraints* [8] must hold among its data objects. A database is said to be *consistent* if the values of its data objects satisfy all of its consistency assertions.

484

19.2.1   Transactions

A user interacts with a database by performing read and write actions on the data objects. The actions of a user are normally grouped together (as a program) to form a single logical unit of interaction, termed a *transaction*. A transaction consists of a sequence of read, compute, and write statements that refer to the data objects of a database. We assume the following properties about a transaction:

- A transaction preserves the consistency of a database.
- A transaction terminates in finite time.

A transaction that does not modify any data object but just reads some of them is referred to as a *read-only transaction*, or a *query*. A transaction that modifies at least one data object is known as an *update transaction,* or an *update.* The term transaction is used in a general sense to stand for either a query or an update.

Note that a transaction T_i can be viewed as a partially ordered set $(S_i, <_i)$ where S_i is the set of read and write actions of the transaction and $<_i$ dictates the order in which these actions must be executed. For the purpose of concurrency control, a transaction T can be considered as a sequence $\{a_1(d_1), a_2(d_2),..., a_n(d_n)\}$ of n steps, where a_i is the action at step i and the d_i is the data object acted upon at step i. Examples of such actions are read and write.

For a transaction, the set of data objects that are read by it are referred to as its *readset* and the set of data objects that are written by it are referred to as its *writeset.* Henceforth, we will denote the readset and the writeset of a transaction T by RS(T) and WS(T), respectively.

19.2.2   Conflicts

Transactions conflict if they access the same data objects. For two transactions T_1 and T_2, T_1 is said to have r-w, w-r, or w-w conflict with T_2 if, RS(T_1) ∩ WS(T_2) ≠ Φ, WS(T_1) ∩ RS(T_2) ≠ Φ, or WS(T_1) ∩ WS(T_2) ≠ Φ, respectively. Also, transactions T_1 and T_2 are said to *conflict* if at least one of these conflicts exists between them.

Example 19.1. For three transactions T_1, T_2, and T_3, shown in Fig. 19.1, T_1 has w-w conflict with T_2 because both modify data object d_6; T_2 has all r-w, w-r, and w-w conflicts with T_3; while T_1 and T_3 have no conflict.

19.2.3   Transaction Processing

A transaction is executed by executing its actions one by one from the beginning to the end. A read action of a transaction is executed by reading the data object in the workspace of the transaction. (The workspace of a transaction is the area, (i.e., pages), in the main memory that is allocated to it.) A write action of a transaction modifies a data object in the workspace and eventually writes it to the database. We assume that a transaction reads a data object (from the database to its workspace) and writes a data

$$T_1: \quad RS(T_1)=\{d_1,d_3,d_5\} \qquad\qquad WS(T_1)=\{d_3,d_6\}$$

$$T_2: \quad RS(T_2)=\{d_2,d_4,d_5\} \qquad\qquad WS(T_2)=\{d_2,d_4,d_6\}$$

$$T_3: \quad RS(T_3)=\{d_1,d_2,d_4\} \qquad\qquad WS(T_3)=\{d_2,d_4\}$$

FIGURE 19.1
Three transactions with their readsets and writesets.

object (from its workspace to the database) only once. Note that a transaction can be considered as a function whose inputs are the values of the data objects in its readset and the outputs are the values of the data objects in its writeset.

19.3 A CONCURRENCY CONTROL MODEL OF DATABASE SYSTEMS

For the purpose of concurrency control, we can view a database system as consisting of three software modules: a transaction manager (TM), a data manager (DM), and a scheduler (Fig. 19.2).

The transaction manager supervises the execution of a transaction. It intercepts and executes all the submitted transactions. A TM interacts with the DM to carry out the execution of a transaction. It is the responsibility of the TM to assign a timestamp to a transaction or issue requests to lock and unlock data objects on behalf of a user. Thus, TM is an interface between users and the database system.

The scheduler is responsible for enforcing concurrency control. It grants or releases locks on data objects as requested by a transaction. The data manager (DM) manages the database. It carries out the read-write requests issued by the TM on behalf of a transaction by operating them on the database. Thus, DM is an interface between the scheduler and the database. A DM is responsible for chores such as failure recovery.

A TM executes a transaction by executing all its actions sequentially from the beginning to the end. In order to execute an action, the TM sends an appropriate request to the DM via the scheduler. Hence, the execution of a transaction at the TM results in the execution of its actions at the DM. So, in general, the DM executes a stream of transaction actions, directed toward it by the TM. Note that to perform concurrency control, the scheduler modifies the stream of actions directed toward the DM.

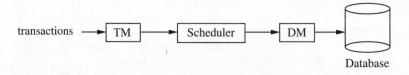

FIGURE 19.2
A model of a database system.

19.4 THE PROBLEM OF CONCURRENCY CONTROL

Typically, in a database system, several transactions are under execution simultaneously. Since a transaction preserves database consistency, a database system can guarantee consistency by executing transactions serially, i.e., one at a time. However, such a serial execution of transactions is inefficient as: it results in poor response to user requests and poor utilization of system resources. Efficiency can be improved by executing transactions concurrently, that is, by executing read and write actions from several transactions in an interleaved manner. Because the actions of concurrently running transactions may access the same data objects, several anomalous situations may arise if the interleaving of actions is not controlled in some orderly way. Such situations are described next.

19.4.1 Inconsistent Retrieval

Inconsistent retrieval occurs when a transaction reads some data objects of a database before another transaction has completed with its modification of those data objects. In such situations, the former transaction faces the risk of retrieving incorrect values of the data objects.

> **Example 19.2.** Suppose customer c_1 transfers $500 from savings account S to checking account C, and teller t_1 concurrently reads both the accounts to compute the total balance. A possible trace of the execution of these transactions is as follows (suppose initially, S = 1000 and C = 500): c_1 reads S into its workspace, subtracts 500 from it, and writes it back to S; t_1 reads S (=500) and C (=500) into its workspace; c_1 reads C (=500) into its workspace, adds 500 to it, and writes it back to C (=1000); t_1 outputs 1000 as the balance. Here, t_1 reads S after c_1 has modified it and reads C before c_1 has modified it, resulting in the incorrect retrieval of the total balance.

19.4.2 Inconsistent Update

Inconsistent update occurs when many transactions read and write onto a common set of data objects of a database, leaving the database in an inconsistent state.

> **Example 19.3.** Suppose two data objects A and B, which satisfy the consistency assertion "(A = 0) or (B = 0)", are concurrently modified by the following transactions [17]:
>
> $$\text{``}T_1 : if A = 0 \text{ then } B := B + 1\text{''}$$
>
> $$\text{``}T_2 : if B = 0 \text{ then } A := A + 1\text{''}.$$
>
> A possible execution trace is as follows (initially A = 0 and B = 0): T_1 reads A (= 0) and B (= 0) in its workspace; T_2 reads A (= 0) and B (= 0) in its workspace; since A = 0 in the workspace of T_1, it increments B by 1 and writes it in the database (B = 1); since B = 0 in the workspace of T_2, it increments A by 1 and writes it in the database (A = 1); the final database state "(A = 1) and (B = 1)" is inconsistent.

Thus, if the interleaving of the actions of transactions is not controlled, some transactions may see an inconsistent state of the database and the database may be left in an inconsistent state. This fundamental problem is referred to as the *concurrency control* problem. In a database system, this problem is handled by a concurrency control mechanism that controls the relative order (or interleaving) of conflicting[†] actions, such that every transaction sees a consistent state of the database and, when all transactions are over, the database is in a consistent state. Nevertheless, the concurrency control mechanism exploits the underlying concurrency.

It is clear that the concurrent execution of transactions must be controlled to ensure database consistency. However, a question arises as to what degree the concurrency must be controlled to ensure that database consistency is maintained (obviously, it is too restrictive to execute transactions serially). We answer this question next and we state restrictions on the concurrency by characterizing the interleavings of transaction actions that produce correct results.

19.5   SERIALIZABILITY THEORY

In this section, we describe the theory of serializability, which gives precise rules and conditions under which a concurrent execution of a set of transactions is correct [4, 7, 15, 16]. A concurrency control algorithm is correct if all of its possible executions are correct. Since the execution of transactions is modeled by a log and the correctness condition is stated in terms of logs, we next introduce the concept of log.

19.5.1   Logs

The serializability theory models executions of a concurrency control algorithm by a history variable called the *log* [7] (also called the *schedule* in [8] and the *history* in [16]). A log captures the chronological order in which read and write actions of transactions are executed under a concurrency control algorithm. Let T = $\{T_0, T_1, ..., T_n\}$ be a transaction system. A log over T models an interleaved execution of T_0, T_1,...,T_n and is a partial order set L = (S, <) where,

1. S = $\bigcup_{i=0}^{n} S_i$, and
2. < $\supseteq \bigcup_{i=0}^{n} <_i$

Condition (1) states that the database system executes all the actions submitted only by T_0, T_1,...,T_n and condition (2) states that the database system executes the actions in the order expected by each transaction.

Example 19.4. Figure 19.3 shows three transactions T_1, T_2, and T_3 and two logs L1 and L2 over these transactions. Notations used are as follows: ri[x] and wi[x]", respec-

---

[†]Recall that two actions conflict if they operate on the same data object, and at least one of them is a write action.

$$T_1 = r1[x] \ r1[z] \ w1[x]$$

$$T_2 = r2[y] \ r2[z] \ w2[y]$$

$$T_3 = w3[x] \ r3[y] \ w3[z]$$

L1 = w3[x] r1[x] r3[y] r2[y] w3[z] r2[z] r1[z] w2[y] w1[x]

L2 = w3[x] r3[y] w3[z] r2[y] r2[z] w2[y] r1[x] r1[z] w1[x]

FIGURE 19.3
Examples of logs.

tively, denote the read and the write operation of transaction T_i on data object x.

19.5.2 Serial Logs

In a database system, if transactions are executed strictly serially, that is, all the actions of each transaction must complete before any action of the next transaction can start, then the resulting log is termed a *serial log* [7]. A serial log represents an execution of transactions where actions from different transactions are not interleaved. For example, for a set of transactions T_1, T_2,..., T_n, a serial log is of the form $T_{i1} \ T_{i2} \ T_{in}$, where $i1$, $i2$,..., in, is a permutation of 1, 2,..., n.

Example 19.5. Log L2 of Fig. 19.3 is an example of a serial log because actions from different transactions have not been interleaved.

Since each transaction individually maintains the database consistency, it follows by induction that a serial log maintains the database consistency.

19.5.3 Log Equivalence

Two logs are equivalent if all the transactions in both the logs see the same state of the database and leave the database in the same state after all the transactions are finished. Let L be a log over a transaction system T = $\{T_0, T_1, ..., T_n\}$ and on a database system D = (x, y, z,...). If $w_i[x]$ and $r_j[x]$ are two operations in L, then we say $r_j[x]$ reads from $w_i[x]$ iff,

1. $w_i[x] < r_j[x]$ and
2. There is no $w_k[x]$ such that $w_i[x] < w_k[x] < r_j[x]$.

Example 19.6. In log L1 of Fig. 19.3, action r1[x] reads x from action w3[x] and action r2[z] reads z from action w3[z].

We call $w_i[x]$ a final write, if there is no $w_k[x]$ such that $w_i[x] < w_k[x]$.

Example 19.7. In log L1 of Fig. 19.3, w3[z], w2[y] and w1[x] are the final writes.

Two logs over a transaction system are equivalent iff

1. Every read operation reads from the same write operation in both the logs, and
2. Both the logs have the same final writes.

Condition (1) ensures that every transaction reads the same value from the database in both the logs and condition (2) ensures that the final state of the database is same in both the logs.

Example 19.8. In Fig. 19.3, log L2 is equivalent to log L1.

19.5.4   Serializable Logs

Note that serial logs are correct because each transaction sees a consistent state of the database and when all the transactions terminate, the database is in a consistent state. However, serial logs result in poor performance. Therefore, there has been a motivation to find out if a log obtained by interleaving actions from several transactions produces the same effect as a serial log. Such logs are called *serializable logs*. Formally, a log obtained by interleaving actions of transactions $T_1, T_2, ..., T_n$ is serializable if it produces the same output and has the same effect on the database as the serial execution of a permutation of $T_1, T_2, ..., T_n$. Thus, a serializable log is equivalent to a serial log and represents a correct execution.

Example 19.9. In Fig. 19.3, log L1 is equivalent to serial log L2, hence, it represents a correct execution.

19.5.5   The Serializability Theorem

It is natural to ask what conditions an interleaved execution (log) should satisfy in order to be serializable. Several researchers (e.g., [15, 16, 18]) have investigated this problem and have stated the condition in terms of a graph, called a *serialization graph*, which is constructed from a log. In this section, we present the results as a theorem (called *the serializability theorem*), which states the required conditions for serializability.

Suppose L is a log over a set of transactions $\{T_0, T_1, ..., T_n\}$. The serialization graph for L, SG(L), is a directed graph whose nodes are $T_0, T_1, ..., T_n$ and which has all the possible edges satisfying the following condition: There is an edge from T_i to T_j provided for some x, either $r_i[x] < w_j[x]$, or $w_i[x] < r_j[x]$, or $w_i[x] < w_j[x]$. Note that an edge $T_1 \rightarrow T_2$ in a serialization graph, SG(L), denotes that an action of T_1 precedes a conflicting action of T_2 in log L.

Example 19.10. The serialization graph for log L1 of Fig. 19.3 is shown in Fig. 19.4.

THE SERIALIZABILITY THEOREM.
Theorem 19.1. A log L is serializable iff SG(L) is acyclic.

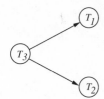

FIGURE 19.4
The serialization graph of L1.

Proof of this theorem is beyond the scope of this book (interested readers should refer to [5] for details). Given an acyclic SG(L), we can determine a serial log corresponding to log L by topologically sorting the SG(L).

Example 19.11. The serialization graph of L1, SG(L1), in Fig. 19.4 is acyclic; therefore, L1 is serializable (which we have already confirmed by showing that it is equivalent to a serial log L2).

19.6 DISTRIBUTED DATABASE SYSTEMS

In a distributed database system (DDBS), data objects are spread over a collection of autonomous sites, say $S_1, S_2,..., S_N$, which are connected by a communication network such that any site can exchange information with any other site [13]. Database at site S_i is denoted by $D_i = (d_i \,|i \in [1...M])$. Note that $D_i \cap D_j = \Phi$ for every i and j, $i \neq j$ and $D_1 \cup D_2 ... \cup D_N = (d_1, d_2, ..., d_M)$. Every data object is stored exactly at one site. Such a database is referred to as *partitioned* DDBS.

There is no globally shared memory and all sites communicate solely via message exchanges. The communication network delivers all messages correctly with a finite delay. For any pair of sites S_i and S_j, the communication network always delivers messages to S_j in the order they were sent by S_i. Sites and the communication network are prone to failures. Communication network failure may result in the partitioning of the system and/or message loss.

The concurrency control model of a DDBS is shown in Fig. 19.5. Each site in a DDBS has three software modules: a transaction manager (TM), a data manager (DM), and a scheduler. Functions of these modules are the same as in a single-site database system. The transaction manager at a site intercepts and processes all the submitted transactions. The TM may have to interact with the appropriate DMs (by sending them requests) to carry out the execution of a transaction. The data manager (DM) at a site manages the database stored at that site. It carries out the requests from TM's by operating them on the database. A DM may communicate with other DM's and is responsible for chores such as deadlock detection.

MOTIVATIONS. A distributed database offers several advantages over a centralized database system [11] such as

Sharing. Program, data, and load can be shared among the sites.
Higher system availability (reliability). The failure of a component does not bring the entire system to a halt.

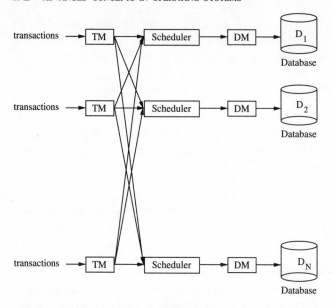

FIGURE 19.5
The model of a distributed database system.

Improved performance. Since a transaction can be decomposed into several subtransactions and these subtransactions can be executed in parallel at different sites, the system can have higher throughput and smaller response time.

Easy expandability. The system can be expanded without disrupting the normal processing.

Large databases. Multiple sites can support a larger database and a higher number of users than a single-site database.

19.6.1 Transaction Processing Model

In a DDBS, a transaction may access the data objects spread over many sites. Thus, a transaction T_i can be viewed to consist of several subtransactions, T_{i_1}, T_{i_2}, ..., T_{i_k}, where subtransaction T_{i_k} represents the processing required by T_i at site S_k. If T_{i_k} is null, then transaction T_i does not require any processing at site S_k.

A TM executes a transaction by executing all its actions sequentially from the beginning to the end. To execute an action, the TM sends an appropriate request to the DM that manages the data object acted upon by that action. Hence, the execution of a transaction at a TM results in the execution of its actions at appropriate DMs. So, in general, a DM executes a stream of actions, directed toward it by many TMs.

19.6.2 Serializability Condition in DDBS

In distributed database systems, transaction execution is represented by multiple logs (one for each site). The serialization condition in DDBS is given by the following theorem [2]:

Theorem 19.2. Let T=$\{T_1, T_2, ..., T_n\}$ be a set of transactions, and E be an execution of these transactions modeled by logs $\{L_1, L_2, ..., L_m\}$. E is serializable if there exists a total ordering of T such that for each pair of conflicting actions a_i and a_j from distinct transactions T_i and T_j, respectively, a_i precedes a_j in any log iff T_i precedes T_j in the total ordering.

Thus, an execution is serial if there is a total order of transactions such that if T_i precedes T_j in the total order, then all of T_i's actions precedes all of T_j's actions in all the logs where they both appear.

19.6.3 Data Replication

In the partitioned DDBS described above, if a site is down, its database is inaccessible to other sites, i.e., all transactions that access (read-write) those data objects are blocked until the site recovers. This problem can be remedied (i.e., system availability can be increased) by storing data objects at two sites. Since the probability of two sites being down simultaneously is very low, all data objects will be available most of the time. If availability of a data object is very critical, its copies can be stored at several sites. In general, a different number of copies can be stored for different data objects.

In addition, multiple copies of data objects reduce the access time for some read operations because data objects can be read locally without exchanging messages. A simple strategy is to store a data object where it is likely to be accessed most frequently.

19.6.4 Complications due to Data Replication

Although data replication enhances system availability and expedites reads, it introduces an additional problem—a system must not only guarantee that each copy is self consistent (called *internal consistency*), but also that all copies of a data object have the same value (called *mutual consistency*) [21].

19.6.5 Fully-Replicated Database Systems

A fully-replicated database is a special case of data replication where every data object is replicated at every site, i.e., if d_{ik} denotes the copy of data object d_k at site S_i, then $D_i = (d_{i1}, d_{i2}, ..., d_{iM})$, for i $= 1, 2, 3, ..., $ N.

Full data replication has overhead due to extra storage and requires complicated synchronization to maintain mutual consistency. Nevertheless, it has several attractive features:

Enhanced reliability. A site can access a data object even if some sites have failed or the network has partitioned.

Improved responsiveness. A query can be executed quickly without any communication.

No directory management. The overhead of managing a directory and a resource locator service is absent.

Easier load balancing. A computation can be readily transferred without moving a data object.

Because of these features, several commercial efforts have been made in this direction, e.g., SDD-1 [6] and distributed INGRES [19].

Since all data objects are available at a site in fully-replicated database systems, a transaction can be completely executed at any site. The following three-step method for executing a transaction T_i has been widely used in fully-replicated database systems:

1. Values of the data objects in RS(T_i) are read;
2. Computation is performed to obtain the values of data objects in WS(T_i); and
3. The computed values are written onto the data objects in WS(T_i) of the database.

Note that the last step must be performed on every copy of the database so that all the copies are mutually consistent.

19.7 SUMMARY

In database systems, concurrent actions of transactions can interfere in unexpected ways to produce undesired results. Examples of such results include inconsistent retrieval and inconsistent update. Inconsistent retrieval occurs when a transaction reads some data objects of a database before another transaction has completed its modification of those data objects, thereby leaving the former transaction with a risk of retrieving incorrect values of the data objects. Inconsistent update occurs when many transactions read and write onto a common set of data objects of a database, leaving the database in an inconsistent state.

Concurrency control deals with the control of concurrent access to database systems to ensure that the correctness of the database is maintained. In this chapter, we discussed theoretical aspects of concurrency control and discussed correctness criterion for concurrency control algorithms. Correctness of concurrency control algorithms is addressed by the theory of serializability, which gives precise conditions under which a concurrent execution of a set of transactions is correct. The execution of transactions is modeled by a log and the correctness condition is stated in terms of logs. A log captures the chronological order in which read and write actions of transactions are executed under a concurrency control algorithm. A concurrent transaction execution is correct if its log has the same effect as a serial log. A precise result is given by the serializability theorem, which states that a log represents correct execution iff its serialization graph is acyclic. Clearly, a concurrency control algorithm is correct if all of its possible executions are correct.

19.8 FURTHER READING

Books by Bernstein et al. [5] and Papadimitriou [14] give a comprehensive discussion on the theory of concurrency control. Serializability theory was first formalized by Papadimitriou in [15]. Kung and Papadimitriou present an optimality theory of concurrency control in [10]. Bernstein and Goodman [3] discuss a theory of multiversion concurrency control in database systems. Hua and Bhargava [9] discuss classes of serializable histories in distributed databases.

PROBLEMS

19.1. Show that the log of Examples 19.2 and 19.3 are not serializable.

19.2. Show that if two logs are equivalent, their serialization graphs are identical [5].

19.3. Show that if there is at most one conflict between any two transactions, then any interleaved execution will be serializable.

19.4. What is the serializability condition for a fully-replicated database system?

19.5. Is serializability the only correctness criterion for concurrent transaction execution?

REFERENCES

1. Abramson, N., "The ALOHA System–Another Alternative for Computer Communications," *1970 Fall Joint Computer Conf.*, vol. 37, 1970.
2. Bernstein, P., and N. Goodman, "Concurrency Control in Distributed Database Systems," *ACM Computing Surveys*, June 1981.
3. Bernstein, P. A., and N. Goodman, "Multiversion Concurrency Control—Theory and Algorithms," *ACM Trans. on Database Systems*, Dec. 1983.
4. Bernstein, P. A., and N. Goodman, "A Sophisticate's Introduction to Distributed Database Concurrency Control," *Proceedings of 8th Intl. Conf. on Very Large Databases*, Sept. 1982.
5. Bernstein, P. A., V. Hadzilacos and N. Goodman, "Concurrency Control and Recovery in Database Systems," Addison Wesley, Reading, MA, 1987.
6. Bernstein, P. A., J. B. Rothanie, N. Goodman and C. A. Papadimitriou, "The Concurrency Control Mechanism of SDD-1: A System for Distributed Databases (The Fully Redundant Case)," *IEEE Trans. on Software Engineering*, May 1978.
7. Bernstein, P. A., D. W. Shipman and W. S. Wong, "Formal Aspects of Serializability in Database Concurrency Control," *IEEE Trans. on Software Engineering,* May 1979.
8. Eswaran, K. P., J. N. Gray, R. A. Lorie and I. L. Traiger, "The Notion of Consistency and Predicate Locks in a Database System," *Communications of the ACM*, Nov. 1976.
9. Hua, C. and B. Bhargava, "Classes of Serializable Histories and Synchronization Algorithms in Distributed Database Systems," *Proceedings of the 3rd Intl. Conf. on Distributed Computing Systems,* Oct. 1982.
10. Kung, H. T. and C. H. Papadimitriou, "An Optimality Theory of Concurrency Control for Databases," *Acta Informatica*, Apr. 1983.
11. Lynch, A., "Distributed Processing Solves Main-frame Problems," *Data Communications*, Dec. 1976.
12. Metcalfe, R. M. and D. R. Boggs, "Ethernet: Distributed Packet Switching for Local Computer Networks," *Communications of the ACM*, July 1976.
13. Ozsu, M. T. and P. Valduriez, "Principles of Distributed Database Systems," Prentice-Hall, NJ, 1991.
14. Papadimitriou, C. H., *The Theory of Database Concurrency Control,* Computer Science Press, Rockville, MD, 1986.
15. Papadimitriou, C. H., "Serializability of Concurrent Updates," *Journal of the ACM*, Oct. 1979.
16. Papadimitriou, C. H., P. Bernstein and J. Rothanie, "Some Computational Problems Related to Database Concurrency Control," *Proceedings of Conf. on Theoretical Computer Science*, 1977.
17. Rosenkrantz, D. J., R. E. Stearns and P. M. Lewis, "System Level Concurrency Control for Distributed Database Systems," *ACM Trans. on Database Systems,* June 1978.
18. Stearns, R. E., P. M. Lewis and D. J. Rosenkrantz, "Concurrency Controls for Database Systems," *Proceedings of the 17th Annual Symp. on Foundation of Computer Science*, 1976.

19. Stonebraker, M., "Concurrency Control and Consistency of Multiple Copies in Distributed INGRES," *IEEE Trans. on Software Engineering,* May 1979.
20. Tanenbaum, A., *Computer Networks*, Prentice-Hall, Englewood Cliffs, NJ, 1981.
21. Thomas, R. H., "A Majority Consensus Approach to Concurrency Control for Multiple Copy Databases," *ACM Trans. of Database Systems*, June 1979.

CHAPTER
20

CONCURRENCY
CONTROL
ALGORITHMS

20.1 INTRODUCTION

A concurrency control algorithm controls the interleaving of conflicting actions of trans-actions so that the integrity of a database is maintained, i.e., their net effect is a serial execution. In this chapter, we discuss several popular concurrency control algorithms. We begin by describing the basic synchronization primitives used by these algorithms.

20.2 BASIC SYNCHRONIZATION PRIMITIVES

20.2.1 Locks

In lock based techniques, each data object has a lock associated with it [8]. A transaction can request, hold, or release the lock on a data object. When a transaction holds a lock, the transaction is said to have locked the corresponding data object. A transaction can lock a data object in two modes: *exclusive* and *shared*. If a transaction has locked a data object in exclusive mode, no other transaction can concurrently lock it in any mode. If a transaction has locked a data object in shared mode, other transactions can concurrently lock it but *only* in shared mode. Basically, by locking data objects, a transaction ensures that the locked data objects are inaccessible to other transactions, while temporarily in inconsistent states.

20.2.2   Timestamps

A timestamp is a unique number that is assigned to a transaction or a data object and is chosen from a monotonically increasing sequence. Timestamps are commonly generated according to Lamport's scheme [17]. Every site S_i has a logical clock C_i, which takes monotonically nondecreasing integer values. When a transaction T is submitted at a site S_i, S_i increments C_i by one and then assigns a 2-tuple $(C_i,$ i) to T. The 2-tuple is referred to as the timestamp of T and is denoted by TS(T). Every message contains the current clock value of its sender site, and when a site S_j receives a message with clock value t, it sets C_j to max($t + 1$, C_j). For any two timestamps $ts_1 = (t_1, i_1)$ and $ts_2 = (t_2, i_2)$, $ts_1 < ts_2$, if either $(t_1 < t_2)$, or $(t_1 = t_2$ and $i_1 < i_2)$.

Timestamps have two properties: (1) *uniqueness* (i.e., they are unique systemwide) because timestamps generated by different sites differ in their site id part and timestamps generated by the same site differ in their clock value part and (2) *monotonicity* (i.e., the value of timestamps increases with time) because a site generates timestamps in increasing order.

Timestamps allow us to place a total ordering on the transactions of a distributed database system by simply ordering the transactions by their timestamps. In concurrency control algorithms for distributed database systems, whenever two concurrent transactions conflict, all sites must agree on a common order of serialization. This can be achieved by assigning timestamps to transactions in the manner described above and then having every site serialize conflicting transactions by their timestamps.

20.3   LOCK BASED ALGORITHMS

In *lock* based concurrency control algorithms, a transaction must lock a data object before accessing it [8]. In a locking environment, a transaction T is a sequence $\{a_1(d_1),$ $a_2(d_2), \dots, a_n(d_n)\}$ of n actions, where a_i is the operation performed in the ith action and the d_i is the data object acted upon in ith action. In addition to read and write, lock and unlock are also permissible actions in locking algorithms. A transaction can lock a data object d_i with a "lock(d_i)" action and can relinquish the lock on d_i by an "unlock(d_i)" action. A log that results from an execution where a transaction attempting to lock an already locked data object waits, is referred to as a *legal* log [8].

A transaction is *well-formed* [8] if it

- Locks a data object before accessing it,
- Does not lock a data object more than once, and
- Unlocks all the locked data objects before it completes.

It is important to note that just being well-formed is not sufficient for correctness (that is, to guarantee serializability). Additional constraints, as to when a lock can be acquired and released, are needed. These constraints are expressed as locking algorithms. Next, locking algorithms are described.

20.3.1 Static Locking

In static locking, a transaction acquires locks on all the data objects it needs before executing any action on the data objects. Static locking requires a transaction to pre-declare all the data objects it needs for execution. A transaction unlocks all the locked data objects only after it has executed all of its actions.

Static locking is conceptually very simple. However, it seriously limits concurrency because any two transactions that have a conflict must execute serially. This may significantly limit the performance of the underlying database system. Another drawback of static locking is that it requires a priori knowledge of the data objects to be accessed by transactions. This may be impractical in applications where the next data object to be locked depends upon the value of another data object.

20.3.2 Two-Phase Locking (2PL)

Two-phase locking is a dynamic locking scheme in which a transaction requests a lock on a data object when it needs the data object. However, database consistency is not guaranteed if a transaction unlocks a locked data object immediately after it is done with it.

Two-phase locking imposes a constraint on lock acquisition and the lock release actions of a transaction to guarantee consistency [8]. In two-phase locking, a transaction cannot request a lock on any data object after it has unlocked a data object. Thus, a transaction must have acquired locks on all the needed data objects before unlocking a data object.

Thus, as the name suggests, two-phase locking has two phases: a *growing phase* during which a transaction requests locks (without releasing any lock); and, a *shrinking phase*, which starts with the first unlock action, during which a transaction releases locks (without requesting any more locks). The stage of a transaction when the transaction holds locks on all the needed data objects is referred to as its *lock point*. A schematic diagram of the execution of a two-phase transaction is shown in Fig. 20.1.

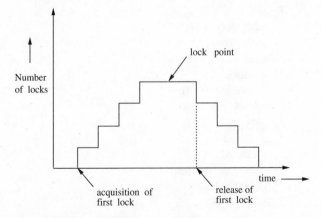

FIGURE 20.1
A schematic diagram of a two-phased transaction.

T_1	T_2
lock A	lock B
A + 100 → A	B + 50 → B
lock B	lock A
unlock A	A − 50 → A
B − 100 → B	unlock B
unlock B	unlock A

FIGURE 20.2
Well-formed, two-phased transactions.

Example 20.1. Figure 20.2 shows two well-formed, two-phased transactions T_1 and T_2. Transaction T_1 transfers \$100 from account B to account A, and transaction T_2 transfers \$50 from account A to account B. In Fig. 20.3, we show a legal schedule of T_1 and T_2, which is serializable.

Eswaran et al. [8] shows that if a set of transactions are well-formed and follow the two-phase structure for requesting and releasing data objects, then all legal logs (legal schedules) are serializable. Minoura [20] shows that if no semantic information on transactions and the database system are available, then two-phase locking is a necessary condition for database consistency.

Two-phase locking increases concurrency over static locking because locks are held for a shorter period. With the help of an example, we next show how 2PL results in higher concurrency.

Example 20.2. Suppose two transactions T_1 and T_2 have the following readsets and writesets:

$$RS(T_1) = \{d_2, d_3\}, WS(T_1) = \{d_3\},$$
$$RS(T_2) = \{d_1, d_2, d_3\}, WS(T_2) = \{d_1, d_2, d_3\}.$$

Transaction	Action	Comments
T_1	lock A	T_1 locks A
T_1	A+100 → A	T_1 adds 100 to A
T_1	lock B	T_1 locks B
T_2	lock B	T_2 tries to lock B, waits.
T_1	unlock A	T_1 unlocks A
T_1	B−100 → B	T_1 subtracts 100 from B
T_1	unlock B	T_1 unlocks B
		T_2 gets lock on B
T_2	B+50 → B	T_2 adds 50 to B
T_2	lock A	T_2 locks A
T_2	A−50 → A	T_2 subtracts 50 from A
T_2	unlock A	T_2 unlocks A
T_2	unlock B	T_2 unlocks B

FIGURE 20.3
A legal and serializable schedule of T_1 and T_2

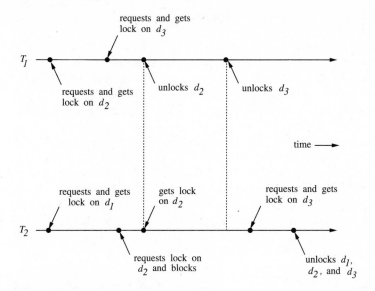

FIGURE 20.4
Concurrent execution of T_1 and T_2.

One possible execution of these transaction is shown in Fig. 20.4. T_1 begins execution first and places a read lock on d_2. T_2 begins by placing a write lock on d_1, performs some computation, and is blocked when it tries to lock d_2. T_1 locks d_3 and can now unlock d_2 since it has locked all data items it will need. This allows T_2 to lock d_2 for write and T_2 can continue computation. After T_1 has unlocked d_3, T_2 can lock d_3 and complete. Thus, T_1 and T_2 can concurrently execute in two-phase locking. In static locking, however, T_2 would not have been able to begin until T_1 had finished. Consequently, 2PL allows more concurrency in transaction execution and has better performance than static locking.

20.3.3 Problems with 2PL: Price for Higher Concurrency

Two-phase locking suffers from the problems of deadlock and cascaded aborts. These problems are not specific to 2PL; in general, any dynamic locking policy will have these problems.

DEADLOCKS. Two-phase locking is prone to deadlocks because a transaction can request a lock on a data object while holding locks on other data objects. A set of transactions are deadlocked if they are involved in a circular wait.

Example 20.3. Suppose a transaction T_1 holds lock on data object d_1 and requests lock on data object d_2 and is blocked because d_2 is already locked by transaction T_2. Later, if transaction T_2, while holding a lock on d_2 requests a lock on d_1, a deadlock will arise between T_1 and T_2.

Example 20.4. In Fig. 20.3, if T_1 locks data object A at step 1 and T_2 locks data object B before T_1 reaches its step 3, a deadlock will arise between T_1 and T_2.

A deadlock may involve more than two transactions. A deadlock persists until it is resolved. A deadlock is resolved by aborting a deadlocked transaction, restoring all the data objects modified by it to their original states, releasing all the locks held by it, and withdrawing its pending lock requests. Deadlocks can be prevented by having each transaction acquire all the needed data objects in the beginning, but this limits concurrency. Deadlocks can also be prevented in 2PL by assigning unique priorities to transactions and having a transaction only wait for higher priority transactions (this scheme is discussed later).

CASCADED ROLL-BACKS. When a transaction is rolled back (for any reason—a user kills it, the system crashes, or it becomes deadlocked), all the data objects modified by it are restored to their original states. In this case, all transactions that have read the backed up data objects must also be rolled back and the data objects modified by them must also be restored and so on. This phenomenon is called the *cascaded roll-back*. Two-phase locking suffers from the problem of cascaded roll-back because a transaction may be rolled back after it has released the locks on *some* data objects and other transactions have read those modified data objects.

Example 20.5. In Example 20.2, if T_1 were to abort after it released the lock on d_2 and after T_2 had read d_2, then T_2 would need to be aborted too, because now T_2 has read a value of d_2 that was never committed (T_1 did not complete).

STRICT 2PL. Cascaded roll-backs can be avoided by making all transactions strict two-phased. In strict two-phase locking, a transaction holds all its locks until it completes and releases them in a single atomic action, often called a *commit*. Strict 2PL eliminates cascaded aborts because transactions can read data objects modified by a transaction only after the transaction has completed. However, strict 2PL reduces concurrency as a transaction holds locks for a longer period than required for consistency.

Clearly, the problems of deadlock and cascaded aborts are created by the two phases of 2PL, the growing and shrinking phases, respectively. To eliminate these problems, it is necessary to avoid these two phases, and consequently return to static locking. Thus, the price of higher concurrency in 2PL are these two problems.

20.3.4 2PL in DDBS

The concurrency control problem is aggravated in a distributed database system because [18],

- Users access data objects stored in several geographically distant sites.
- A site may not have instantaneous knowledge of the state of other sites.

Two-phase locking can be implemented in a distributed database system in the following way. A DM (data manager) at a site controls the locks associated with objects stored at that site. A TM (transaction manager) communicates with the appropriate DM to lock or unlock a data object. If a request for lock cannot be granted, the DM puts it on the waiting queue of the object. When a lock on an object is released, one of the waiting requests for the lock on that object is granted. If all the transactions are two-phased or a TM acquires locks for a transaction in the two-phased manner, then it implements two-phase locking in a distributed database system.

20.3.5 Timestamp-Based Locking

Rosenkratz et al. [22] propose two locking based algorithms for concurrency control in a distributed database system that avoid deadlocks by using timestamps. When a transaction is submitted, it is assigned a unique timestamp. The timestamps of transactions specify a total order on the transactions and can be used to resolve conflicts between transactions. When a transaction conflicts with another transaction, the concurrency control algorithm makes a decision based on the result of the comparison of their timestamps. The use of timestamps in resolving conflicts is primarily to prevent deadlocks. Conflicts are resolved uniformly at all sites because conflicting transactions have the same timestamps systemwide.

Recall that a conflict occurs when (1) a transaction makes a read request for a data object, for which another transaction currently has a write access or (2) a transaction makes a write request for a data object, for which another transaction currently has a write or read access.

CONFLICT RESOLUTION. A conflict is resolved by taking one of the following actions.

Wait. The requesting transaction is made to wait until the conflicting transaction either completes or aborts.

Restart. Either the requesting transaction or the transaction it conflicts with is aborted (all data objects modified by the aborted transaction are restored to their initial states) and started afresh. Restarting is achieved by using one of the following primitives:

Die. The requesting transaction aborts and starts afresh.

Wound. The transaction in conflict with the requesting transaction is tagged as wounded and a message "wounded" is sent to all sites that the wounded transaction has visited. If the message is received before the wounded transaction has committed at a site, the concurrency control algorithm at that site initiates an abort of the wounded transaction, otherwise the message is ignored. If a wounded transaction is aborted, it is started again. The requesting transaction proceeds after the wounded transaction completes or aborts.

WAIT-DIE ALGORITHM. The WAIT-DIE algorithm is a nonpreemptive algorithm because a requesting transaction never forces the transaction holding the requested data object to abort. The algorithm works as follows. Suppose requesting transaction T_1 is in conflict with a transaction T_2. If T_1 is older (i.e., has a smaller timestamp), then T_1 waits, otherwise T_1 dies (and starts afresh).

WOUND-WAIT ALGORITHM.   The WOUND-WAIT algorithm is a preemptive algorithm and works as follows. Suppose a requesting transaction T_1 is in conflict with a transaction T_2. If T_1 is older, it wounds T_2, otherwise it waits.

Both these algorithms produce serializable logs and guarantee that no transaction waits forever to prevent deadlocks.

COMPARISON BETWEEN THE ALGORITHMS

Waiting Time.   In the WAIT-DIE algorithm, an older transaction is made to wait for younger ones. Hence, the older a transaction becomes, the higher the number of younger transactions it waits for and the more it tends to slow down.

In the WOUND-WAIT algorithm, an older transaction never waits for younger ones and wounds all the younger transactions that conflict with it. Hence, the older a transaction becomes, the less it tends to slow down.

Number of Restarts.   In the WAIT-DIE algorithm, the younger requester dies and is restarted. If this younger transaction is restarted with the same timestamp, it might again conflict with the older transaction (if still running) and again die. Thus, a younger transaction may die and restart several times before it completes.

In the WOUND-WAIT algorithm, if the requester is younger, it waits rather than continuously dying and restarting.

20.3.6   Non-Two-Phase Locking

When the data objects of a database system are hierarchically organized (i.e., hierarchical database systems [29]), a non-two-phase locking protocol can ensure serializability and freedom from deadlock [24]. In non-two-phase locking, a transaction can request a lock on a data object even after releasing locks on some data objects. However, a data object cannot be locked more than once by the same transaction.

In order to access a data object, a transaction must first lock it. If a transaction attempts to lock a data object that is already locked, the transaction is blocked. When a transaction unlocks a data object, one of the transactions waiting for it gets a lock on it and resumes. When a transaction T_i starts, it selects a data object (denoted by $E(T_i)$) in the database tree for locking and can subsequently lock the data objects only in the subtree with root node $E(T_i)$. Moreover, a transaction can lock a data object only if its immediate ancestor is also currently locked by it.

> **Example 20.6.**   Figure 20.5 shows a hierarchical database system and Fig. 20.6 shows two non-two-phased transactions T_1 and T_2. Transaction T_1 must lock the node B first so that it can lock all the required data objects (D, G, and I). Likewise, T_2 must lock node A before accessing any other node. Before T_2 can lock node H, it must first lock node C.

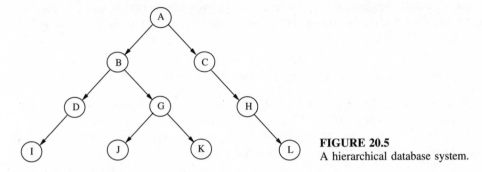

FIGURE 20.5
A hierarchical database system.

THE LOCKING PROTOCOL

1. T_i can lock data object R $\neq$ E(T_i) iff T_i is holding a lock on R's ancestor.
2. After unlocking a data object, T_i cannot lock it again.
3. T_i can only access those data objects for which it is holding a lock.

Silberschatz and Kedem [24] show that the non-two-phase locking protocol guarantees serializability and is deadlock free. Intuitively, serializability is achieved because data objects are locked in ascending order (i.e., from the root to leaves) in a tree that is acyclic. Deadlocks are avoided because the tree structure puts an order on data objects and the first rule of the protocol guarantees that data objects are requested (locked) in ascending order.

ADVANTAGES. Non-two-phase locking has two advantages over two-phase locking. First, it is free from deadlocks and hence, no transaction is aborted to resolve deadlocks. Second, a lock can be released when it is no longer needed (rather than waiting for a moment when all the required locks are set). Hence, the availability of data objects to other transactions is higher. However, the database must be organized as a tree and

T_1	T_2
lock D	lock H
D+100 $\rightarrow$ D	H+200 $\rightarrow$ H
lock I	unlock H
I$-$50 $\rightarrow$ I	lock D
unlock D	D$-$100 $\rightarrow$ D
lock G	unlock D
G*2 $\rightarrow$ G	
unlock I	
unlock G	

FIGURE 20.6
Non-two-phased transactions T_1 and T_2.

a super set of all the data objects to be accessed by a transaction must be known in advance. Singhal and Joergensen [14] have qualitatively compared the performance of 2PL and N2PL algorithms.

20.4 TIMESTAMP BASED ALGORITHMS

In timestamp based concurrency control algorithms, every site maintains a logical clock that is incremented when a transaction is submitted at that site and updated whenever the site receives a message with a higher clock value (every message contains the current clock value of its sender site). Each transaction is assigned a unique timestamp and conflicting actions are executed in the order of the timestamp of their transactions. Recall that a timestamp is generated by appending the local clock time with the site identifier [17].

Timestamps can be used in two ways. First, they can be used to determine the currency or outdatedness of a request with respect to the data object it is operating on. Second, they can be used to order events (read-write requests) with respect to one another. In timestamp based concurrency control algorithms, the serialization order of transactions is selected a priori (decided by their timestamps) and transactions are forced to follow this order.

We next describe a series of timestamp based concurrency control algorithms [4]. We assume that the TM attaches an appropriate timestamp to all read and write operations. All DMs process conflicting operations in timestamp order. The timestamp order execution of conflicting operations results in their serialization.

20.4.1 Basic Timestamp Ordering Algorithm

In the basic timestamp ordering algorithm (BTO), the scheduler at each DM keeps track of the largest timestamp of any read and write processed thus far for each data object. Let us denote these timestamps by R-ts(object) and W-ts(object), respectively. Let read(x, TS) and write(x, v, TS) denote a read and a write request with timestamp TS on a data object x. (In a write operation, v is the value to be assigned to x.)

A read(x, TS) request is handled in the following manner: If $TS < W\text{-ts}(x)$, then the read request is rejected and the corresponding transaction is aborted, otherwise it is executed and R-ts(x) is set to $\max\{R\text{-ts}(x), TS\}$. A write(x, v, TS) request is handled in the following manner: If $TS < R\text{-ts}(x)$ or $TS < W\text{-ts}(x)$, then the write request is rejected, otherwise it is executed and W-ts(x) is set to TS.

If a transaction is aborted, it is restarted with a new timestamp. This method of restart can result in a cyclic restart where a transaction can repeatedly restart and abort without ever completing. This algorithm has storage overhead for maintaining timestamps (note that two timestamps must be kept for every data object).

20.4.2 Thomas Write Rule (TWR)

The Thomas write rule (TWR) is suitable only for the execution of write actions [28]. For a write(x, v, TS), if $TS < W\text{-ts}(x)$, then TWR says that instead of rejecting the write, simply ignore it. This is sufficient to enforce synchronization among writes because the effect of ignoring an obsolete write request is the same as executing all writes in their timestamp order. However, an additional mechanism is needed for synchronization between reads and writes because TWR takes care of only write-write synchronization. Note that TWR is an improvement over the BTO algorithm because it reduces the number of transaction aborts.

20.4.3 Multiversion Timestamp Ordering Algorithm

In the multiversion timestamp ordering (MTO) algorithm, a history of a set of R-ts's and < W-ts, value > pairs (called *versions*) is kept for each data object at the respective DM's. The R-ts's of a data object keep track of the timestamps of all the executed read operations, and the versions keep track of the timestamp and the value of all the executed write operations. Read and write actions are executed in the following manner:

- A read(x, TS) request is executed by reading the version of x with the largest timestamp less than TS and adding TS to the x's set of R-ts's. A read request is never rejected.

  Example 20.7. In Fig. 20.7(a), a read(x, 18) is executed by reading the version <12, V2> and the resulting history is shown in Fig. 20.7(b).

- A write(x, v, TS) request is executed in the following way: If there exists a R-ts(x) in the interval from TS to the smallest W-ts(x) that is larger than TS, then the write is rejected, otherwise it is accepted and a new version of x is created with time-stamp TS.

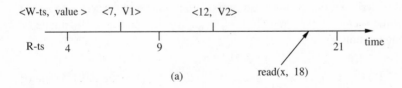

(a)

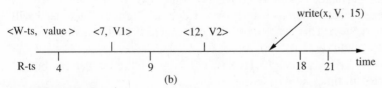

(b)

FIGURE 20.7
An example of MTO.

Example 20.8. In Figure 20.7(b), write(x, V, 15) is rejected because a read with timestamp 18 has already been executed. However, a write(x, V, 22) is accepted and is executed by creating a version <22, V> in the history.

It can be shown that the MTO algorithm is correct; i.e., every execution is equivalent to a serial execution in timestamp order. The MTO algorithm reduces the number of transaction aborts over the BTO and TWR algorithms. It does, however, require a huge amount of storage, as a set of R-ts's and multiple versions of data objects are kept for data objects. It is not practical to keep all versions of data objects—techniques exist to delete old versions.

20.4.4   Conservative Timestamp Ordering Algorithm

The conservative timestamp ordering algorithm (CTO) altogether eliminates aborts and restarts of transactions by executing the requests in strict timestamp order at all DM's. A scheduler processes a request when it is sure that there is no other request with a smaller (older) timestamp in the system.

Each scheduler maintains two queues—a R-queue and a W-queue—per TM. These queues, respectively, hold read and write requests. A TM sends requests to schedulers in timestamp order and the communication medium is order preserving. A scheduler puts a new read or write request in the corresponding queue in timestamp order. This algorithm executes read and write actions in the following way:

1. A read(x, TS) request is executed in the following way. If every W-queue is nonempty and the first write on each W-queue has a timestamp greater than TS, then the read is executed, otherwise the read(x, TS) request is buffered in the R-queue.

2. A write(x, v, TS) request with timestamp TS is executed in the following manner. If all R-queues and all W-queues are nonempty and the first read on each R-queue has a timestamp greater than TS and the first write on each W-queue has a timestamp greater than TS, then the write is executed, otherwise the write(x, v, TS) request is buffered in the W-queue.

3. When any read or write request is buffered or executed, buffered requests are tested to see if any of them can be executed. That is, if any of the requests in R-queue or W-queue satisfies condition 1 or 2.

PROBLEMS WITH CTO.   Conservative timestamp ordering technique has two major problems.

- Termination is not guaranteed. This is because if some TM never sends a request to some scheduler, the scheduler will wait forever due to an empty queue and will never execute any request. This problem can be eliminated if all TMs communicate with all schedulers regularly.

- The algorithm is overly conservative; That is, not only conflicting actions but all actions are executed in timestamp order.

These problems have been addressed in [4] in detail.

20.5 OPTIMISTIC ALGORITHMS

Optimistic concurrency control algorithms are based on the assumption that conflicts among transactions are rare. In optimistic algorithms, no synchronization is performed when a transaction is executed, but at the end of the transaction's execution, a check is performed to determine if the transaction has conflicted with any other concurrently running transaction. In case of a conflict, the transaction is aborted, otherwise it is committed. When conflicts among transactions are rare, very few transactions need to be rolled back. Thus, transaction roll-backs can be effectively used as a concurrency control mechanism rather than locking.

20.5.1 Kung-Robinson Algorithm

Kung and Robinson were the first to propose an optimistic method for concurrency control [16]. In their technique, a transaction always executes (tentatively) concurrently with other transactions without any synchronization check, but before its writes are written in the database (and become accessible to other transactions), it is validated. In the validation phase, it is determined whether actions of the transaction have conflicted with those of any other transaction. If found in conflict, then the tentative writes of the transaction are discarded and the transaction is restarted. The basic algorithm is as follows:

THE ALGORITHM. The execution of a transaction is divided into three phases: read phase, validation phase, and write phase. In the read phase, appropriate data objects are read, the intended computation of the transaction is done, and writes are made on a temporary storage. In the validation phase, it is checked if the writes made by the transaction violate the consistency of the database. If the check passes, then in the write phase, all the writes of the transaction are made to the database. A typical transaction execution in the optimistic approach is shown in Fig. 20.8.

THE VALIDATION PHASE. In the validation phase of a transaction T, it is checked if a transaction exists that has its write phase after the beginning of the read phase of T, but before the validation phase of T, and which has its writeset intersected by the readset of T. If there exists such a transaction, a conflict occurs and T is restarted. Formally, each transaction is assigned a unique (monotonically increasing) sequence number after it passes the validation check and before its write phase starts. Let t_s be

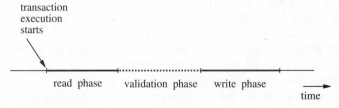

FIGURE 20.8
Transaction execution in the optimistic approach.

the highest sequence number at the start of T and t_f be the highest sequence number at the beginning of its validation phase. After the read phase of transaction T, the following algorithm is executed in a mutually exclusive manner [16] (which consists of the validation phase and a possible write phase of T):

<valid: = true;
for t:= $t_s + 1$ to t_f do
    if (writeset[t] ∩ readset[T] ≠ Φ) then
        valid: = false;
if valid then {write phase; increment counter,
    assign T a sequence number} >

A read-only transaction does not have a write phase, but it still has to be validated using the above validation algorithm. The optimistic approach is suitable only in environments where conflicts are unlikely to occur, as in a query dominant system.

Schlageter proposed an improvement to the Kung-Robinson method wherein a read transaction always proceeds without validation check and thus without the risk of restarts [23]. In the Kung-Robinson method, read transactions are treated in the same way as update transactions, and thus, are subject to a validation check with the risk of restart [16].

20.6 CONCURRENCY CONTROL ALGORITHMS: DATA REPLICATION

In this section, we discuss concurrency control algorithms for fully-replicated database systems. That is, data objects are replicated at all sites.

20.6.1 Completely Centralized Algorithm

In the completely centralized algorithm (CCA) [10], a site is designated as the "central" site, which executes all update transactions. When a transaction arrives at a site, it is forwarded to the central site for execution. (All transactions are assumed to be updates.) The central site either queues the requests and executes them sequentially, or executes them in parallel using some local concurrency control, ensuring that the net effect is as if they were executed serially. If it is acceptable for read-only transactions to access data which may not be current, it is possible for queries to be executed locally at other sites.

After executing an update, the central site assigns it a sequence number and broadcasts the new values for the data objects to all other sites in a *perform update* message (which contains the sequence number). Sites apply new values in the order in which they were produced by the central site. That is, when a site receives a perform update message, it does not apply its updates to its local database copy until it has processed all perform update messages with lower sequence numbers.

An advantage of this scheme is its simplicity. The assumption of atomic reads and writes eliminates the possibility of deadlock. Only local concurrency control is required at the central site. There are, however, several disadvantages to this scheme. First, it has poor reliability because if the central site crashes, no further updates can be processed.

This problem can be mitigated by including a protocol to elect a new central site if the current central site crashes [11]. Second, the central site can become a bottleneck. The capacity of the system is limited by the capacity of the central site.

20.6.2 Centralized Locking Algorithm

The centralized locking algorithm (CLA) strives to eliminate the bottleneck created in the CCA by allowing transactions to be processed in distributed manner (at their home sites). However, the lock management is centralized [10].

Before a site executes an update transaction, it requests locks from the central site via a *lock request* message for the data objects it accesses. If all the locks can be granted, the central site responds with a *lock grant* message, including a sequence number. Otherwise, the request is queued and a lock grant message is sent when the transaction can be granted all its locks. There is a queue for each data object and a request waits in only one queue at a time. To prevent deadlock, all transactions request locks in a predefined order.

A site executes a transaction when it has received its lock grant message by reading data objects from its local database and computing update values. It then broadcasts a perform update message to all other sites. When the central site receives the perform update message, it releases all the locks set by the corresponding transaction. Sites process perform update messages in the order of their sequence numbers.

OPTIMIZATIONS. Several optimizations are possible to minimize unnecessary waits, which can be caused by a more recent transaction (i.e., higher sequence number) having to wait for a perform update from an older transaction that does not conflict with it [10]. One possibility is for the central node to keep track, for each data object, of the last transaction that locked it. In this manner, the central node can inform a transaction of the last earlier transaction it must wait for. This *wait for* list can be appended to each *lock grant* message.

Alternatively, the central site can prepare a *don't wait for* list by keeping track of all transactions holding concurrent locks [10] (and therefore not conflicting). This data is more easily accessible at the central node and therefore requires less overhead to implement, although it does not eliminate all of the unnecessary delays. Still another method would require the central site to keep locks on a site-wise basis. This would permit concurrent execution of nonconflicting transactions, although it would require more messages.

All of the algorithms presented so far in this section are not crash resistant. However, it is possible to make all of the algorithms crash-resilient, and the cost of doing so is roughly the same for all of the algorithms.

20.6.3 INGRES' Primary-Site Locking Algorithm

Concurrency control in distributed INGRES is based on the *primary site* method [27]. In an effort to eliminate the bottleneck caused by the central site in the previously discussed algorithms, lock management here is distributed among all sites. For each object of the database, irrespective of its number of copies, a single site is designated as its primary site. All updates for an object are first directed to its primary site.

A transaction consists of a series of actions (RETRIEVEs and SENDs) that might take place at different sites. For a query, a series of RETRIEVE and SEND requests are directed to either the local copy (with some possible loss of consistency) or to the primary copy. For an update, the data access requests must be directed to the primary copy of each data object. This activity is coordinated by a master INGRES process at the site, where the transaction originated.

Local RETRIEVEs and SENDs are performed by slave processes created by the master. A local concurrency controller runs at each site, which views a transaction as consisting of a collection of local actions, received one at a time from the master. The lock tables created and used by each concurrency controller are local to its site.

When an update is processed it generates a deferred update list, which is sent to the primary site for the data objects that are to be updated. Each site at which a copy of a data object to be updated resides, receives a deferred update list from the slave process that prepared it. At the local site, the update is performed (either by the slave process or by a special copy process created for that purpose) when the transaction is committed. INGRES uses a two-phase commit protocol.

A deadlock is possible in this system. Local deadlocks are handled by the local concurrency control mechanism. If, however, more than one machine is involved in a deadlock, the master for the deadlocked transaction is notified and it handles the deadlock by rolling back the entire transaction. In addition, INGRES includes facilities to maintain consistency in the face of site crashes and communication failures, including network partitions.

20.6.4 Two-Phase Locking Algorithm

Recall that two-phase locking has two phases—a growing phase in which a transaction acquires locks and a shrinking phase during which a transaction releases locks. Two-phase locking allows for greater concurrency than static locking, which locks all data objects that will ever be needed in the beginning.

Two-phase locking can be applied for concurrency control in replicated database systems by locking (in exclusive mode) all copies of a data object to be modified, and by locking (in shared mode) any one copy of a data object to be read [5].

Since two-phase locking is prone to deadlocks, some mechanism must be used to detect and resolve them (this is not a simple task in a distributed environment [26]). Since the algorithm requires that data objects in the writeset of an update be locked at every site, it requires a large number of messages and causes an additional delay for each write lock since it must wait for a reply from each site. There is also a potential for cascaded roll-backs.

Site failure is also a problem. If a transaction has a read lock on a data object d_i at site S_j (recall that a read lock needs to be placed only on one site) and site S_j crashes, another transaction can put a write lock on d_i since all available sites do not have a lock on d_i. Consequently, a transaction has a read lock and another transaction has a write lock on d_i, leading to inconsistency. However, Bernstein and Goodman [5] proposed an algorithm that is effective in the presence of site failures and crash recovery. The basic idea behind this algorithm is that when a transaction reaches the point at which it has all of its locks, it checks to make sure that all the data objects it read are still available and locked. If a site at which it holds a read lock has gone down, then the data object is considered unavailable and the transaction aborts. If the data object is available, it unlocks the data object.

20.7 SUMMARY

In this chapter, three types of concurrency control algorithms were discussed, viz., locking, timestamping, and optimistic. In static locking, a transaction acquires locks on all the needed data objects before it starts execution and unlocks them only after it has completely executed. Thus, it requires a transaction to predeclare all the data objects needed for execution. It may limit the performance of the underlying database system because any two transactions that have a conflict must execute serially. Two-phase locking handles this problem by allowing transactions to acquire data objects on demand. However, a transaction is not allowed to request a lock on any data object after it has unlocked a data object—a transaction must have acquired locks on all the needed data objects before unlocking a data object. Two-phase locking has two phases. First, a growing phase, during which a transaction requests locks (without releasing any lock). Second, a shrinking phase, that starts with the first unlock action, during which a transaction releases locks (without requesting any more locks). The price of higher concurrency in 2PL are the problems of deadlocks and cascaded roll-backs. The problem of deadlock is introduced by the growing phase and the problem of cascaded roll-backs is created by the shrinking phase.

In hierarchical database systems, a non-two-phase locking protocol can ensure serializability and freedom from deadlock. In non-two-phase locking, a transaction need not have two phases. When a transaction starts, it selects a data object (say d) in the database tree for locking and can subsequently lock any data object in the subtree with root node d. A transaction can lock a data object only if its direct ancestor is also currently locked by it.

In timestamp based concurrency control algorithms, a transaction is assigned a unique timestamp and conflicting transaction actions are executed in the order of the timestamp of their transactions. We discussed four timestamp based concurrency control algorithms. In the basic timestamp ordering algorithm, a read(x, TS) request is accepted for execution only if no transaction with timestamp greater than TS has written x; A write(x, v, TS) request is accepted only if no transaction with timestamp greater than TS has read or written x. The Thomas write rule (TWR) is suitable only for the execution of write actions and states that execute a write(x, v, TS) request by simply ignoring it if a transaction with timestamp greater than TS has written x. The multiversion timestamp ordering algorithm reduces the rejection of requests by keeping multiple versions of data objects. The conservative timestamp ordering algorithm altogether eliminates the rejection of requests by executing the requests in strict timestamp order.

The Kung-Robinson optimistic concurrency control algorithm was discussed, wherein the execution of a transaction is divided into three phases: read phase, validation phase, and write phase. In the read phase, appropriate data objects are read, the intended computation of the transaction is done, and writes are made on a temporary storage. (The read phase is executed without any synchronization against concurrent transactions.) In the validation phase, a check is performed to see if the writes made by the transaction violate the consistency of the database. If the check passes, then in the write phase, all the writes of the transaction are made to the database.

20.8 FURTHER READING

Two survey articles by Bernstein and Goodman [3] and Kohler [15] provide an excellent overview of concurrency control algorithms for database systems. A book by Bernstein et al. [6] contains a comphrensive discussion on locking and timestamp based concurrency control algorithms for database systems. Treatment of concurrency control problem in distributed database systems is given by Ozsu and Valduriez [21].

Badal [2] discusses the degree of concurrency provided by locking based algorithms. Two papers by Yannakakis [30, 31] discuss the theory of deadlock-free locking policies. Silberschatz and Kedem [25] have generalized non-two-phase locking algorithm for database systems, where data objects are organized as a directed acyclic graph. Leu and Bhargava [19] extend timestamping algorithms to multidimensional timestamp algorithms where timestamp is a vector of several elements. Farrag and Ozsu [9] proposed a generalized concurrency control algorithm such that locking and timestamping algorithms are two special cases of it.

Gifford [13] proposed a weighted voting algorithm for concurrency control in replicated database systems. Recently, this idea has been taken to quorum, votes, and logical structures to increase efficiency as well as fault tolerance [1, 7, 12].

PROBLEMS

20.1. What is the difference between concurrency control and mutual exclusion?

20.2. Show that only being "well-formed" does not guarantee serializability.

20.3. Two-phase locking increases concurrency in transaction execution relative to static locking. However, what problems are associated with two-phase locking?

20.4. Show that in 2PL, a serialization order of a set of transactions is the same as the order of their lock-points in a log.

20.5. Show by an illustration that two-phased locking can have cascaded aborts. Prove that if deadlock resolution is the only reason to abort a two-phased transaction, there will not be any cascaded aborts.

20.6. Why are timestamp-based concurrency control algorithms free from deadlock? List basic, multiversion, and conservative timestamp ordering algorithms in increasing order of transaction aborts.

20.7. Consider two concurrent transactions T_1 and T_2, which write the same data object X and perform concurrency control using two-phase locking. Show that if T_1 wrote X before T_2 wrote it, then the lock-point of T_1 must precede the lock-point of T_2. (The lock-point of a transaction is the stage at which it has acquired all needed locks.)

20.8. Show that N2PL algorithm is deadlock free.

20.9. Show how the use of timestamps in locking algorithms (i.e., WAIT-DIE and WOUND-WAIT) prevent deadlocks.

20.10. Does the N2PL algorithm have the problem of cascaded aborts? Provide an example.

20.11. Discuss how static locking can be implemented in DDBS. Is it deadlock free? If message delays are high (as compared to the computation time of an action), show that static locking can outperform 2PL in DDBS.

20.12. Give an example of "cyclic restart" in the BTO algorithm.

20.13. Discuss a scheme to discard obsolete data versions in the MTO algorithm.

REFERENCES

1. Agrawal, D., and A. E. Abbadi, "The Generalized Tree Quorum Protocol: An Efficient Approach for Managing Replicated Data," *ACM Trans. on Database Systems*, 1992.

2. Badal, D. Z., "On the Degree of Concurrency Provided by Concurrency Control Mechanisms for Distributed Databases," *Distributed Databases*, 1980.

3. Bernstein, P., and N. Goodman, "Concurrency Control in Distributed Database Systems," *ACM Computing Surveys*, June 1981.

4. Bernstein, P. and N. Goodman, "Timestamp Based Algorithms for Concurrency Control in Distributed Database Systems," *Proceedings of 6th Int. Conf. on Very Large Databases*, Oct. 1980.

5. Bernstein, P. A., and N. Goodman, "An Algorithm for Concurrency Control and Recovery in Replicated Distributed Databases," *ACM Transactions on Database Systems*, Dec. 1984.

6. Bernstein, P. A., V. Hadzilacos, and N. Goodman, "Concurrency Control and Recovery in Database Systems," Addison Wesley, Reading, MA, 1987.

7. Cheung, S. Y., M. H. Ammer, and M. Ahamad, "The Grid Protocol: A High Performance Scheme for Maintaining Replicated Data," *Proceedings of 6th Intl. Conf. on Data Engineering*, February 1990.

8. Eswaran, K. P., J. N. Gray, R. A. Lorie, and I. L. Traiger, "The Notion of Consistency and Predicate Locks in a Database System," *Communications of the ACM*, Nov. 1976.

9. Farrag, A., and M.T. Ozsu, "Towards a General Concurrency Control Algorithm for Database Systems," *IEEE Trans. on Software Engineering*, Oct. 1987.

10. Garcia-Molina, H., "Performance Comparison of Two Update Algorithms for Distributed Databases," *Proceedings of 3rd Berkeley Workshop on Distributed Data Management and Computer Networks*, Aug. 1978.

11. Garcia-Molina, H., "Elections in a Distributed Computing System," *IEEE Trans. on Computers*, Jan. 1982.

12. Garcia-Molina, H., and D. Barbara, "How to Assign Votes in a Distributed System", *Journal of the ACM*, 1985.

13. Gifford, D. K., "Weighted Voting for Replicated Data," *Proceedings of the 7th Symposium on Operating Systems*, 1979.

14. Joergensen, G., and M. Singhal, "A Comparative Analysis of Two-Phase and Non-Two-Phase Locking Algorithms for Database Systems," *Proceedings of the 11th Annual Intl. Computer Software and Applications Conf.*, Oct. 1987.

15. Kohler, W., "Survey of Techniques for Synchronization and Recovery in Decentralized Computer Systems," *ACM Computing Surveys*, June 1981.

16. Kung, H. T., and J. T. Robinson, "On Optimistic Methods for Concurrency Control," *ACM Trans. on Database Systems*, June 1981.

17. Lamport, L., "Time, Clocks and Ordering of Events in Distributed Systems," *Communications of the ACM*, July 1978.

18. LeLann, G., "Distributed Systems—Towards a Formal Approach," *Information Processing 77*, 1977.

19. Leu, P.J., and B. Bhargava, "Multidimensional Timestamp Protocol for Concurrency Control," *Proceedings of the 3th Intl. Conf. on Data Engineering*, 1986.
20. Minoura, T., "Maximally Concurrent Transaction Processing," *Proceedings of 3rd Berkeley Workshop on Distributed Data Management and Computer Networks,* Aug. 1978.
21. Ozsu, M.T., and P. Valduriez, "Principles of Distributed Database Systems," Prentice-Hall, NJ, 1991.
22. Rosenkrantz, D. J., R. E. Stearns, and P. M. Lewis, "System Level Concurrency Control for Distributed Database Systems," *ACM Trans. on Database Systems*, June 1978.
23. Schlageter, G., "Optimistic Methods for Concurrency Control in Distributed Database Systems," *Proceedings of 7th Intl. Conf. on Very Large Databases*, Oct. 1981.
24. Silberschatz, A., and Z. Kedem, "Consistency in Hierarchical Database Systems," *Journal of the ACM*, vol. 27, Jan. 1980.
25. Silberschatz, A., and Z. M. Kedem, "A Family of Locking Protocols for Database Systems that are Modeled by Directed Graphs," *IEEE Trans. on Software Engineering*, Nov. 1982.
26. Singhal, M., "Deadlock Detection in Distributed Systems," *IEEE Computer*, Nov. 1989.
27. Stonebraker, M., "Concurrency Control and Consistency of Multiple Copies in Distributed INGRES," *IEEE Trans. on Software Engineering*, May 1979.
28. Thomas, R. H., "A Majority Consensus Approach to Concurrency Control for Multiple Copy Databases," *ACM Trans. on Database Systems*, June 1979.
29. Tsichritzis, D. C. and F. H. Lockovsky, "Hierarchical Database Management," *ACM Computing Surveys*, Mar. 1976.
30. Yannakakis, M., "A Theory of Safe Locking Policies in Database Systems," *Journal of the ACM*, 1982.
31. Yannakakis, M., "Freedom from Deadlocks in Safe Locking Policies," *SIAM J. on Computing*, 1982.

INDEX